Spells
and
Charms

Spells
and
Charms

The complete guide to
magical enchantments

Pamela Ball

This edition published in 2021 by Arcturus Publishing Limited
26/27 Bickels Yard, 151–153 Bermondsey Street,
London SE1 3HA

AD008819UK

Printed in the UK

And we harm no one

Lest we be accused of undue influence, as have others before us, we hereby take responsibility for the words written within the pages of this book. We do not however take any responsibility for your performance of the spells and rituals herein nor for the results of the use of the Powers. Such performance and result is a transaction between you and those Powers, for which you yourself must take responsibility.

Do what ye will.

We trust that this book will help you in your search for understanding and offer a blessing to help you on your way.

May your God be with you.
May He guide, guard and protect you.

CONTENTS

CONTENTS

CONTENTS

PREFACE

From the time humans first stood upright upon the Earth, felt the wind in their hair, the rain on their face and the Sun on their back, to the time when they pushed beyond the boundaries of the Earth on which they lived in order to conquer the vastness of the skies above, they have used magic. During their search for an identity, they discovered that they possessed some powers but that other powers were beyond them. Having discovered their own capabilities, they wondered, watched and learned. They learnt that if they and their companions performed certain actions and made certain sounds, things around them changed, sometimes for better, sometimes for worse. This is the first principle of manifestation.

No matter how sophisticated we have become, this first principle still applies. There are some powers we can call on for assistance and some we must protect ourselves against. Whether we call them energies or powers does not really matter; still we must reach both inside ourselves and beyond to tap into the immensity of what is available to us.

This book is intended to help you do just that. In making use of the information available here, you will begin an exploration that can take you in many directions. We start very simply with some basic traditions of belief and schools of thought that have their origins in antiquity. We take a brief look at the various types of magic available – involving herbs, colour, candles, knots, etc – before we explain the basic tools and how to achieve a desired result by applying both physical and mental techniques. By this point in the book, you should have an understanding of what a spell truly is, the various types of spell and why it is so important to keep records of what you have done in your spell-making.

For practice, and to show you how to link many aspects of your working, we give you some techniques for protecting your home. By practising a few simple spells in the fields of relationship and prosperity – areas of life that intrigue everyone – you will learn some more about the various types of magic. When you then gain knowledge of how to create a sacred space, both inside and outside your home, you protect yourself and others from the misuse of power, and it is this step which you take next on your journey of discovery. This means that you can have an appreciation of the power and beauty in rituals.

We then move on to meet the deities of many different religions. Your rituals and spells can take on a new and deeper meaning when you bring them into your working. The natural objects that occur in the physical world can also be used in spell-making. There is a resurgence of appreciation of the world in which we live, and going back to basics allows us to appreciate Mother Nature in a different way. By linking with her essential rhythms, we permit ourselves to be at one with her rather than simply existing on Earth. This naturally turns us to a consideration of that other symbol of femininity – the Moon.

Then we delve more fully into the various forms of magic, where we draw together what we have learned in our excursion into spell-making. In the next section, on charms, amulets and talismans, we see how the Ancients cleverly used correspondences and simple signs to represent very complex ideas, ideas that are still in use today and can help us to live successful lives. You learn how to bless charms, dedicate amulets and create talismans. Finally, you learn how to dismiss (let go) and thank the Powers you have called upon, and to close the space you have used for your workings.

This book has been devised to encourage you to dip into it as the mood takes you, and to take what you need from it. It doesn't have to be read from cover to cover. However, thorough perusal and use of its contents will provide the foundation for a personal magic that is both fun and rewarding. We offer this first spell to set you on your path:

To Learn Spell-making

YOU WILL NEED
This book
Your two hands
Your mind

METHOD
Allow the book to open at any point.
Begin reading.
Enjoy whatever you do.

1
THE TRADITIONS
OF MAGIC

While we might make an attempt at defining ancient beliefs as applied to the modern day, magic, as contemporary scholars admit, is much less amenable to categorization. No definition of magic has ever found universal acceptance, and countless attempts to separate it from religion on the one hand and science on the other have never been truly successful, because what one group of people may label magic, another would label religion, and another science. By choosing only one of these classifications for magic, we close our minds to other possibilities. We also run the risk of imposing a limiting system of categorization upon societies that would quite simply never have recognized themselves within such a framework.

Given these difficulties, it is sometimes best not to attempt any definition of ancient magic and magical belief. However, in any discussion of magic and its practitioners, we must take account of a period in which the magical traditions of several different cultures coalesced and merged into a type of international and even multicultural magical practice, with its own rituals, symbols and words of power. This occurred in the Mediterranean basin and the Near East from the 1st to the 7th centuries AD, and is the basis of most of the more intellectually based systems of magic.

Magic is, in some ways, a manifestation of the innate human desire for control, and in this period there was a need to control the natural environment, the social world and, eventually, to attempt to control destiny. This underlying desire comes to the surface most often in times of change, as has repeatedly been the case over the last 15 centuries. During this time, the techniques may have been modified but the goals have remained the same. The basic laws of magic still apply today just as they have always done.

One of most interesting characters from this very early period was Abraham Abulafia (1240–95), who made available much arcane knowledge which ultimately formed the basis of the esoteric Jewish system of theology called Kabbalah. Believing in the divine nature of the Hebrew alphabet, he held that God cannot be described or conceptualized using everyday symbols. He therefore used abstract letter combinations and permutations (*tzeruf*) in intense meditations lasting for hours to reach ecstatic states. These were spells in the real sense of the word, since literally they 'spelt out' the keys to altered states of consciousness – failure to carry through these keys correctly could have a far-reaching effect on the careless practitioner. Again, these beliefs have been brought through to the modern day and used to great effect.

The Renaissance period in Europe saw the coming to prominence of many secret societies and scholar-magicians, and because of the burgeoning natural curiosity encouraged by Renaissance principles, a new importance was placed on the actual controlling of the forces of nature. The basis of magic working had previously been seen as harnessing the power of spirits and demons. Now, additionally, the human mind was a factor to be considered, and magical working was geared to gaining power over all of these elements. Much good work was done in understanding the interaction between the spiritual realm and the physical, and how changes can be brought about within the latter. Both Kabbalah and alchemy, a system whose objective was to transform baser metals into gold, became very popular.

By the 17th century, folk magic and witchcraft were being used side by side, often with little differentiation between them. Most people were alternately fascinated and frightened by energies that offered control of nature coupled with opportunities for enormous wealth. James I had himself fallen foul of Scottish witches in that they had tried to control his behaviour during his time as King of Scotland, and as a result he did his best to control pagan belief in his countries. Witchcraft then became more widely identified with demonic or satanic entities opposed to God and therefore wholly evil. A heretic, therefore, was defined as a traitor – an offence punishable by death – and the persecution of those who did not conform to the so-called religious thought of the day became relentless. This caused the practice of witchcraft to go underground, not just in terms of secrecy but in actuality, for example in the use of caves and secret places, such as Wookey Hole in the West Country.

The practice of magic survived, however, and by the 19th century there is evidence that many secret societies, each surrounded by its own unique mysteries, still survived. Often they were formed by highly creative people who were searching for new and different ways of self-expression. Many of the beliefs of these societies were based on the old traditions, though some differed widely from those of the old alchemists. Rituals and invocations were developed which were supposedly based on the ancient rites, often with a very strong bias towards melodrama. Secret societies have also survived into the present day, though not always with full awareness of the fact that their rituals are based on magical practice.

Today there is a rich heritage of magical practices and beliefs on which we can call to satisfy our need for control over our environment and circumstances. Where conventional religion no longer offers a structured outlet for our sense of belonging, we can turn to magical rituals and spell-making to honour our origins. We can make use of the knowledge and practices that have been handed down to us over the centuries and have survived throughout, often in the face of adversity. The principles that form the basis of magical practice still operate today, as do the various belief systems associated with them.

Many of these belief systems take their names from the Greek word *theo*, meaning God. One can be polytheistic (belief in all Gods) yet see all things as being part of one Great Mystery, can be monotheistic (belief in one God) yet recognize that for others there may be many Gods. Alternatively, one might be atheistic (with no belief in God). In the working of magical spells, no one can tell you what to believe – you must make your own decisions. The words 'paganism' and 'pagan' come from the Latin *paganus*, meaning 'rustic' or 'belonging to the country'. Ancient paganism was largely pantheistic, but nowadays the word has come to mean someone who does not recognize the God of the main religions of the world – Christian, Jewish or whatever. We look at paganism in more detail later, but now we give brief explanations of the various theisms to help you decide on a focus for your magic.

POLYTHEISM

Polytheism means that a belief in and respect for all Gods in whatever way they may manifest and in whatever culture. When we begin to work with magic, we rapidly begin to realize that no one way is better than another. There is only one 'right' way, and that is the way that works for each of us as individuals. Some of us, after a little thought and study, may wish to work with Gods, Goddesses, energies and powers from many and diverse religions or belief systems.

Quite frankly, it does not always do to be too fanatical about one system, because often an entity or spiritual energy belonging to another system may be more appropriate to the achievement of our particular goal. So, if you wish to link in to all the wonderful power and energy that is available, you may like to use a kind of general invocation that calls on all of the Gods and Goddesses. You might, for instance, use a form of words such as:

I hereby call upon the Powers that Be to aid me in my task.
May whatever deity from whatever religion which is appropriate to the
task in hand grant me the assistance to complete the work I do tonight.

At the same time, you should be aware of those beliefs in you which are likely to prevent you from using the energy you have available. You might recognize, for instance, that you dislike the idea of Voodoo or are fearful of the more vengeful Hindu Gods. Provided that you acknowledge these fears and are respectful of them, you will not prevent the energy being used. You should also, of course, be aware of other people's beliefs and fears, and be equally respectful of them.

If you are truly a polytheist, then your watchword in everything you do will be 'tolerance' – all you need do is to remember that Divine Energy has made itself manifest through many deities in many ways and in different places and at different times, nor would a true polytheist have it any other way. No single deity can express the totality of the Divine. This can truly be called polytheism – it does not prevent you from calling on your own favourite Gods, Goddesses or powers with whom you have built up a special relationship to help you in your spiritual awareness.

PANTHEISM

Pantheism derives from the idea that the Divine is present in Nature and in each one of us. This is the life force which is cyclical and moves from the beginning through growth to a point of 'blossoming', when it begins to decay, disintegrate and return back to the beginning. It then rests for a time, renews itself and once again grows to fruition. This life force is in everything, and many people like to honour this force and celebrate it in whatever way they feel is appropriate.

This belief was much simpler in days gone by when the ordinary man's life was intimately linked to the stars and planets and their effect on nature. His life was ruled by the weather, the Moon and what he must do to live in harmony with these forces. He quickly learnt that by doing so, he prospered, and that there was a power greater than himself. This energy was honoured in whatever way was appropriate. He would leave an offering for the corn Goddess, carry out rituals to propitiate the storm Gods and worship the spirit of the tree.

Today we can often blind ourselves with scientific knowledge and forget that the energy that is the life force also needs to be cared for. Most pantheists also recognize that we must return to a simpler life if we are to put ourselves back in harmony with nature. They are prepared to revere their own bodies and processes as part of their worship of the Divine.

Although the world has moved on considerably since the days when pantheism was the norm, the power and energy within life today can still be honoured. We can do this by recognizing the beauty of a small urban garden, by taking time to walk among managed woodland and not to 'rape' the Earth by harvesting rocks and crystals mindlessly. You may wish to say a short prayer whenever you deal with the gifts that come from the Earth, maybe using words similar to the following:

Mindful of the goodness of the Earth
and the gifts that are given me,
I give praise to nature and ask guidance
to use them wisely and well.

To work truly with nature, you will need to be aware of the power that is inherent in all living and earthly things. You may well find that you have a different appreciation of the elements and are drawn to different places and areas that are more in tune with your own energy. For instance, you may find that you are constantly drawn to a particular tree or area in woodland, or perhaps to the sea with its many moods. Be guided by your inner self.

Initially, as you put yourself more in touch with nature, you may feel rather silly and somewhat embarrassed by the force of your reactions; this is a time when you need to be tolerant of yourself and recognize that you are putting yourself in touch with your own life force. Pantheism is wholly about the worship of nature and is in many ways the most spontaneous of all the belief systems under consideration here.

MONOTHEISM

Monotheism is usually taken to mean belief in one God – often personalized and usually paternalistic. Rather, it is the existence of a Universal power. The very word 'universe' should make us aware of the power behind this concept and that in the beginning there was only one energy or sound from which everything emanates.

This notion is not so far away from the idea that there is a life energy which exists via the courtesy of a power greater than ourselves. The difficulty arises when we fall into the error of believing that, in the beginning, this Universal power manifested as either masculine or feminine. When we view monotheism in this way, we are making one half of the human race less than the other half. Since we are all equal in the eyes of God, it is irrelevant whether we believe that God was masculine or feminine.

Simple monotheism means that everyone has the opportunity to live as closely as they can to their own ideal. In theory, living in this way would mean there would be no wars and no difficulties between people. Being what we are, we humans cannot often aspire to such purity of thought or indeed reach such heights. If, however, we hold to the belief that there is a power greater than ourselves, albeit one still working on our behalf, then we come close to the idea of one power. Returning to the idea of Universal power having a single 'sound', petitioning or working with that power entails naming it.

A modern-day petition might consist of a form of words such as the following:

Universal God,
Grant me now the right to make use of your power (goodness, etc)
To the Greater Good and in your name.

When you have a belief in one God, this will be the only power that you wish to work with, though you will often work through an intermediary such as Jesus or Mohammed. It is unlikely that you will wish to invoke the power; you are most likely to ask for a blessing or to pray; neither are you likely to feel that it is your energy that has had very much to do with making your actions count.

Probably the greatest discovery that you will make is of your own humility. While it is very true that believers in one God can become fanatical and arrogant, the quality most needed is humility. In the granting of any petition, you will become aware that, however much you have studied, your own knowledge and information is infinitesimal in relation to greater knowledge.

ATHEISM

Atheism is defined as the theory or belief that God does not exist. An atheist, quite simply, has no belief in any deity. However, hidden in that simplicity is a difficulty, in that some atheists will assert that God does not exist while others who claim to be atheists will state that they have no belief that God exists. It is this question of belief that permeates the use of magic and spells for an atheist.

• First, if there is no God, he or she must believe implicitly in their right and ability to call on their own inner energy and power in order to perform spells.
• Second, they must believe in their ability to manipulate the energy.
• Third, they must believe that they are justified in so doing. The smallest hint of uncertainty in any of these areas can alter the mind's ability to function properly on the levels necessary for this work. If the energy is tapped into inappropriately or without the

correct preparation, the subtle energy used can be harmed beyond repair.

A suitable form of words to use might be:

I summon the power that is mine in order to bring about my purpose.
May the result be as I wish.

If the intent is honest and the action totally dispassionate, such a magician takes full responsibility for their actions. It cannot be said, if the spell did not work, 'It was not my fault' or ' It was not meant to be'. The practitioner will act within the knowledge that they are manipulating energy on the physical plane of existence. They would need extensive training and initiation to become adept at believing in, and making efficient use of, the more subtle energies around them.

PAGANISM

This term was often used in a derogatory way by the early Christians. It is this aspect which gives us a clue to the real beliefs held by the original pagan people, for in the early days they would believe implicitly in the power of the Earth and the blessings of the Sun. Their lives were ruled by the vagaries of the seasons and they developed their own ways of placating and supplicating the powers which they perceived as much mightier than themselves. Whether they called them Gods or spirits did not matter; it was important that they developed a relationship with them. Sometimes the powers could be tamed, sometimes they were made angry and would not co-operate. There were times when one power could be called upon to intercede on a person's behalf and other times when one must accept the fate meted out.

NEO-PAGANISM

The most relevant form of paganism to practitioners of magic today is probably neo-paganism. (For the record, the other forms of paganism are shown in the panel opposite.) In their attempts to reconnect with nature, neo-pagans often use the ancient forms of imagery and ritual, but adjusted so that they are more relevant to the needs of modern people.

VARIOUS OTHER FORMS OF PAGANISM

Paleo-paganism: The more remote Australian Bushmen, the ancient Celtic Druids, the pre-patriarchal religions of ancient Europe, including Scandinavia, and those of the Native American peoples can all be described as paleo-pagan. None of these were influenced by other beliefs, and all retained their basic forms of practice and ritual.

Civilo-paganism: In societies where changes in culture and thinking fed into the belief system – for example, in classical Greece and Rome, ancient Egypt and in the sophisticated Aztec religion – the forms of paganism so influenced are described as civilo-pagan.

Meso-paganism: This is a group which has been influenced by a conquering culture but has in turn had an influence on that culture. It usually succeeds in maintaining a separate culture and a separate religious practice; many Native American nations have succeeded in doing this.

Syncreto-paganism: Similar to meso-paganism, this defines a group which has submerged itself into the dominant culture and adopted the external practices and symbols of that culture's religion – thus, voodoo adopts many of the Christian saints as part of its hierarchy.

Many neo-pagan groups developed in the 20th century as a backlash against organized religion. Some of them are shown below.

ASATRU AND OTHER FORMS OF NORSE NEO-PAGANISM

Traditionally there were three races of deities in this polytheistic religion. All are regarded as living beings who are involved in human life:

The Aesir These are the Gods of the tribe or clan, representing kingship, order, craft and so on.

The Vanir These represent the richness of the earth and forces of nature. They are associated with the clan and its wellbeing, but are not part of it.

The Jotnar These are giants who are in a constant state of war with the Aesir. They represent chaos and destruction. On the final day of reckoning, all Gods will die and then be reborn.

CHAOS THEORY

By this notion, all things are unpredictable but can be influenced. The idea arose initially from the ancient myth of Gaea springing from Chaos and becoming the mother of all things. In a later development of the theory, Chaos is the formless matter from which the cosmos, or harmonious order, was created. This matter is ultimately unpredictable, even in the absence of random influences. In chaos magic, change is effected in a sometimes apparently random fashion.

DRUIDISM

In ancient times, druids were the sole possessors of esoteric knowledge. They were reputed to be great magicians capable of all sorts of magic, and it is in this role that they are most often perceived by lay people. Largely Celtic, they seem to have worshipped many Gods and Goddesses, particularly those of nature.

NATIVE AMERICAN PRACTICES

These show a strong bias towards Earth worship and the use of herbs and mind-altering substances. Smudge sticks, sweat lodges and other such practices are employed to enable different perspectives on life. The various beliefs often follow tribal custom.

THE SABAEAN ORGANIZATION

A modern version of the ancient religion of the Chaldeans, who believed that the stars are the celestial homes of the heavenly bodies. It is based on the worship of the outpouring of occult teachings of archaic Mysteries.

MEN'S SPIRITUALITY MOVEMENTS

As women have begun their own search for autonomy, so men also have recognized that there is a spiritual side to themselves and have begun to research and develop their own ways of expressing this, leading to an awareness of a personal magic.

SHAMANISM

The distinguishing characteristic of Shamanism is its focus on an ecstatic trance state in which the soul of the Shaman is believed to leave the body and ascend to the sky (heavens) or descend into the earth (underworld). Shamanism ultimately gives each individual the potential to contact the powers of the Universe for himself without the interference of an intermediary. The truly initiated Shaman possesses genuine humility about his power, recognizing it as a gift that enables him to act as a messenger between two worlds.

THELEMA

This practice is based on the work of Aleister Crowley and his associates, and dates from the early 20th century. Its basic tenet is 'Do what thou wilt is the whole of the law'. It is a way of studying the Mysteries, part of which means understanding the Kabbalah.

WOMEN'S SPIRITUALITY MOVEMENTS

Various movements have arisen as women search for their own ways of expressing their power and dynamism. Often such movements are based on a fresh understanding of the notion of the Triple Goddess and the recognition of the stages of development which women go through as they understand the concept of Maid, Mother and Crone.

WICCA (IN ALL ITS MANY FORMS)

The main traditions and beliefs in the craft include Gardnerian Wicca, Alexandrian Wicca, Dianic Wicca, the Faery tradition, many branches of Celtic-based Wicca and other forms which are often called Eclectic Wicca. Wiccans draw their practices and information from many different sources. They may call themselves Witches, with a capital 'W'.

FOLK MAGIC

Practitioners who incorporate many core magical beliefs in their work with traditional remedies may also be called witches, but this time without the word having a capital letter.

HIGH AND LOW MAGIC

Whichever 'ism' – belief – we subscribe to, and whether we use a specific form of words to put ourselves in touch with subtle power and energy or not, we have to understand – and be able to differentiate between – 'high' and 'low' magic, the two types of magic considered within the pages of this book.

The technical term for that aspect of magic popularly called 'low magic' is Thaumaturgy. This is the use of magic for what might be called non-religious purposes, and is designed to actually change things on the Earth or Material Plane. Many experienced practitioners will not perform such magic because they believe they have no right to interfere with the laws of nature. Others believe that low magic is permissible if the skill is used responsibly and harms no one. Practitioners who choose to use their knowledge indiscriminately must be prepared to take the consequences of their actions and be aware that the laws of cause and effect, or karma, may well catch them out at some future date.

Theurgy, the use of magic to attain a higher state of being, salvation or for personal soul development is often referred to as 'high magic'. It is usually used for religious and perhaps psychotherapeutic purposes or to achieve enlightenment, and it is thought that it is this intent which makes it the best use of magic. Many practitioners of high magic consider it to be the magic of harmony because it uses the idea of the union of positive and negative forces in perfect balance and with supreme control. The results achieved through theurgy may also achieve thaumaturgical ends. In other words, while the intention may be to work for the good of all, the effect may actually be to change things on the physical plane. Practitioners of this kind of magic are fully aware that they must take responsibility for what they do, trusting that they are working in harmony with the forces and energies they are using.

An easy way of differentiating between the two types of magic is perhaps to think of thaumaturgy as using commands, and theurgy as using requests. Such a classification is not totally accurate, but does make it easy for the beginner to make a distinction when deciding on the form of words to use:

'As I will, so be it!'

'I ask in the name of [Goddess and God or The All]
that I [put in your own name] be granted my request ...
I ask that this be fitting and for the Greater Good.'

HERMETICISM

The aim of this belief system, which might be said to form the cornerstone of Western culture, is spiritual growth and the search for spiritual meaning. It is polytheistic in that it arises from many expressions of the Divine, and yet is also ultimately monotheisitic – coming from one source.

Hermeticism takes its name from Hermes Trismegistos (meaning 'Thrice-Greatest Hermes'), the Greek name given by Neoplatonists to the Egyptian God, Thoth, who is said to have dictated 42 books detailing the philosophy of the ancient Egyptians and how they lived. These were translated into Latin by the 15th-century scholar Ficino and called the *Corpus Hermeticum*. In the early 17th century, however, it was discovered that the *Corpus* was a collection of writings of scholars from Alexandria active in the 2nd and 3rd centuries AD.

The basic tenets of the religion are still that:
• The whole of mankind is on a spiritual journey designed to return it to a state of unity with the Mind of God; this is its sole purpose.
• Spiritual growth cannot be achieved without human effort. Therefore, if humanity is to reach the Divine, it must aspire to the Divine.
• The Divine is both within and yet beyond everything.
• The Divine creation of the Universe is ultimately good.
• The Divine can be found in the Mysteries of Nature.

Hermeticism encourages regular use of spiritual and magical practices such as theurgy, meditation and ritual in order to attain access to the higher realms of knowledge.

KABBALAH

Whereas Hermeticism is essentially a belief founded in Graeco-Egyptian thought, Kabbalah belongs to the Jewish tradition. The word 'Kabbalah' comes from the Hebrew root *kbl* which means 'to receive'. The most influential Kabbalistic document, the *Sepher ha Zohar* ('Book of Splendour') was published for popular consumption by Moses de Leon (1238–1305), a Spanish Jew, in the latter half of the 13th century. In some Jewish communities it was ranked as highly as texts such as the *Talmud* as a source of interpretation of the *Torah*. The *Zohar* is a series of documents covering a huge variety of subjects, from esoteric interpretation to discussions on the nature of God. It was – and indeed, still is – highly significant in mainstream Jewish thought.

There was a time when science, philosophy, metaphysics, theology and so-called 'occult sciences' intermingled in a way that is totally beyond our comprehension today. Only recently have we again begun to realize that understanding gained in one discipline can often be applied in other areas. As key texts of the Kabbalah were being translated, it was also being adopted by many Christian mystics, magicians and philosophers. There was a great deal of argument as to whether the Kabbalah held keys that would reveal mysteries hidden in the Scriptures, or whether it contained dogma that might be used to convince Jews of the validity of Christian belief.

In many ways this was a pointless exercise, because Kabbalah held many themes that were recognizable in Hermeticism and Neoplatonism, and were probably therefore part of a greater body of awareness. Part of the problem in understanding was that study of Kabbalah outside the Jewish community tended to concentrate only on the magical and not on other more spiritual aspects. It could be said that from the Renaissance onwards a working knowledge of some aspects of Kabbalah was necessary for virtually all European occult philosophers and magicians, although it has been heavily adulterated at times by other systems of belief.

The most important medieval Kabbalistic magical text is the *Key of Solomon*. It contains all the techniques of classic ritual magic – names of power, the magic circle, ritual implements, consecration and evocation of spirits, among other instructions. It is not known how old it is, but there is reason to believe that its contents preserve techniques that might well date back to King Solomon. In Judaism, it was accepted that a true magician had to have an extensive knowledge of *all* aspects of Kaballah and not just the magical parts.

This knowledge was jealously guarded up until relatively recently, and was only revealed more fully through the work of the French magician Éliphas Lévi and the early 20th-century *Order of the Golden Dawn*. S. L. Mathers and A. E. Waite, popularists of magical practice and Tarot respectively, were knowledgeable Kabbalists. Three Golden Dawn members have given impetus to the modern-day movement: Aleister Crowley, Israel Regardie and Dion Fortune. Dion Fortune's Order of the Inner Light has also produced a number of authors: Gareth Knight, Walter Butler and William Gray, to name a few.

Some of the originators of modern witchcraft (e.g. Gerald Gardner and Alex Sanders) drew heavily on medieval ritual and Kabbalah for inspiration, and many modern practitioners of magic teach some form of Kabbalah, although the intrinsic spiritual knowledge is not always properly integrated into practical technique.

To summarize, Kabbalah is a mystical and magical tradition that originated nearly 2,000 years ago. It has been practised continuously during that time by Jews and also by non-Jews for about 500 years. It has created a rich mystical and magical tradition with its own validity, and also forms the bedrock of much philosophical thought that is still relevant today. Without its wisdom, humanity would be much the poorer.

2

TECHNIQUES OF MAGIC

We have talked of Kabbalah as the root of most modern-day magic. There are many different types of magic which have developed over time, and as a modern practitioner you are fortunate to have so many choices as you undertake your journey. These are 'forms' or different 'techniques' that are applied in order to achieve the end you require. You can use any of them in isolation, or can combine them in ways of your choosing. The only thing you do have to remember is that everything should be appropriate to the work in hand and you should not use a technique if you have any doubts about your own ability regarding that particular aspect of magic.

COLOUR MAGIC

Perhaps the simplest form of magic is that involving colour. This technique is also used in various other forms of magic. Colour can enhance, alter and completely change moods and emotions, and can therefore be used to represent our chosen goal. At its simplest, it can be used alone and in dressing an altar. We give some colour correspondences elsewhere in the book (see pages 96–7 and 189).

HERB MAGIC

To back up the use of colour, we can use Herb Magic. This can also be employed alongside many other forms of magic. Used as talismans and amulets – for example in a pouch or bag – herbs become protective; the oil from herbs can also be used in candle magic. There are many different types of herbs available for use in this way. Each herb has its own specific use, but can also be used in synergy with many other herbs and oils to produce a desired result.

The following is a charm that uses both colour and herbs.

Herbal Charm to Attract Love

YOU WILL NEED

A circle of rose or red-coloured cloth with any of the following: acacia, rose,
myrtle, jasmine or lavender petals, in any combination or singly
Red felt heart
Copper coin or ring
Blue thread or ribbon

METHOD

As you fill the cloth with your items, visualize the type of lover you are looking for.
Tie the cloth with blue thread or ribbon, in seven knots.
As you tie the knots, you may chant an incantation, such as:

Seven knots I tie above,
Seven knots for me and love.

Hang this at your bedhead and await results.

CANDLE MAGIC

As soon as man recognized the power of fire, he found the need
to control it. He eventually found this in the use of Candle Magic,
one of the oldest forms of magic, as well as one of the most simple.
Using candles to symbolize himself and his beliefs meant that he
had access to a power beyond himself. Candle Magic formed an
effective back-up for most other forms of magical working.

CRYSTAL MAGIC

Every stone or gem has its own attribute which can be used
in magic. Crystals are used extensively in healing because of
the vibrational impact they can have. Because of this, they lend
themselves to the enhancement of any spell-making or magical
working. Even ordinary stones have their own power and can be
used as repositories for all sorts of energies and powers.

This next working utilizes Herb, Colour, Candle and Crystal Magic.
(Specific information on the use of each type of magic touched on
here is given throughout the book.)

To Bring Romantic Love to You

YOU WILL NEED
Sprig of rosemary (for remembrance)
A piece of rose quartz crystal
Rose or vanilla incense
1 pink or red votive candle
Small box
Red marker/pen

METHOD
Sit in your own most powerful place (that might be inside, outside, near your favourite tree or by running water).
First, write in red on the box, 'Love is mine'.
Light the incense – this clears the atmosphere and puts you in the right mood.
Put the rosemary and the rose quartz in the box.
Put anything else that represents love to you in the box
(drawings of hearts, poems, or whatever – be creative).
This spell is to attract love to you, not a specific lover,
so don't use a representation of a particular person.

Be in a very positive state of mind.
Imagine yourself very happy and in love.
Burn the candle and say:

I am love, love I will find
True love preferably will soon be mine.

Love is me, love I seek
My true love I will soon meet.

Now sit for a little while and concentrate again on being happy.

Then pinch out the candle and add it to the box.
Let the incense burn out.
Seal the box shut and don't open it until you have found your true love.

When you have found your lover, take the rose quartz out of the box and keep it as a reminder.
Bury the entire box in the earth.

KNOT MAGIC

Knot Magic is both an intriguing and unobtrusive method of working. It works partly with the principle of binding, which is a type of bidding spell but also with that of weaving, as the Three Fates are said to weave our lives. It utilizes ribbon, rope, string, yarn, or anything that can be knotted or plaited to signify our aspiration. It is a type of representational magic, and is used in conjunction with many of the other forms. You might carry the tied desire around with you, wear it as necessary and untie it to represent release. The techniques of colour, form and use of energies are all combined when practising this type of magic.

REPRESENTATIONAL MAGIC

Representational Magic owes a great deal to the practice of voodoo, and involves utilizing an object that represents someone or something for which you are working the spell. It helps in concentrating the energy and visualizing the desire and the end result. Poppets – small dolls – are often used in this type of magic. They are easily made. As you fashion the poppet, think of the person concerned. It often helps to include personal objects or a lock of hair to give the right vibration. Such objects should never be used for negative purposes.

SYMBOLIC MAGIC

Symbolic Magic arises out of Representational Magic. In this system, different symbols are used to represent various ideas, people or goals. These symbols can be personal to you or things such as Tarot cards, Runes, Hebrew letters or numerology. You will often use Symbolic Magic in your rituals and will develop your own symbolic language.

ELEMENTAL MAGIC

In this type of magic, the Elements of Fire, Earth, Air and Water are given their own directional focus to create added power. You will no doubt find that you tend to favour one particular direction, but should be able to use all of them.

Here is a simple ritual to help you to focus. We discuss these Elements more fully later in the book.

To Summon Help from the Elements

YOU WILL NEED
1 white candle (to represent Fire)
Small bowl of salt or sand (to represent Earth)
Small bowl of water
Incense such as bergamot

METHOD
Light the incense and the candle.
Bear in mind as you do so that you are now making use of the Elements of
Fire and Air.
Call upon the power of these Elements (using words such as those given in
the Incantation for the Four Elements on page 63).
Ask for their help in the work you are about to do.

Lift the bowl of salt and likewise invoke the powers of the Earth Element.
Do the same with the water.

When you have finished:
Pour the water on to the Earth.
Bury the ashes of the incense.
Snuff out the candle.

TALISMANS, AMULETS AND CHARMS
These devices use all the other forms of magic in their formation, but principally Representational and Symbolic Magic. They are 'charged' (given power) magically and are usually worn or carried on the person for protection or good luck. Many are worn around the neck, perhaps as jewellery or carried in a pouch, and incorporate crystals, herbs or other magical objects. There are many types of each of these objects, and you will gradually learn to differentiate between them.

CHOOSING YOUR MAGIC
Magic is a highly personal art and sometimes the above categories will become blurred and what you choose to do will defy description. This is absolutely fine, because it suggests that there are no limits to what can be done.

To pique your curiosity, below is a spell that uses many of the types of magic we have been looking at here. Several actions, ingredients or techniques described in the spell may not appear to make much sense at this stage – for example, the instruction to 'cast a circle with the willow wand'. We shall explain this and other techniques shortly. Many of the ingredients are easily found, and you should be able to purchase the herbs from a good herbalist, chemist or even over the internet.

To Ease a Broken Heart

YOU WILL NEED
(Be sure to charge all the ingredients before you begin):

Strawberry tea (one bag)
Small wand or stick from a willow tree
Sea salt
2 pink candles
Mirror
Pink drawstring bag
Quartz crystal
Copper coin
Bowl made of china or crystal that is special to you
1 teaspoon dried jasmine
1 teaspoon orris root powder
1 teaspoon strawberry leaves
1 teaspoon yarrow
10 drops (at least) apple blossom oil or peach oil
10 drops (at least) strawberry oil

METHOD

On a Friday morning or evening (the day sacred to the Goddess Venus), take a bath in sea salt in the light of a pink candle.
As you dry off and dress, sip the strawberry tea.
Use a dab of strawberry oil as perfume or cologne.
Apply make-up or groom yourself to look your best.

Cast a circle with the willow wand around a table on which the other ingredients have been placed.
Light the second pink candle.
Mix all oils and herbs in the bowl.

While you stir, look at yourself in the mirror and say:

Oh, Great Mother Earth,
Nurture and protect me now.
Let me use the strengths I know I have.

Look into the mirror after you have finished mixing the ingredients and say:

Mother of all things,
All that is great is mine,
Help me now to be the person I can be
And let me overcome my difficulty.

Put half the mixture in the pink bag and add the coin and crystal.
Carry the bag with you until you feel you no longer need it.
Leave the other half of the potion in the bowl in a room where you will smell
the fragrance.
Repeat this ritual every Friday, if you so wish.

CONSECRATING A SACRED SPACE

You can see that it is possible to employ aspects from all of the systems of magic or decide to concentrate on only one. It is your choice. However, if you are going to be carrying out a fair number of rituals or spells, you will really need a sacred space or altar along with various other altar furnishings.

Whether your altar is inside or outside does not matter. To set it up indoors, your altar and/or sacred space should preferably be in a quiet place in the home, where it will not be disturbed and where candles can be burned safely.

The space first needs to be dedicated to the purpose of magical working. You can do this by first brushing the area clean, concentrating your thoughts on cleansing the space as you work physically to bring this about. Mentally cleanse the space three times, imagining doing it once for the physical world, once for the emotional space and once spiritually. If you wish, you may sprinkle the whole area with water and then salt (which represents the Earth). You might perhaps also burn incense such as jasmine or frankincense to clear the atmosphere. Think of the space as somewhere you would entertain an honoured guest in your home – you would wish the room you use to be as welcoming as it can be.

If you travel a lot or are pushed for space, you might dedicate a tray or special piece of wood or china for ceremonial working. This, along with your candles and incense, can then be kept together in a small box or suitcase. Otherwise, you could dedicate a table for the purpose. Ideally, you should not need to pack up each time.

You will also need a 'fine cloth' – the best you can afford – to cover the surface. Place your cloth on your chosen surface and spend some quiet time just thinking about its purpose. You may, if you wish, have different cloths for different purposes, or perhaps have one basic cloth which is then 'dressed' with the appropriate colour for each ritual.

SETTING UP AN ALTAR

To turn your dressed table into a proper altar, you will need as basics the following objects:

1. Two candles with candle holders – you might like to think of one representing the female principle and one the male. You may also choose, in addition, candles of a colour suitable for the ritual or spell you are working.

2. An incense holder and incense suitable for the working.

3. A representation of the deity or deities you prefer to work with. An image of the Goddess, for instance, could be anything from a statue of the Chinese Goddess of Compassion, Kuan Yin, to seashells, chalices, bowls or certain stones that symbolize the womb or motherhood.

4. A small vase for flowers or fresh herbs.

Other objects appropriate for ceremonial working, according to your beliefs, are:

• An athame, which is a sacred knife for ceremonial use; it should never be used for anything else.

• A white-handled knife (called a boline) for cutting branches, herbs, etc.

• A burin, which is a sharp-pointed instrument for inscribing magical objects such as candles.

• A small earthenware or ceramic bowl, or a small cauldron, for mixing ingredients.
• A bowl of water.
• A bowl of salt or sand, representing Earth.
• A consecrated cloth, or a pentacle (see below), on which to place dedicated objects.

(For a full explanation of these objects, see pages 44–6.)

Some people additionally use bells for ringing in and ringing out the ritual – some have additional candles with the colours representing both themselves and the work they wish to do. You can also have other items on your altar, such as crystals, amulets and talismans, and perhaps your Book of Shadows or holy books.

A pentacle

You can do what you wish with your own altar, provided you have thought through very carefully your logical or emotional reasons for including whatever you have there. You might, for instance, choose to have differing representations of the Earth Mother from diverse religions or include a pretty gift to establish a psychic link with the person who gave it to you.

DEDICATING AN ALTAR

Now you have turned your space into an altar, dedicate it in such a way that it will support any workings you may choose to do. One good way is to dedicate it to the principle of the Greater Good – that none may be harmed by anything that you may do. (Remember that traditionally any harm you instigate deliberately will return to you threefold, particularly when it comes from such a sacred space.) It will depend on your basic belief just how you choose to dedicate the altar further, perhaps to the Moon deity and all her manifestations, perhaps to the Gods of power.

Try to put as much passion and energy into the dedication as you can, and remember to include a prayer for protection of your sacred space. Some people will need to cast a circle each time they do a working, while others will feel that just by setting the altar up in the way suggested that that space is consecrated henceforth. If you wish to follow the principles of feng shui rather than Wicca within your work, your placings will be slightly different, as they will also be if you choose to follow the tenets of other religions.

However, whatever you do, you should take care to dedicate all of your tools and altar furnishings to the purpose in hand. You are empowering them in a very special way and making them usable only in ritual and magical work. If you try to use them for any other purpose, you will negate that magical power.

CONSECRATING ALTAR OBJECTS

If you are not using completely new objects on your altar – here we are referring to the basic 'furnishings' of candle holders, etc – you should take care to cleanse them first before you dedicate them to your purpose. You should treat them in the same way as you would any crystals you use, by soaking them overnight in salt water to remove anyone else's vibrations and then perhaps standing them in sunshine (or moonshine) to charge them with the appropriate energy.

When you are ready, hold each object and allow your own energy to flow into it, followed by the energy of your idea of Ultimate Power. (That way, you make a very powerful link between yourself, the object and the Ultimate.) Ask this Power to bless the object and any working you may do with it, and perceive yourself as truly a medium or channel for the energy. Hopefully, each time you use any of the objects, you will immediately be able to reinforce that link rather than having to re-establish it. It is like a refrain continually running in the background. Now place the objects on your altar however it feels right for you.

Finally, if appropriate, create and charge your circle so that it includes yourself and your altar, as is shown in Casting a Circle and Forming a Ritual. The magic circle defines the ritual area, holds in personal power and shuts out all distractions and negative energies. You now have a sacred space set up which is your link to the powers that be. It is a matter of personal choice as to whether you choose to rededicate your altar and what it contains on a regular basis.

CASTING A CIRCLE
Purify yourself first. You can do this by meditating or you might take a ritual bath. If you can, try to keep the water flowing, possibly by leaving the bath plug half in, or by having a shower. This reinforces the idea of washing away any impurities so you are not sitting in your own psychic 'rubbish'. (Scent your bath water with your selection of a sacred or special herb or oil.) Ideally, your towel – if you choose to use one – should be clean and used only for the purpose of ritual.

• Wear something special if you can. You might buy or make your own robe (see page 97) or, if not, choose something that you only wear during a ritual or working. You can always add a pretty scarf or a throw in the correct colour for your working. This sets apart rituals from everyday confusion.
• Decide on the extent of your circle, which should be formed in front of your altar. Purify this space by sprinkling the area with

water followed by salt – both of these should have been blessed in a similar way to the blessing of the crystal.

• Meditate for as long as you can inside the area that will become your circle.

• Imagine a circle of light surrounding you. This light could be white, blue or purple. If you are in a hurry and cannot purify and cleanse fully, then also reinforce the circle of light by visualizing it suffused with the appropriate colour for your ritual.

• Circle the light around, above and below you in a clockwise direction, like the representation of an atom. Feel it as a sphere around you or as a cone of power. Sense the power of the sphere or cone and create them to your own design. You might also remember to leave a 'doorway' through which your magic energy may exit, though you can also 'puncture' the energy as suggested below. You should always feel warm and peaceful within your circle.

• Use your own personal chant or form of words according to your own belief system to consecrate your circle and banish all evil and negative energy, forbidding anything harmful from entering your space. Remember, you are always safe within your circle if you command it to be so.

• If appropriate, invite the Gods and Goddesses to attend your circle and ritual.

• Relax and be happy.

If you wish, you can use objects on the ground to show the boundaries of the circle, such as candles, crystals, cord, stones, flowers or incense. The circle is formed from personal power. This may be felt and visualized as streaming from the body to form a bubble made of mist or a circle of light. You can use the athame (ritual dagger) or your hands to direct this power.

The cardinal points of the compass may be denoted with lit candles, often white or purple. Alternatively, place a green candle at the North point of the circle, a yellow candle at the East, a red candle at the South and a blue candle at the West, or use the ritual tools assigned to each point (see pages 44–6). The altar stands in the centre of the circle, facing North in the direction of power.

An Alternative Method of Circle Casting

This method probably owes more to Wicca than any other way, though you do not have to be Wiccan to use it.

YOU WILL NEED
Broom
Candle snuffer
Heatproof dish
Your usual ritual tools
1 red candle (if not using directional candles)

METHOD
Cleanse the sacred space symbolically with the broom.
Place the altar in the centre of the circle facing North.
Set up the altar as already suggested.

Light the candles on the altar.
Start with the Goddess candle (representing the feminine element),
then the God (masculine).
Follow with whichever other candle you may be using.

Light the incense.
Move towards the northern edge of the area you are enclosing.
Hold the left hand out, palm down, at waist level.
Point your fingers toward the edge of the circle you are creating.
(You can, of course, if you wish, use your athame if you have consecrated it.)
See and feel the energy flowing out from your fingertips (or the athame), and slowly walk the circle, clockwise. Think of the energy that your body is generating.

Continue to move clockwise, gradually increasing your pace as you do so.
Move faster until you feel the energy flowing within you.
The energy will move with you as you release it.
Sense your personal power creating a sphere of energy around the altar.
When this is firmly established, call on the rulers of the four directions.

Your circle is now consecrated and ready for you to use.

CONSECRATING YOUR TOOLS

Most magical traditions make use of the familiar magical Elements of Earth, Air, Fire and Water. Some traditions have specific tools that are important to them, such as the scourge used in the Gardnerian tradition, which must also be consecrated. There is also a fifth magical element – that of spirit. The simplest consecration that can be made is to offer each of the objects to spirit so that they may be used for the best purpose possible. You can specifically dedicate any tool using a short invocation such as, 'I dedicate this magical tool to the purpose for which it is intended'. You can, of course, be as creative with your speech as you desire. Anything else that is done will be according to the traditions of your own belief. Below are listed some of the most common tools.

Athame Your athame (or ritual knife) may be purchased new, the shape and size depending on what appeals to you. It is usually black-handled with the blade sharp on both sides to remind us of the power inherent in magic. The athame is used only as a ceremonial tool and never for anything else. Many practitioners inherit their athame, or find that it has come to them in some way.

Cleanse and consecrate your athame before you use it, dedicating it to the Fire Element and the South. It should be noted that some witches attribute it to Air and the East. When placing the athame on your altar, choose whichever direction is appropriate for you.

Besom The besom is used to cleanse the ritual area and keep it sacred. It is a bundle of twigs or hay attached to a handle and often made from woods of known magical significance, such as hazel or ash. Recognize that its presence within the sacred space keeps the latter clear at all times.

Boline This is usually a white-handled knife – a practical working tool used to cut herbs, waxes, resins and so on. It is not used in ritual magic, but to prepare for it. To dedicate it for its purpose, you will use the same correspondences as for the athame. A burin is used to etch candles with symbols and magical signs.

Cauldron or bowl A cauldron is usually thought of as a large cast-iron pot, owing much to the herbal traditions of folk magic. Cauldrons for ceremonial purposes are now being made of various materials, though a simple bowl will also suffice. In the Wiccan tradition, it is said to be associated with the womb of the Goddess. It represents the Element of Water and is essential in Celtic magic. It is often dedicated to the Goddess (usually Ceridwen) and is associated with magical happenings. Its position is usually in the West. During certain spells, candles are set in it and allowed to burn out.

Chalice This is a drinking vessel which is usually used as a ceremonial tool. It is often used to represent femininity. It can range from a very simple design to the more elaborate. The material from which it is made can also vary – from highly decorated precious metals to simple materials such as earthenware. Associated with the element of Water, its natural place is the West. In ceremonies it may hold wine, water or fruit juice, but is sometimes used empty.

Pentacle The word 'pentacle', sometimes erroneously substituted for pentagram, actually refers to a shallow dish (which is usually inscribed with a pentagram – a five-pointed star) and is used as an altar tool by modern Witches. It has a similar use to the 'patten' at a Roman Catholic Mass. Common variations of the pentacle include a dish of earth or silver, or a disk of copper or wax.

When a pentagram is placed within a circle as a symbol of unity and completeness, it highlights our connection with the universe as a whole. This is therefore symbolized by the pentacle. It is used as a power point for consecrating ritual objects, such as water or wine in a chalice, amulets and tools; it is associated with the Earth Element and aligned with the North. It can also be used for grounding stray energy in a room.

If you do not have a pentacle, a white cloth can be used to serve the same purpose. This should also be consecrated first.

Sword Like the wand, the sword is a tool of command. It is like the athame, ruled by the Element of Fire and therefore belongs to the South. It is not used often, but can be necessary for certain spell-workings.

Wand and staff Traditionally, both a wand and staff should be of a wood known for its magical qualities (see pages 162–72). It is better if they are fashioned by the person who will use them. As with all your tools, if you purchase them or have them made, cleanse them before use, then dedicate them by filling them with your own energy as you did with your altar objects. You might also offer them to the appropriate deity (see pages 110–26). Your wand should be no longer than your forearm, and your staff should come to at least shoulder height. Both wand and staff are of the Element Air and are aligned with the East (although some traditions hold that the wand is an instrument of Fire and aligned with the South).

ENDING YOUR RITUAL

When you have finished your ritual or working, remind yourself that you are as pure a channel for the energies that you have called upon as possible. These energies must be returned whence they came, so visualize them passing through you and being returned to where they belong. At the same time, remember that you are blessed by these energies and that you have used them with good intent.

Closing a Circle

Thank the rulers, if you have called upon them, for attending the ritual.

If you use ritual tools, holding your athame, stand at the North.
Pierce the circle's wall with the blade at waist level.
If you wish, simply use your index finger to achieve the same end.

Move clockwise around the circle.
Visualize its power being sucked back into the knife or your finger.
Sense the sphere of energy withdrawing and dissipating.

Let the outside world slowly make itself felt in your consciousness.
As you come back to the North again, the energy of the circle should have disappeared. If it has not, repeat the actions.

If you have laid items to mark out the circle, remove them.
If you have used salt and water, you may save the excess salt for future uses,
but pour the water on to the bare earth.
Bury the incense ashes.

Finally, put out the candles.
Never ever blow them out (some say this dissipates the energy).
Either snuff or pinch them out.

Start with the candles that mark the cardinal compass points,
followed by any others that you might have used.
Put out the one representing the God energy, and finally the Goddess candle.

You can leave the candles to burn out on their own if you wish.
If you wish, put away your tools.

FINDING YOUR SPOT

Each time you perform a ritual, you are putting yourself in tune with the energies that surround you. Always bear in mind that any adjustment that happens in performing magic – or any ritual for that matter – is on the inner planes initially. This adjustment is far more subtle than whatever happens on an outer level; what occurs there is as a result of the changes you make internally. Becoming aware of what is happening on both levels will give you a much better perception of everything around you and how the various interactions take place. Hopefully, you will not feel that you have to have power over these interactions but will approach everything you do in a spirit of co-operation. Ultimately as you become more proficient at making your own personal adjustments, you may even achieve a strong sense of collaboration – that you are very much part of a greater whole. Your own consciousness will become sensitive to the subtle energies available to you and there will be more evidence that you are living in harmony with all aspects of Nature.

Should you wish to work outside, you will become much more conscious of other energies in operation. Working with the power of Nature, you will become aware that each plant, animal, rock and other entity has a particular vibration or resonance. For magic of this type to work properly, you need to be in tune with these particular resonances. The vibrations are capable of uniting in a sort of composite energy that expresses the spirit or power of a particular natural area.

They are not the Elementals, which tend to be a much more raw, untutored energy and therefore more difficult to control. Nature Spirits can be extremely powerful allies; they can include real natural intelligence and are psychically powerful. You should be able to sense Nature Spirits and determine whether they are receptive to a planned ritual. They may well actively participate in magical workings and often will channel tremendous amounts of power into the magic being performed. You will soon get used to the idea that they are there because they want to be, and that this is Nature channelling her power into the magic in her own way. Never try to command Nature Spirits – rather invite their participation – and you may be surprised at the results.

TO SENSE THE NATURAL SPIRIT OF A PLACE

When entering an area of woodland or looking for a site for a ritual, find a place first of all which feels right. It is not possible to describe that feeling; you will simply 'know' that it feels good.

Then do the following, either individually or, if in a group, as a guided meditation.

• Feel the air all around you, relax and put yourself in tune with it.
• Breathe deeply and allow your inner spirit to respond to the subtle energies. At this point you may experience a heightening of perception.
• Picture, if you can, a glow around your solar plexus. As you breathe, begin to feel the glow expand, purifying your body and energizing you. Then allow it to reach beyond you to fill your aura – your energy field.
• Feel yourself glowing, balanced, purified and full of power, becoming at one with the energies around you.
• Seek out and make a connection with your inner or higher self, and begin to feel your intuition operating more fully.

Now become aware of the Elements around you and experience yourself as each of these in turn. You will find that you will adopt your own order. Feel yourself as –

• The Earth, noting how your physical body belongs to but is separate from Mother Earth.
• Fire, the light of the Sun, warm, alive, energizing, allowing everything to live and channelling the power to communicate with Nature.

• The Air, full of life, movement and intelligence, touching everything with which it comes into contact.
• Water, life-giving, refreshing, cleansing, emotional and intuitive, a part of every living thing.
• Finally accept yourself as a blend of all of these Elements.

Now, concentrating on yourself as this completely whole being –

• Experience the glow you worked with previously as love or power.
• Expand the light and love beyond your own immediate boundaries to the surrounding area and feel yourself as part of it.
• Ask permission of the place to use it for your ritual or spell and invite the Nature Spirits to join you.

Realistically, you may feel nothing at all, in which case you may assume that you can continue. Any unease means that you should stop, whilst if the area goes still and seems to be waiting, you may continue –

• Communicate why you have come, either by thought or words spoken aloud. Invite the spirits to join in sharing with you and the work you intend to do.
• Visualize the energy you are channelling extending out as far as it can go and merging with the energies that belong to the rest of the cosmos.
• Feel the power of the Earth flowing up through your feet and body.
• Feel the power from the sky and channel this power outwards, combining it with the power of the Earth, if you can. This can happen together or separately, and is used for communicating with Nature.
• See the energy expanding and merging with the other energies around.

Now become even more aware –

• Close your eyes; sit on the Earth, if you can, and sense your deep connection with it while allowing more light, love and energy to flow through you.

• Invite receptive spirits to join you and to make themselves known. Be alert to signals that may vary from inner feelings to physical senses or perceptions. The experience is yours and unique to you.

• If you are part of a group, someone might start playing a drum at a rate of about one beat per second, or a flute or similar instrument; you should listen to the rhythm and let it take you deeper.

• Let the rhythm and the connections you have made awaken the part of you that most naturally communicates with other life forms.

• Confirm that you work with natural forces, that you are one who knows, understands and communicates with Nature.

• Let this part of yourself become part of your consciousness. Let it awaken your inner senses and allow yourself to receive as well as give out information.

When you feel ready, slowly open your eyes and look around, while remaining aware of the energy flowing both from and to you. You will probably sense light or a powerful energy coming from certain areas that have responded to your awareness. It is difficult to say what to expect, but you may test your perception by requesting a different signal for positive and negative responses. The light might become brighter or dimmer, for instance. You may get other signals, such as a feeling of power or love returning from a certain direction. Perhaps the type of response to this work will be unexpected; simply follow your intuition in interpreting it.

You are now ready to begin with your chosen ritual. Do not be too surprised, however, if it no longer seems necessary. The stating of the intent is often enough to have it taken care of by the Nature Spirits and your energy is better used elsewhere. Do not be disappointed; simply acknowledge the help you have had and promise to return another time. Simply use your intuition, for the more you use the particular spot, the more powerful it can become.

NATURE SPIRITS

As you become more proficient, you may find you can actually see as well as sense Nature Spirits. Dryads are the principal Nature Spirits, mainly of forests and trees. Each category of Dryad has a particular magical significance and tends to work with only one aspect of Nature, though they will also take responsibility for what surrounds their own particular domain. Thus, some will work with groves, valleys and trees, but will protect the source of water which helps to nurture their charges, such as grottoes, streams and lakes.

Dryads were known in all the Celtic countries. The Celts believed them to be spirits who dwelt in trees, and were very careful to pay them respect. The Druids believed they were inspired by Dryads, particularly by those that lived in oak trees. The Greeks and Romans believed that flocks and fields were protected by them and that they could give the gift of prophecy.

Nymphs and Dryads were companions of the God Pan, particularly in his aspect of Nature God. You can also make them your companions, either in your own garden or your special place. You have already become aware of the energy within a particular place. Now you can begin to learn a little more about the Dryads.

Calling the Dryads

YOU WILL NEED
Birthday cake candles of different colours
Ice cream sticks or nutshells such as walnuts
Water in a natural pool, pond or bowl

METHOD
Use different-coloured candles to attract different 'families' of Dryad.
Fix the candles into the half shells or on to the slivers of wood with hot wax.
(This can be very fiddly, but be patient. Use half candles if this is easier.)
Light each candle with a blessing and float your boats on the surface of the water.
Send loving thoughts to the Nature Spirits and ask them to join you.

You might use an invocation such as:

Awake you spirits of the forest green
Join me now
Let yourselves be seen.

Now sit quietly and just listen.
Shortly you will sense the presence of the Dryads, often as there are strange rustlings in the trees or vegetation.

You may feel them as they brush past you or play around you.
Initially, you will probably not be able to differentiate between them, but as time
goes on, you will sense subtle differences.

Half close your eyes and see if you can see them.
Don't be too disappointed if nothing happens immediately; just accept that
you will be aware of them eventually.

Now invite them to play with you:

Come, Dryads all, come join with me
Explore Earth, Sky, Sand and Sea
Show me, guide me, take my hands
Together thus, we see new lands
New vistas, new horizons and knowledge of old
Come together, in power enfold.

When they are comfortable with you, and you with them, thank them for coming
and leave the area tidy.

You can leave the candles to burn out if it is safe to do so.

FORMING A RITUAL

The ritual given above has been used for calling on the Dryads. You
do not have to use rituals that have been prepared by someone
else, nor do they have to be according to one set of beliefs, unless
you so choose. Indeed, in many ways the broader your focus, the
more knowledge you will gain and the more successful your spell-
casting will be. If you have developed your own rituals, they will
have more meaning. Anything given in this book may be altered
according to your own understanding. If you bear in mind the rules
of magic, you can do almost anything you want to. The practical
suggestions given below to construct a ritual are only ideas to give
you a framework in which to operate.

Type of ritual Decide what kind of ritual you are initiating. You
will learn more about this as you progress through the book. Let us
suppose, for instance, that you wish to rid your house of negative
influences. This would be a banishing ritual or one to create a good
atmosphere that would be an invocation or blessing.

Purpose of the ritual Use your imagination to its full extent and have a very clear concept of what you want to do and how you want to do it. Also think about what tools, if any, you will need – tools such as candles and herbs you might require are discussed later in the book. For a simple spell, you will need only yourself and the energies at your disposal.

Ritual preparation A well thought-out spell or ritual is like a piece of music that you have just learned to play. You know what you are doing and are not likely to make mistakes. Attempting to cast a spell without having thought it through or planned it properly can have unforeseen reactions. These could rebound on you, just as using muscles without warming them up can be very painful. Prepare the words you intend to use carefully; it is often easier if you write them down. Make sure they express your intention fully and ensure no negative words are included. Words do not have to be in rhyme, unless you prefer it that way.

Open the circle Perceive your energy as being contained in the centre of your being – in your solar plexus initially, though this may change as you become more proficient. To cast a circle, either for magical working or to protect yourself, simply enlarge the field from your centre to whatever size is needed for the task you plan to perform. To protect your home, for instance, you would see your influence spreading in a circle to the boundaries, whether that is simply the walls of your home or your garden. As time goes on, you will find that you are developing a sensitivity to what is positive and what is negative energy. Permit only positive energy in, and push away from yourself any negatives that you may sense. You may find that a spontaneous image arises – such as a conduit or filter –that allows you to do this.

Invocation to deities, spirits or helpers Here you call on deities or spirits that are relevant to the work in hand. In the case of your home, you might, for instance, call on the Roman household Gods, the Lares, for their assistance, or invoke the Spirit of the Household to keep a happy atmosphere. Suitable deities are discussed on pages 110–26.

Statement of purpose The repetition of the purpose of the ritual is important and it should be done with feeling. You must repeat it at least three times – and preferably nine – in order to gain maximum benefit (incidentally, the novena prayer used in the Catholic Church follows the same principle of nine repetitions). Repeating the request three times means also that any negative spirit or influence has been challenged and that everything is done with the best intention.

Actual working The power raised in rituals is contained within the circle until it is released as a spell or a gift to the Gods. In working to create the circle, you have become aware of how to manipulate energy and asked for additional help and energy from the Gods and helpers; you now have to apply yourself to sending the energy out of your body instead of using it in a self-involved manner. You might do this by allowing it to flow through you and reach out to the edges of your circle and beyond, to where you want it to reach. To bless your home, you would allow the energy to flow out and fill the circle you created as far as its boundaries, whereas to make your home attractive to others you would reach out beyond the boundaries to encompass those with whom you wish to share your home.

Meditation At this time, it is good to contemplate quietly what you have done in working your ritual. Send the energy on its way with love and respect, recognizing that things must now change. Be prepared to take responsibility for your actions. Be ready at this point to let go of the past and to accept the future with all its joys and sorrows. Visualize, if you can, the outcome of your spell or ritual and be content with what is happening. In the case of your home, you will recognize the changes as they begin to happen, perhaps as people are happy to stay with you or go away from your house refreshed.

Thanking the deities By raising the energy ourselves, we show the Gods that we are willing to work for what we want. In any ritual it is wise to thank the deities or spirits who have assisted you. In blessing your house, you might perhaps have called upon the ancestors to help you. Now is the time to acknowledge them if you wish, to thank them for having given you life and to ask for their protection in the future as you go about your everyday business.

Closing the circle Close the circle by shrinking it back within yourself, almost like drawing a huge bubble of energy back in to your centre. Sit quietly for a few moments and become aware of your surroundings in the ordinary everyday world. Because you have been in an altered state of consciousness, make sure you are properly grounded within your own body by touching the ground or running your hands over your own body from head to feet to settle your energies down.

You can change these steps around or add some as you see fit.

WORKSHEETS FOR RITUALS, SPELLS AND FORMULAE

Traditionally, spells, formulae and rituals were recorded in the Grimoire which, of late, has become known as the Book of Shadows. There is often controversy over whether one's magical books should be called a Grimoire or a Book of Shadows. Really it depends on which traditions of magic you have been taught.

The word 'Grimoire' simply means 'a book of learning'. It came to mean the records kept by true practitioners of magic as they wrote down the secret keys they discovered as they progressed along the path of initiation. The best-known Grimoire was the translation of one made widely available at the beginning of the 20th century – that of King Solomon. This book was of great antiquity and traditionally is seen as the magical key to the Kabbalah. In truth, it was the key to the Mysteries and has since formed the basis of other magical systems as we have seen when considering neo-paganism.

The first Book of Shadows is said to have been written by Gerald Gardner as he developed modern Wicca in the 1920s. It does not serve as a diary, but reflects religious rituals, their modifications and any other workings that need to be recorded.

Both books were traditionally secret writings. Particularly in the case of the Grimoire, they might be written in Runes, pictures or magical alphabets so that the contents were hidden from the uninitiated. The Book of Shadows follows the same principle, although obviously with modern communication much of what used to be hidden is more readily available.

Most solitary practitioners will treasure the records of their workings, whether they choose to call it a Book of Shadows or a Grimoire. Either book becomes part of a rich tradition.

Any self-respecting practitioner will both want and need to keep a record of all of these aspects of magic for future reference. You will need to find an easy way of remembering what you have done.

Utilizing the worksheets and the respective headings below will help you to do this.

These can also be used, should you wish, with modern technology. Computer or phone apps can be tremendously helpful to the modern-day witch in keeping a Grimoire in a fashion that is suitable for passing on to other people.

SPELLS AND FORMULAE RECORD SHEET

Type of spell or formula This should state very clearly what the type of spell is, e.g. blessing, binding, protection, etc. When developing formulae for lotions and potions, for instance, you need to be clear as to the exact purpose.

Date and time made This gives a cross-reference if you wish to use the correct magical days or planetary hours (see pages 131–33).

Reference You should develop your own system of reference; this might be, for instance, according to the time of year or alphabetically. Do remember to keep safely somewhere a record of how you have developed your reference system so that others may benefit from your experience.

Astrological phase If you have an interest in astrology, you will probably want to record where the planets are when you prepare the spell or formula. A decent ephemeris (list of planetary positions) can be of great help here, though there are also many sources of information online.

Specific purpose You should always state the specific purpose of the spell or formula very clearly. This is partly because it helps to focus your own mind, but also because it leaves no one in any doubt as to your intentions. Should you have more than one main purpose, you should also record these.

List of ingredients and/or supplies needed Having all your ingredients to hand within that space ensures that you are working with maximum efficiency and not misusing or needing to adjust the energy by leaving the sacred space. Also, when you repeat a working you will need to replicate what you did the first time; even one small change in ingredients can make a tremendous difference to the outcome.

Specific location required You may well need to perform some rituals and spells within a certain area or setting – the spell associated with Nature Spirits, for instance, is obviously best performed in the open air. Also, you may discover that your own energy responds to some locations better than others.

Date, time and astrological phase when used In all probability you will not want all your spells to take effect at the time you cast them. Let us suppose you have applied for a job and wish your spell to work at the time of interview. When casting your spell, probably the night before the event, you would need to carefully calculate the date, time and astrological phase of the interview, as well as the time you are actually casting your spell and incorporate both sets of information into your working. Here you would be using planetary hours, which you will learn about later.

Results Carefully record all aspects of results you feel are associated with your working. This record should include how successful you consider the spell to be and how it might be improved.

Deities invoked during preparation and/or use Knowledge of the Gods and Goddesses helps you to choose the ones most appropriate for the purpose in hand. More specifically, knowing which deities are the most powerful for you gives you the opportunity to be a good practitioner.

Step-by-step instructions for preparations and/or use Often when spell-working, movements and words are intuitive and instinctive; the more you are able to remember what you did, the more likely you are to achieve similar results. Also, should you require them for someone to work on your behalf or to undertake someone else's magical training, you will have an exact record.

Additional notes Here you should record for each occasion anything that seems strange, bizarre or noteworthy so that you know what to expect next time.

RITUAL RECORD SHEET

Type of ritual There are many types of ritual, as we have seen, and here you will record whether it is one of invocation, honouring, supplication (asking a favour) or thanks.

Date and time made It will help if you are consistent in how you record this, e.g. time (am or pm)/date/month/year.

Moon phase and astrological correspondences As you become more proficient, you will wish to become more accurate and will want to be sure that you have drawn in all the power that you can. In the making of talismans and amulets, particularly creating the best conditions for success means knowing the Moon phases and astrological correspondences.

Weather The weather conditions can have a profound effect both on your mood and on the way in which your ritual is carried out. A ritual honouring Thor or Mars (both Gods of war) would have more energy done during a thunderstorm, for instance.

Physical health Your health is important in any magical working. You owe it to yourself to make sure you are as well as you can be. Remember that you are as much an instrument or tool as articles such as your incense holder or athame. You would not, after all, wish to use a contaminated incense holder during your workings.

Purpose of ritual This should always be stated very clearly, along with any secondary purpose or agenda. You might, for instance, wish to honour Brigit on her day of 1 February, but also wish to gain her help for a pet project. Both intents should be stated and a suitable form of words chosen.

Tools and other items required You should list carefully how you laid out your sacred space and what you used for this particular ritual. You might well find yourself motivated to use a particular herb or object, for instance, and unless you record it, you may not remember why in future.

Deities or energies invoked You should start off any ritual with a clear idea of the specific energies you require for success. According to your own beliefs, that may require the presence of a particular God or Gods. If you find yourself invoking or calling on a specific energy, then acknowledge that by keeping a record of it. Even a simple candle lit to help someone uses energy and requires dedication.

Approximate length of ritual This is recorded so that you know, should you wish to repeat the ritual, that you have enough time in which to carry out your allotted task. If a ritual takes half an hour and you only have 20 minutes, you are not treating yourself, the ritual or the powers you are calling upon fairly if you hurry the process.

Results of ritual Carefully record the results of your ritual, how you felt, how the energy has changed and so on.

Ritual composition Again, record in your own words exactly what you did and how. Most rituals have a basic form, but your input is important, and what you do intuitively is just as important as the basic form. During your rituals, do not be surprised if you find yourself performing an action you would not expect. Just go with the flow, but remember that you are in charge.

Additional notes Note down anything else you need to remember; for example, how you might improve the ritual the next time, peculiar feelings or occurrences and specific thoughts and ideas that might come to you.

WHAT IS A SPELL?

With a little thought, it can be seen that casting a spell is, in essence, very similar to saying a prayer. Indeed, it is more than probable that the latter arose from the former. In early Shamanistic societies, for instance, the elders of the community had access to certain knowledge (and therefore power) that was not available to the ordinary individual. As a consequence, their words would have more power. So it was initially with the priests and clerics of other religions.

Words spoken with intensity and passion have a power of their own. The speaker also has a power and an energy which, with practice, they may learn to focus. The forces and powers belonging to that which is beyond the human being are – according to the beliefs of the supplicant – called upon, utilized or directed for a specific purpose. The use of all three of these aspects gives a very powerful spell. There are several kinds of spell, each of which requires a different approach.

The invocation This calls on what is believed to be the ultimate source of power, which differs from spell to spell. Quite literally, it calls up that power and asks for permission to use this influence for a stated purpose. Such invocations are an important part of ritual and ceremonial magic, and are most feared in the calling up of malign and powerfully negative forces.

Meddling with these forces is very unwise unless the practitioner is in control of both themselves and the forces they unleash. Spells for personal power or to gain power will often backfire on the unwary and may cause damage to the individual who casts them.

This is why a practitioner of the black arts is supposed to be totally dispassionate (not care about the results of their actions) in their use of power, since they cannot afford to have any fear at all lest the negative energy comes back to give them trouble.

This book hopefully will help you to recognize the tremendous propensity for good – both in yourself and others – which makes the use of the black arts redundant. Invocations of positive forces can do no real harm, except the results can be highly disconcerting due to the sheer energy created, although the eventual outcome may be good.

The incantation This second type of spell prepares the practitioner and his helpers for further work by heightening their awareness. It does not set out to call up the powers. Chanting, prayer and hymns are in many ways incantations, particularly when the intent is stated with some passion. An incantation is often very beautiful and rhythmic.

Love spells Many people, when thinking of spells, think of love spells – ways of making another person find one sexually attractive and desirable. By their very nature, this third type should be entirely unselfish and free from self-interest, and yet most of the time obviously cannot be so unless they are performed by a third party, someone outside the longed-for relationship. To try to influence someone else directly may well go against the ethics of many practitioners and magicians, though such spells do tend to be the stock-in-trade of many Eastern practitioners. These spells are often accompanied by gifts or love philtres that are also meant to have an effect on the recipient. Really such spells come under the heading of 'bidding spells' and therefore must be used carefully.

Bidding spells These are spells where the spell-maker commands a particular thing to happen, without the co-operation of those involved. Trying to make someone do something they do not want to do, or which goes against their natural inclination, obviously requires a great deal of power and energy and can possibly misfire, causing the originator of the spell a good deal of difficulty. For this reason it is probably wise to preface such spells, where they are perceived as being necessary, with words to signify that the occurrence will only be in accord with the Greater Good – that is, that in the overall scheme of things no one will be harmed in any way whatsoever. This nullifies any possibility that the intent behind the spell is not of the purest, or that there is any maliciousness within the practitioner. It does mean that an able and responsible practitioner must choose their words carefully, even when they are not casting a spell.

One type of bidding spell that is allowable is when a curse or 'hex' is being removed. A hex is a spell that ill-wishes someone and in many cases binds the recipient in some way. A curse is a spell with a much more generalized effect. Many curse tablets – which were often made of lead – unearthed in archeological excavations show this admirably. Here is part of one such example:

'I conjure you, holy beings and holy names; join in aiding this spell, and bind, enchant, thwart, strike, overturn, conspire against, destroy, kill, break Eucherius, the charioteer, and all his horses tomorrow in the circus at Rome.'

To remove such a negative spell, it is usual to turn it around and send the malign energy back to the person who summoned it in the first place! You simply command the energy to return from whence it came.

Blessings These might be counted either as prayers or spells, and need a passionate concentration on bringing, for instance, peace of mind or healing to the recipient. They cannot damage the practitioner but are often more difficult to operate, since they tend to be more general than other types of work. They may be thought of in terms of a positive energy from beyond the practitioner being channelled towards a specific purpose.

Saying Grace is a form of blessing preceded by an offer of praise and a prayer of thankfulness, an acknowledgement of a gift of food. The food is enhanced by the act and the blessing is given by drawing on the power vested in the knowledgeable expert. Thus, one practitioner may call on the Nature Gods, whereas another might call on the power of Jesus Christ.

Healing spells and charms In the case of such spells and charms, various objects such as crystals are charged with energy and power to focus healing or other energies in a quite specific way, often to remind the patient's body of its own ability to heal itself. Within this type of spell, it is wise to go beyond the presenting symptoms and to ask for healing on all levels of existence – physical, mental and spiritual – because the practitioner may not have the knowledge or correct information to enable them to diagnose a condition correctly. The natural energies and specific vibrations are enhanced by invocations, incantations and blessings, wherever appropriate.

To understand the difference between the various actions, let us assume that you have decided to protect the place where you live from all harm, to bless it and to make it a pleasant place for someone to share it with. You also wish to leave it secure when you go away.

Invoking the Household Gods

This ritual is best performed during the waxing Moon. It could be considered a kind of birthday party, so feel free to include food and drink as part of it, if you so wish.

YOU WILL NEED
An incense that reminds you of herbs, forests and green growing things
A green candle in a holder
Your wand
Small statues of deer or other forest animals
Pine cones, ivy, holly, or something similar
Symbol appropriate to your guardian (e.g. a crescent Moon for
the Moon Goddess)

METHOD
Decorate the area around the symbol of your guardian with the greenery.
Clean the guardian symbol so that there is no dust or dirt on it.
If the symbol is small enough, put it on the altar, otherwise leave it nearby.

Light the incense and candle.
Stand before your altar and say:

Guardian spirits, I invite you to join me at this altar.
You are my friends and I wish to thank you.

Take the incense and circle the guardian symbol three times, moving clockwise
and say:

Thank you for the help you give to keep this home clean and pleasant.

Move the candle clockwise around the symbol three times and say:

Thank you for the light you send to purify this space and dispel the darkness.

With the wand in the hand you consider most powerful, encircle the symbol again
three times clockwise and say:

I now ask for your help and protection for me, my family and all who live herein.
I ask that you remove trouble-makers of all sorts, incarnate and discarnate.
I thank you for your love and understanding.

Stand with your arms upraised.
Call upon your own deity and say:

[Name of deity], I now invoke the guardian of this household whom I have invited
into my home.
I honour it in this symbol of its being.
I ask a blessing and I add my thanks for its protection and friendship.

Incantation for the Four Elements

Drumming and chanting help to raise the vibration in any incantation.
Always keep your words simple. A good example would be:

Spirit of Fire
Spirit of Earth
Spirit of Air
Spirit of Water
Join with me now.

Then state the purpose of your ritual. You might also use the names of the
Gods or Goddesses (see pages 110–26).

Love Spell to Bring Someone into Your Life

This spell can be used to attract love or to draw a companion closer. It should be started on the night of a New Moon.

YOU WILL NEED
1 salt shaker and 1 pepper shaker (or two objects which obviously make a pair)
A piece of pink ribbon about 3 feet (1m) long

METHOD
Assign one article as the feminine person and one as masculine.

Take the piece of pink ribbon and tie the female object to one end and the male to the other, leaving a good length of ribbon between them.

Every morning, untie the ribbon, move the objects a little closer together, and retie the knots.
Eventually the objects will touch.

Leave them bound together for seven days before untying them.
By this time, love should have entered your life.

Bidding Spell — Cleansing a Place of Old Influences

This spell incorporates methods used in American Indian rituals. A smudge stick is a bundle of dried herbs that cleanse and clear the atmosphere to make it suitable for a different purpose (see page 176). There is a knack to lighting a smudge stick, so we suggest long-stemmed matches (and a healthy pair of lungs!).

YOU WILL NEED
Smudge stick
An oyster or seashell (to help waft the smoke)

METHOD
Light the smudge stick and blow on it gently until it is well alight.
(It should be kept alight throughout the ceremony.)
Move clockwise around the house and clockwise around each room in turn.
Waft the smoke in front of you as you go.

(Make sure you do this thoroughly, ensuring that all the corners are included.)
Repeat this action three times in each room:

I command negativity, fears, problems, habits and bad influences to be gone.

A Blessing – A Crystal for the Home

You can use your altar for this blessing, but you can also simply use your own power coupled with the energy of the environment and of your particular deity (see pages 110–26). The crystal becomes like a generator of spiritual power within the home, so we suggest that you stand in a spot that you estimate is as close to the centre of your home as possible.

YOU WILL NEED
A suitable crystal (e.g. rock crystal or rose quartz)

METHOD
Holding the crystal, imbue it first with your own energy, then the power of your particular deity.
Ask for a blessing for both the crystal and your home.
(It is best if you use your own form of words for this and keep it as simple
as possible.)

When you have finished, place the crystal somewhere prominent where its beauty and energy can be appreciated.

Ring of Protection

In this method of working, you place a protective shield around your home so that no harm can come to either it or the people therein.

YOU WILL NEED
The power of your own mind

METHOD
Visualize a ring of light surrounding your property.
Ask your guardians or deities to protect it and its occupants for as long
as necessary.

Reinforce the circle of light whenever you go away, or whenever you think about it.

3
LOVE, MONEY AND JOB SPELLS

Earlier we defined 'low' magic as the use of magic for what might be called 'non-religious' purposes, and stated that it is designed to bring about change on the earth or material plane. We also warned against using love spells as a way of influencing someone in an inappropriate way. Spells to attract love or money are so appealing to the majority of people, however, that it would be somewhat remiss of us not to include a section on them. So, beyond imploring you to question your motives to the nth degree to prevent your becoming caught up in an irresponsible cycle of change for change's sake, here is a selection of spells and techniques to satisfy your curiosity.

Much of what is included here comes from Romany lore. Any itinerant population, such as the Romanies, develop customs to help bind them together. Many of their magical ideas are also seen in agricultural communities or those associated with the natural cycles of birth and death. People used materials that were to hand – such as apples or leaves – to find out information or produce an effect. Little was required in the way of altars and tools. Where candles, herbs and fruit are specified here, you will find fuller explanations of their various properties later in the book.

Colours are also important in spell-making, but for now it is enough to know that pink signifies love, red passion and green money. You also need to know that Friday is the day sacred to Venus, the Roman Goddess of Love, and therefore has added power when performing love spells.

LOVE SPELLS
This section covers most aspects of love relationships. Found here are spells to attract a person, ostensibly to bewitch them,

to strengthen attraction, reign in an errant lover and get rid of an unwanted lover, and there are even ones to deal with a broken heart. The passion with which you perform the spells is important, so feel free to use your own words or herbs.

Discovering a Lover's Initials

If you wish to find out the initials of a future partner's first or last name, use this Romany custom. (The rhyme or charm commemorates two Christian saints. It is possible that the references are ironic.)

Take an apple and peel it, without allowing the peel to break.
Holding the peel in your right hand, say the following:

Saint Simon and Saint Jude,
On you I intrude,
With this paring, to discover,
The first letter of my own true lover.

Turn around three times in a counter-clockwise direction before throwing the peel over your left shoulder.
The peel is said to fall in the shape of your future lover's initial.

Another technique to bring about the same result is to hang the peel inside the entrance to your home.
The first person who enters will bear the same initial as your future lover.

True Love or Illusion?

Another custom is to take an apple seed and give it the name of your lover.
Place it in the embers of a fire.
If it pops, the person loves you; any other reaction and it isn't true love.

To divine if a couple will stay together – remembering that Romany marriage was for life – drop two apple seeds together into the embers of a fire.
If they both fly off in the same direction, the relationship will be a lasting.

To Find a New Lover

This spell works best if is performed at the time of a New Moon. All the materials you use should be new, so that you change the basic vibration and can look forward with hope to new and better times.

YOU WILL NEED
A heart-shaped rose petal or a red heart cut out of paper
Clean sheet of white paper
A new pen
A new candle (preferably pink)
A new envelope

METHOD
On the day of a New Moon, cut a red heart out of paper or card.
Take a clean sheet of white paper and write on it with the new pen:

As this heart shines in candlelight,
I draw you to me tonight.

Bathe and change into nightclothes.
When ready, light the candle and read the spell out loud.
Hold the heart in front of the flame and let the candlelight shine on it.

Place the heart and spell in a new envelope.
Seal it with wax from the candle.

Conceal the envelope and leave it untouched for one cycle of the Moon (28 days).
By the time the Moon is new again, there should be a new love in your life.

To Beckon a Person

This is a simple method of putting out a vibration which, if the relationship has a chance of succeeding, will make the other person aware of you. It does not force the other person to do anything; it simply paves the way.

METHOD
Say the following:

Know I move to you,
As you move to me.

As I think of you,
Think also of me.

As I call your name,
Call me to you.
Come to me in love.

Say the person's name three times (if known).
You may need to recite the whole spell several times in order to feel the proper effect.

For a Lover to Come to You

This spell is reputed to work very quickly. Red candles represent passion, so you must take responsibility for whatever happens when you call your lover to you.

YOU WILL NEED
2 silver pins
A red candle

METHOD
Stick two silver pins through the middle of a red candle at midnight.
Concentrate on your lover.
Repeat their name several times.

After the candle burns down to the pins, your lover will arrive.

To Achieve Your Heart's Desire

This is quite an effective spell and does give you something to do while you are waiting for true love!

YOU WILL NEED
A fresh rose – preferably red and perfumed
2 red candles

METHOD
Find out the time of the next sunrise.
Just before going to sleep, place a red candle on either side of the rose.

The next morning at sunrise, take the rose outside.
Hold the rose in front of you and say:

This red rose is for true love.
True love come to me.

Now go back inside and put the rose between the candles again.
Light the candles and visualize love burning in the heart of the one you want.

Keep the candles burning day and night until the rose fades.
When the rose is dead, pinch out the candles and then bury the rose.

To Strengthen Attraction

If you love someone but feel that they are not reciprocating, try this spell. Be aware, though, that by doing this you are trying to have a direct effect on the other person. Before you perform it, you should have tried to work out why they seem indifferent and consider whether what you are proposing is appropriate.

YOU WILL NEED
A few strands of the person's hair
Rose-scented incense stick

METHOD
Light the incense.

Repeat the name of the one you long for, saying each time:

[Name], love me now.

Hold the hair on the burning incense until it frizzles away.
As the hair burns, think of the person's indifference dissipating and being replaced
by passion.
Leave the incense to burn out.

To Have Your Love Returned

This spell is more complicated because it requires an understanding of
symbolism. The objects you use need not be the real things; they can be
miniaturizations such as cake decorations (see charms on pages 200–15).
The horseshoe represents luck in love, the key represents the key to your
heart, and the gold candle represents the relationship. Traditionally, the
pink candle represents the female and the blue the male, so adjust your
colours accordingly.

YOU WILL NEED
1 pink candle
1 blue candle
1 gold candle
Horseshoe
Key
2 roses
An article of the person's clothing (failing that, use something of your own)

METHOD
On a Friday, light the pink and blue candles (pink first if you are female,
blue if male), followed by the gold.
Place the horseshoe and key on either side of the candles, with the roses
between them.

When the candles have burnt down, wrap the flowers, key and horseshoe
in the clothing.
Place the items in a bedroom drawer and leave them alone for 14 days.

If the flowers are still fresh, this is a good sign.
Then bury them or put them (along with the horseshoe and key) in a potpourri.

To Bring a Loving Relationship to You

This spell is looking for true love, not a particular person. It is a very gentle working that uses natural rhythms to achieve its ends.

YOU WILL NEED
Rose petals (preferably wild)
A natural source of moving water (not a household tap)

METHOD
Visualize a person with the qualities of your ideal mate.
Collect the petals.
Take the petals to any source of moving water.

Throw the petals into the water and say:

As this rose moves out to sea,
So true love will come to me.

Repeat the incantation, again visualizing your ideal mate.

To Enhance Your Attractiveness

This spell is as much about changing your attitude to yourself as it is about influencing someone else. The better you feel about yourself, the easier you will find it to attract others.

YOU WILL NEED
3 candles (red, pink or white)
A clean bathroom (to give you a fresh start)
Salt
White or pink cloths or towels (to cover the mirrors)
Special lotions, potions or incense that please you
Relaxing music

METHOD
Clean your bathroom very well.
If you have any mirrors in your bathroom, cover them with the cloth or towels.
(You are creating a new image and do not wish to fall into the old one.)

Light your incense (if using).
Run a warm bath.
Add a handful of salt and any other cleansing potions to it and say:

I am renewed from today,
Negativity washed away,
The one I desire will choose to stay.

Light the candles.
Concentrate on your good points.
If there is someone you have in mind, then also concentrate on them.
Play your music, immerse yourself in the water and relax.

Stay in the bath as long as you can.
Make sure at some point you are completely immersed.
When you feel ready, repeat your opening words, adding others you feel are
appropriate in the circumstances.

Partnership Spell

This love spell is a little bit more complicated in that you have to cast a
circle of protection (see pages 41–3) and also call upon the Goddess of
Love (see pages 127–8).

YOU WILL NEED
1 white candle
1 coloured candle in your favourite colour
2 candle holders
A rose-coloured cloth
A piece of red chalk

METHOD
Cast your circle of protection, then ground and centre yourself.
Meditate on your idea of a perfect partner.
(Do not have a particular person in mind, although you might have previously
listed all the qualities you are looking for in a partner.)

When your mind is clear and open, hold the coloured candle (this represents you).
Meditate and then say aloud all the qualities and energies you personally are
willing to bring to an intimate relationship.

Replace that candle on the rose-coloured cloth.
Pick up the white candle (this represents your ideal partner).
Say out loud the essential qualities you desire in a mate.
Ask Aphrodite (Goddess of Love) to bring you together.

Place the two candles in their holders at opposite ends of the cloth.
Draw a heart in the centre of the cloth with the red chalk.
Make sure the heart is big enough to accommodate both candle holders.

Each day, meditate on the perfect loving relationship for a few minutes, moving
the two candles an inch closer together each time.
When they meet, draw two more hearts around the first one.
Burn the candles right down.

To Create Opportunities for Love

This is not a spell to draw a person to you, but more to 'open the way' – to alert the other person to the possibility of a relationship with you. Let's assume there is someone in whom you are interested, but the interest does not seem to be reciprocated. This spell ensures there are no hindrances, but there has to be at least some feeling for it to stand a chance of working. The spell should be performed on a Friday.

YOU WILL NEED
Wine glass
A ring (traditionally your mother's wedding ring would be used)
A red silk ribbon about 30 inches (80cm) long

METHOD
Put a wine glass right way up on a table.

Make a pendulum by suspending the ring from the red silk ribbon.

Hold the pendulum steady by resting your elbow on the table, with the ribbon
between your thumb and forefinger.

Let the ring hang in the mouth of the wine glass.

Clearly say your name followed by that of the other person.

Repeat their name twice, i.e. three times in all.

Then, thinking of them, spell their name out loud.

Allow the ring to swing and tap against the wine glass, once for each letter of their name.

Tie the ribbon around your neck, allowing the ring to hang down over your heart.

Wear it for three weeks, and repeat the spell every Friday for three weeks.

By the end of the third week, the person you have in your sights will show an interest, unless it is not meant to be.

To Win the Heart of the One You Love

You do need patience for this spell, and you may well find that you lose the impetus for the relationship before the spell is complete. This would suggest that the relationship may not be right for you.

YOU WILL NEED
Onion bulb
A new flowerpot

METHOD
Scratch the name of the one you love on the base of the bulb.
Plant it in earth in the pot.
Place the pot on a windowsill facing the direction in which your sweetheart lives.

Over the bulb, repeat the name of the one you desire morning and night until the bulb takes root, begins to shoot and finally blooms.
Say the following incantation daily:

May its roots grow,
May its leaves grow,
May its flowers grow,
And as it does so,
[Name of person]'s love grow.

To Have a Person Think About You

This is another spell that works over time. A relationship that grows slowly generally has more chance of success than a whirlwind romance, and that is what is represented here.

YOU WILL NEED
Packet of seeds
Pot of soil (to grow them)
A small copper object, such as a coin

METHOD
On a night when the Moon is waxing, go outside and hold the coin in the moonlight.

Bury the coin in the soil in the pot.
Sprinkle the seeds on top to form the initial of the other person's name.

As the seeds germinate, love should also grow.
Remember that just as plants need nurturing, so does love.

To Rekindle Your Lover's Interest

This technique is worth trying when your lover is not paying you enough attention. You are using the laurel leaves to back up the energy that you are putting into making the relationship work.

YOU WILL NEED
A large quantity of laurel leaves
A fire

METHOD
Sit in front of the embers of a fire and gaze into them, concentrating on your lover.
Keep your gaze fixed on the fire.

With your left hand, throw some laurel leaves on to the embers.
As they burn, say:

Laurel leaves burn in the fire.
Bring to me my heart's desire.

Wait until the flames die down,
then do the same again.

Repeat the action once more.
It is said that within 24 hours your lover will come to you.

To Focus Your Lover's Interest

If you find that your partner's attention seems to be wandering, try this spell. It is best performed on a Friday, the day sacred to Venus the Goddess of Love. Note that she will not assist if there is any intrinsic reason for the relationship not to work out – if your partner no longer loves you, you may be unsuccessful in your aim. This you must accept, knowing you have done the best you can.

YOU WILL NEED
Clean piece of paper
A pen that you like

METHOD
Taking your pen, write your first name and your lover's surname on the paper.

Draw either a square or a circle around them.
(Use the square if you decide all you want is a physical relationship, but the circle if you are utterly convinced this person is right for you.)

With your eyes closed, say:

If it be right, lover come back to me.

Cut the square or circle out and place it inside your pillowcase.
Your lover will show renewed interest.

To Get Someone to Call

This spell is a good one to use if you have had an argument with someone you love and would prefer them to make the first move towards reconciliation. It is probably best done when the Moon is in its expansive waxing phase, since more energy is available at this time, but it doesn't matter if you can't wait until then.

YOU WILL NEED
A photograph or something that represents the other person
A photograph of yourself
Paper clip

METHOD
Use a paper clip or something similar to fix the two objects together.

Place the linked objects in a dark place or at the bottom of a drawer.

Leave them there until the person responds.

If you are to make the best of this situation, as you perform the above actions you should really give some consideration as to why the two of you argued in the first place. That way, you are more open to taking your share of the blame.

Nether Garment Spell for Fidelity

This spell uses the combination of nutmeg and intimate garments in a form of sympathetic magic. It is said to keep a partner faithful.

YOU WILL NEED
2 whole nutmegs
A pair of your and your partner's clean underwear
A wide red ribbon
Large white envelope
A pin

METHOD
Take two nutmegs.
Carefully scratch with the pin your partner's full name on one and your own on the other.

Tie the two nutmegs together with the ribbon.
Wrap them in the underwear and then place in the envelope.

Sleep with the envelope under your pillow if your partner is away or you are separated from them.

To Decide between Two Lovers

You need infinite patience for this spell, and the problem may well have resolved itself before the flowers have grown. It is the very fact that you have taken action that will have an effect on the people concerned.

YOU WILL NEED
2 tulip bulbs
A new pin

METHOD
With the pin, scratch the name of one suitor on each bulb.

Plant the bulbs beside each other.

The bulb that blooms first will reveal the best option.

Apart from patience, this spell also requires a good memory, because you have to remember which bulb represents which lover.

To Clear the Air between Lovers

When communication between you and your partner seems difficult, you can forge a new link using this spell. You need to have confidence in your own power, though.

YOU WILL NEED
Crystal ball or magnifying glass
Your partner's photograph

METHOD
Place the crystal or magnifying glass over the image of your partner's face. Because the features are magnified, the eyes and mouth will appear to move and come to life.

Simply state your wishes or difficulties and what you feel your lover can do about them.

They will get the message.

To Rid Yourself of an Unwanted Admirer

Occasionally, people get into a situation where they are being pursued by someone whose attentions are a nuisance. Rather than reacting in anger, it is often easier to open the way for the unwanted suitor to leave. This spell, done on a waning Moon – that is, after the Full Moon and before the next New Moon – often does the trick. Preferably this should be done outside, but it can also be performed indoors if conditions are not right. Strictly, one is supposed to gather the vervain leaves, though with urban living this is a bit of a tall order. Make sure you have at least a couple of handfuls of the dried herb.

YOU WILL NEED
Vervain leaves
A fierce fire

METHOD
Light a fire.

As you pick up the herb, call out the name of the offending person.

Fling the leaves on the fire and say, for instance:

Withdraw from me now.
I need you not.

Repeat the action three nights in a row.

To Disengage Gently

This spell can be used when you want to let someone down gently. Perhaps you have recognized that a relationship will not work. By setting the person free and not pushing them away, you are finishing on a good note rather than a sour one.

YOU WILL NEED
Small square piece of paper
Black ink pen (preferably a fountain pen)
A white candle
Container for ashes

METHOD
Write the name of the unwanted person on the paper.
Let the ink dry.

Light the candle.
Burn the paper while visualizing the person moving away from you.
Make sure you catch the ashes for later disposal.

Go up to a high place.
Place the ashes in the palm of your right hand and say:

Winds of the North, East, South and West,
Carry these affections to where they'll be best.
Let [Name]'s heart be open and free,
Let [Name]'s mind be away from me.

Blow the ashes in the direction of the prevailing wind.

To Forget about an Ex-Lover

This spell is best done at the time of the waning Moon or at New Moon. It is not done to get rid of an old partner, but to exorcize your bad feelings about them. For this reason, it is sensible to finish the spell by sending loving thoughts to your former partner. You can substitute other herbs; woody nightshade is poisonous and you may not care to use it.

YOU WILL NEED
Photograph of your ex-partner
Suitable container for burning the photograph (one in which the ashes can be saved)
Root of bittersweet (woody nightshade, which is poisonous)
A red cloth or bag

METHOD
Place the picture of your ex-partner in the container.
Set it alight.

Gather up all your hurt and pain as the picture burns down.
Feel them flowing away from you as you say these words or similar:

Leave my heart and leave me free,
Leave my life, no pain for me.
As this picture burns to dust,
Help me now, move on I must.

Repeat the words until the picture is burnt out.
Taking the herb root, hold it first to your solar plexus.
Allow the bad feelings to flow into the root.

Then touch the root to your forehead, indicating that you have converted
the bad feelings into good.

Wrap everything, including the container of ashes, in your red bag or cloth.
As soon as convenient, bury it as far away from your home as possible.

To Heal a Rift

Divorce is disliked among the Romanies even today. When action is
required to heal a seemingly irreparable rift, this spell can begin a process
of reconciliation. To finish off the spell, Romanies use their campfire to
bake the apple until it appears whole.

YOU WILL NEED
A fresh apple
Clean sheet of white paper
Pen
Knife
2 pins or cocktail sticks

METHOD
Cut the apple in half.
Tradition says it is a helpful, but not vital, if the seeds remain whole.
If they don't, reconciliation may be a little more difficult to bring about.

Write one person's full name on the paper.
Next to it, write the other person's name.
Ensure that the space taken up by the names doesn't exceed the width of the
halved apple.

Cut out the names.

Place the paper with the names between the two halves of the apple.

Visualize the marriage or relationship being healed.

Skewer the apple halves together, inserting the pins diagonally from right to left and then vice-versa.

When you have positioned the pins, send your love to the person concerned and ask to receive their love in return.

MONEY AND JOB SPELLS

Most people's main concerns, other than love, are money and career. In this section we include spells designed to attract money towards you, and also ways of achieving the correct employment for you. Do remember that, as with anything in life, the effort you put in equals the effort you get out. All these spells need to be backed up by correct procedures, such as looking after your money when you have got it, and thoroughly researching a company with whom you hope to gain employment.

Attracting Extra Money

Use this working only at the time of a New Moon and make sure you are in the open air. It is said that the spell is negated if the Moon is seen through glass.

METHOD
Gaze at the Moon.

Turn your money over in your purse or pocket.

Repeat the following three times:

Goddess of Light and Love, I pray,
Bring fortune unto me this day.

You will know that it has worked when you find extra money in your pocket or purse, or find money unexpectedly.

Money Charm

This is more properly a charm (see pages 195–6) rather than a spell, because you have formed a different object – the bag – and given it power through the incantation. Once you have made the bag, meditate daily on what you want. Be as realistic as possible, imagining what you will do with the money and how best it will be used.

YOU WILL NEED
A square of green cloth
Allspice, borage, lavender and saffron
Some suitable crystals or rock salt
3 silver coins
Gold and silver-coloured thread

METHOD
Gather up the three silver coins.
Breathe on them four times and say:

To the spirits of Air I say,
Bring some money my way.

Put the ingredients on the cloth.

Tie the cloth into a bag.

Use eight knots in the thread.
(It is probably easiest to fold the thread into two and tie the knots around the neck of the bag.)

Hide the bag in a safe, cool, dark place, away from prying eyes for eight days.

After eight days, money should be coming in.

(You will have noticed a lot of eights in this spell. The significance of the number 8 is explained on pages 248–9.)

Silver Spell

The ritual for this spell takes a week to perform. Before you begin, believe that you have prosperity and that you have no money worries. Be aware that the more you need money, the more it will be attracted to you. Deeply consider your attitude to money – the fears and doubts that you have over money transactions, how you spend it, what you do with it and so on.

YOU WILL NEED
Small bowl
7 coins
A green candle and holder

METHOD
Place the bowl, the candle and its holder on a flat surface in your home,
where it will be passed every day.

For the next seven days, put a coin in the bowl.

After the seven days, take the candle in your hands and imagine prosperity
passing through you.
Sense the opportunities that you will have with money.
Be aware of the energy that has been given to money.

Place the candle in the holder.
Pour the seven coins into your left hand.
Make a circle around the candles with the coins.

Put the first coin right in front of the candle.
As you place it, say these or similar words:

Money grow, make it mine.
Money flow, Money's mine.

Repeat this six more times until you have created a circle around the candle with
the seven gleaming coins.

When you've completed this, light the candle.
Strike a match.
Touch its tip to the wick.

See the power of money flowing out from the seven coins up to the candle's flame
and then out to the atmosphere.
Blow out the match.

Settle down before the glowing candle and money.
Reconsider your attitude to money.

After ten minutes or so, leave the area.
Let the candle burn itself out in the holder.

Afterwards, collect the coins, put them back in the bowl and 'feed' the bowl a few
coins in loose change every day for as long as seems right.

Money will come to you, but always make sure you have at least seven coins
in the bowl.

Eliminating Personal Poverty

Based on a New Orleans voodoo formula, this spell will guarantee that you
always have the basic requirements in life – a roof over your head, food in
your stomach and so on.

YOU WILL NEED
Small bowl
Salt
Sugar
Rice
An open safety pin

METHOD
Fill a bowl with equal parts of sugar, salt and rice.

Place the open safety pin in the centre of the mixture.

Keep the bowl out in the open.

Refresh the ingredients when you feel the time is right.

Want Spell

Since Mother Nature supplies our most basic needs, this spell uses the cycle of her existence to help fulfil your wants.

YOU WILL NEED
Marker pen
A fully grown leaf

METHOD
Write or draw on the leaf a word, picture or letter that represents the thing that you want.
Lay the leaf on the ground.

As the leaf withers, it takes your desire to the earth.
In thanks, Mother Nature will grant your wish.
You may also throw the leaf into running water or place it under a stone,
if you wish.

Money Bottle

This spell owes a lot to hoodoo. It is a bottle spell for money-drawing and can be 'fixed' – that is, given the opportunity to work – by burying it close to your home, as an alternative to actually keeping it in the house.

YOU WILL NEED
5 cloves
5 cinnamon sticks
5 kernels of dried corn
5 kernels of dried wheat (or 5 teaspoons wheat flour)
5 pennies
5 10p pieces
5 20p pieces
5 sesame seeds
5 pecans
5 whole allspice

METHOD
Put all the ingredients into a tall, thin glass bottle, making sure the top
is secured tightly.

Shake the bottle with your power hand for five minutes while
chanting words such as:

Money gain, silver and herbs,
Copper and grain hear my words.

Place the money bottle on a table somewhere in your house.

Leave your purse or wallet near the bottle when at home.

When money comes to you, it is a good idea to pass on some of your good
luck to a charity or the needy.

A Spell for Employment

Unless you particularly want specific skills to be utilized, do not try to
force the issue by imagining names of firms or other details of your job,
because this may limit your choices. This spell will help to keep your
energy positive and focused.

YOU WILL NEED
A stone or crystal (to represent the job you want)
(You may like to have further prepared by writing out the sort of advertisement you
would reply to. This needs careful thought and is a mental preparation only.)

METHOD
Hold the stone.
Visualize the kind of job you want and the feelings of satisfaction you want.

Say aloud the qualifications you have for holding such a job.

Raise power by letting your energy build up and flow through you to
charge the stone.

The following day, make sure you have the stone or crystal with you as you contact
six potential employers.

Make precisely six contacts each day, until you have the job you desire.

Wishing Spell

The bay leaf possesses powerful magical properties and is used for granting wishes. This spell can be used to fulfil a range of desires.

YOU WILL NEED
3 bay leaves
Piece of paper
Pencil or pen

METHOD
During a New Moon, write your wish on a piece of paper and visualize it coming true.

Fold the paper into thirds, placing the three bay leaves inside.

Again, visualize your wish coming true.

Fold the paper into thirds a second time, thus forming an envelope.

Keep it hidden in a dark place.

Reinforce your wish by repeatedly visualizing it coming true.

When the wish comes to fruition, burn the paper as a mark of thanks.

Achieving a Dream Job

Candles always work well when dealing with aims and aspirations. This spell introduces some of the techniques beloved of those who believe in using the Element of Fire, which represents drive. This particular spell is best begun on the night of a New Moon.

YOU WILL NEED
2 brown candles (to represent the job)
Green candle (for prosperity)
A candle to represent yourself (perhaps your astrological colour)
Prosperity incense such as cinnamon
Prosperity oil

METHOD
Light your prosperity incense.
Anoint the candles with the prosperity oil from wick to end.

Place one of the brown candles in the centre of your chosen space.
Place the green one on the right
Place your personal candle on the left.
(These candles should be in a safe place; they have to burn out entirely.)

As you light your own candle, say:

Open the way, clear my sight,
Bring me chance, that is my right.

Light the green candle and say:

Good luck is mine and true victory,
Help me Great Ones, come to me.

Light the brown candle and say:

Openings, work, rewards I see,
And as I will, So Must it Be.

Leave the candles to burn out completely.

Each night for a week, or until the candle is used up,
light the second brown candle for nine minutes while meditating on the job
and the good to come out of it.

4

RITUALS OF MAGIC

The dictionary definition of 'spell' is 'to name the letters of'. This immediately gives us a link with the Kabbalistic belief that the name of God had an intrinsic power. We need to understand that Hebrew letters represent so much more than simple representations which together form words. Both letters and numbers have magical properties which, when combined, make powerful vibrations. A spell, therefore, was the sounding of this combination, used to affect the present or the world in general – as we have seen in both thaumaturgy and theurgy (high and low magic). When you add significant movements (rituals) to such words, you have an even more powerful energy. This energy needs to be given focus lest it goes out of control, so the movements used in the rituals became an important part of the whole process.

These rituals, therefore, took on both a religious and magical aspect and could probably be more properly called 'rites'. In order for rites to survive, the rituals were taught very carefully to those who chose, or dared, to work with magic.

Many rituals are particularly beautiful because they show an inherent appreciation of the world in which we live. Particularly in the pagan and neo-pagan belief systems, they have achieved a new lease of life. Creativity of all sorts is, however, an important part of spell-making and magic, and other magical systems that rely on an awareness of a more cosmic spiritual philosophy also retain their own magical power and energy. Rituals may be thought of as offerings to Ultimate Power. Most of the rituals included in this section owe their origin to the turning Wheel of the Year and the acknowledgement of the power of nature. The first one acknowledges the four cardinal points (points of the compass) and the duality that is an integral part of our being.

A Ritual of Gestures

This simple ritual acknowledges the four 'directions' and the Elements they rule. It needs little special knowledge; just remember that the Goddess represents the feminine principle and the horned God the masculine.

METHOD
Stand in your sacred space and quieten your mind as far as you can.
Breathe deeply for a while, trying to breathe out a little longer than you breathe in.
Turn your attention to the deities you are going to ask for assistance.

FACE NORTH:
Put your hands out in front of you, palms facing the Earth.
Use your hands to sense the solidity and fertility of the Earth.
Invoke the powers of the Earth as you do so.

TURN TOWARDS THE EAST:
Raise your hands slightly higher with elbows bent, your hands with palms
facing away from you.
Spread your fingers fairly wide and hold this position.
Invoke the forces of Air and sense movement and communication.

NOW FACE SOUTH:
Keeping your elbows straight, make your hands into tight fists.
Raise your hands above your head and feel the energy flow through you.
Invoke the forces of Fire: power, creativity and necessary destruction.

TURN TO THE WEST:
Extend your cupped hands in front of you as though they are carrying water.
Sense all the qualities of water and invoke the forces of water.

FACE NORTH AGAIN:
Raise both hands to the sky, with the palms upwards and the fingers spread wide
as though you were throwing your whole self at the sky.
Pull towards you the energy of the universe with all its mystery.
Acknowledge Ultimate Power.

With your receptive hand held high, make the shape of the crescent Moon with
your thumb and forefinger. (Tuck the other fingers into the palm of your hand.)
With this action, acknowledge the reality of the Goddess and her presence with you.
Sense all her qualities and power and make an act of reverence.

With your projective hand held high, create an image of the horned God by bending down the middle and fourth fingers toward the palm, holding them with the thumb.
Lift the forefinger and little finger up to the sky.
Acknowledge the energy and power of the Sun.
Sense the presence of the God with you.
Make an act of reverence.

Now, if you can, lie down flat on the ground.
Stretch your legs and arms in the shape of Perfect Man, arms out sideways and legs outstretched until you feel you have created the pattern of a pentagram.
Sense the energies and powers of all the Elements coursing through your body, becoming part of you and you part of them.
Recognize them as coming from the One, the Goddess and God combined.

Now do whatever you have to do from a mental standpoint: meditate, ask for help or make a dedication.

Your ritual is finished when you feel complete.
Now stand up.

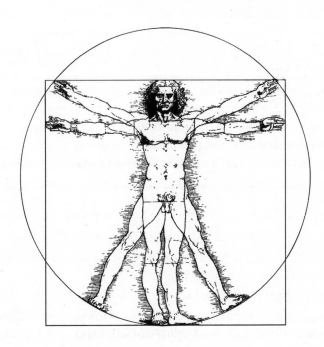

Perfect Man

USING COLOUR

Colour is something which, over time, you will use as a natural adjunct in your rituals. It can be used in your robes, to dress your altar, or in your candles as representative of the vibration you wish to introduce. By and large, the colours you choose for your workings will be those appropriate to your intention or the purpose of your spell.

There are other uses of colour in magic as well. To create a talisman bag, for instance, you should always remember to choose a colour that represents an energy appropriate for the task you wish the talisman to perform. Some simple colour symbolism is listed below.

COLOUR SYMBOLISM

Black is essentially the absence of both light and colour. It can therefore be used to banish negativity. It is often seen as the colour of the Goddess in her Crone form.

Brown promotes the healing of the Earth, symbolizes the hearth and home, and is connected with the animal kingdom. It can also be used for the blending of several intentions.

Gold and yellow represent vitality, strength and rejuvenation, and are therefore used to promote physical healing, hope and happiness. Related to the Sun Gods and the Element of Air, they may be used for protection.

Green belongs to Venus and promotes love, fertility, beauty, prosperity and wealth. Associated with the Earth in its guise of the Green Man and with the Great Mother in her nurturing form, it suggests emotional healing and growth.

Orange is used as a healing vibration, particularly of relationships. It is also associated with material success and legal matters. A highly creative vibration, it often relates to childhood and emotional stability.

Pink is the colour associated with the Goddess as Maiden and signifies friendship, love, fidelity and the healing of emotions. It also symbolizes creativity and innocence.

Purple, indigo and violet are the royal colours and are therefore associated with wisdom and vision, dignity and fame. Often used when remembering the Goddess in her aspect of Crone (Wise

Woman) and the God as King, they command respect and promote psychic and mental healing.

Red is associated with passion and sexual potency, and also with intensity. It is usually associated with fire, the quality of courage and healing of the blood and heart.

Silver is almost always associated with the Moon Goddesses (see Deities on pages 110–26) and workings with the Moon. Should you wish to work with the energy of the High Priestess as representative of the Goddess, you would use silver.

Sky blue signifies communication in all its forms, not just between people but also between the realms. It is therefore good for meditative practices and also for help with study and learning. This colour is also used to symbolize water.

White symbolizes purity, chastity and spirituality, and is said to contain within it all the other colours, so always use it if you have nothing else available. Use it also when you want focus and a protective influence.

ROBES AND CLOTHING

Using special robes for your rituals and spell-making adds a nice touch, although it is not strictly necessary. Many magicians of old would use simple robes of black or white – white symbolizing purity and black conveying the idea that the personality of the practitioner should be disregarded, since they are being used simply as a channel for the energy. This tradition is carried on even today in the workaday garb of priests and nuns. Nowadays, magical practitioners would far rather blend into the world at large than stand out because of the way they dress.

As there is such a richness of material available, today's spell-makers can do as they like and make use either of their own creativity or that of others when deciding how best to honour their calling. Wearing a robe during your ritual sets it apart both in thought and energy from the mundane, enabling you to be as quiet and restrained in your decoration or as flamboyant and over the top as you want to be. Some people like single colours and little decoration, while others prefer many shades and much ornamentation. As always, it is your choice.

HOW TO DRESS CANDLES

Just as preparing yourself and your altar appropriately is important, so is choosing the colour of the candles for your workings. You can do this in accordance with the previous list. Equally necessary is the 'dressing' of your candle for any spell or ritual.

Dressing a candle performs two functions. By anointing it with oil, you ensure that it burns safely and you also have the opportunity to infuse it with the required vibration. Any oil can be used for the purpose, but initially it is usual to use either your favourite essential oil, such as frankincense, or perhaps an oil infused with a suitable herb appropriate to the task in hand. (A list of oils is given on pages 180–2.) There are various ways to dress a candle, but what is important is the direction in which you anoint it. Working from the top down draws in power from spiritual sources, and working from the bottom up draws in energy from the earth. If you remember this, it is very easy to work correctly for your purpose. Never rub the candle with a back-and-forth movement. If you do, you will end up with a confusion of energies.

TECHNIQUE FOR CANDLE DRESSING

First, sit quietly and think carefully about your intent. If you have learned to meditate, then enter a meditative state and allow the energies to build up within you. Now dress your candle:

• If your intention is to bring something to you, rub oil on the candle in a downward motion from the top to the middle and then from the bottom to the middle.

• If your intention is to send something away from you, rub the oil from the middle of the candle out to the ends.

• Continue with either movement until you have a sense that you have done enough. If you have any oil left on your hands, either rub your hands together until the oil is absorbed or dab the remaining oil from your fingers on to the centre of your forehead; this is your 'third eye' and the seat of vision.

• Now say the following, or something similar:

I cleanse and consecrate this candle.
[In the name of your chosen deity if you choose to use one],
May it burn with strength in the service of the Greater Good.

Charging Your Candle

This is a quick, uncomplicated method of more fully charging a candle. It is designed to fix your intent and dedicate the candle to the appropriate purpose. You can use this method without having to set up your altar completely. It can also be used to charge your altar candles.

YOU WILL NEED

A candle or candles of the appropriate colour (if preferred, mark them with appropriate symbols)
Candle holder
Matches (preferable to a lighter)

METHOD

Hold the candle in your 'power hand' (the hand with which you consider you give out energy).
Open the other hand and turn that palm towards the sky.
Breathe deeply and visualize your goal.

Now perceive whatever you think of as Universal Energy flowing through the palm that is turned skyward filling your body.
Visualize that Universal Energy mixing within you with the energy of your intention.
Now allow that mixed energy to flow into the candle.

Be conscious of the energy as it builds up.
Feel the energy streaming into the candle.
Fill it from bottom to top as though the candle was an empty vessel.
If you are comfortable doing so, speak your intention out loud.
As you place the candle in its holder, stabilize the thought within the candle so that it will be converted into pure, clear intent.

Strike a match above the candle.
Draw down the flame towards the candle, lighting the wick.
Extinguish the match flame, but do not blow it out in case you blow out the candle.
Stay with the candle for a few moments, visualizing your intention, feeling its energy moving into the Universe.

Leave the area and let the candle burn right down as it does its work.

RITUAL HERBS

Most magical practices make use of herbs in various ways, often in rituals and magical workings. Often they are used as incense, when they are crushed and powdered, or as oils. Their properties mean that they create a type of forcefield that intensifies the vibration needed. Additionally, when the practitioner calls upon the power of the Gods and spirits, the herbs become even more effective. Some of the main uses are given below.

THE USES OF HERBS

Protection Some herbs guard against physical and psychic attacks, injury, accidents and wicked spirits. They usually offer protection in a general sort of way. They should be used as preventatives and as a back-up for rituals and spells – a kind of insurance.

Love magic The vibration of these herbs is such that they can help you to meet new people, overcome shyness and let others know that you are open to new relationships. They put out a particular vibration so that those who are interested will answer the call. Such herbs will not usually bring about an increase in lust, so are not used to coerce others against their will. The safest way to use them is to recognize that several people may be attracted to you and you can then make an informed choice.

Fidelity Some herbs and plants can be used to ensure fidelity. Since their use takes the practitioner into the realms of a binding spell, they should be used with responsibility. It is unwise to hold anyone in a relationship against their will.

Healing Many herbs have healing properties which can help both from a physical and a magical viewpoint. A practitioner working from both points of view can be of tremendous help. However, always remember to advise anyone you work with to seek medical assistance, particularly if the condition is serious. Never allow yourself to be drawn into being a substitute for medical help. That was the way witches got themselves a bad name in days of old.

Health Not only the smell of herbs and plants but also their vibration can help to prevent illness and restore good health. So if you are prone to illness, carry healthy herbs with you and make sure they are always as fresh as possible. This was the principle of the nosegays carried in the past.

Luck The meaning of 'luck' is the knack of being in the right place at the right time and being able to act on instinct. Luck herbs help you create your own good fortune. Once you have such a foundation, you can build upon it.

Lust If the object of your desire is interested, then certain herbs might be used to enhance love-making. Many herbs are said to have aphrodisiac qualities and to have a subtle effect on sexual enjoyment.

Manifestations For spirits and apparitions to appear, they must have some sort of substance to manipulate. Smoke has often been used for this purpose. The smoke from certain herbs can also be used to work clairvoyantly.

Money It is sometimes easier to visualize the outcome of having money – i.e. what you are going to spend the money on – than visualizing actual money coming to you. Certain herbs create an environment in which things can happen. They enable the creation of the means to fulfil your needs – perhaps a gift or a pay rise.

SPECIFIC APPLICATIONS FOR HERBS

So that you can experiment a little, we have included a list of potential applications and suitable herbs that can be used. Simply having the herbs in your sacred space or having them about your person is sufficient to begin the process of enhancing the area or your personal vibration. Later, you can use them in incense and dedicate them to the appropriate Elements and Deities (see pages 110–26). Many of the herbs mentioned can be obtained from a good herbalist, though for those of you who are truly interested it would be worthwhile creating a small herb garden or growing them on your windowsill.

Attracting men Jasmine, Juniper (dried berries worn as a charm), Lavender, Lemon Verbena, Lovage, Orris Root, Patchouli.
Attracting women Henbane, Holly, Juniper (dried berries worn as a charm), Lemon Verbena, Lovage, Orris Root, Patchouli.
Banishing Hyssop, Lilac, St John's Wort.
Cleansing Cinnamon, Clove, Lovage (powdered root), Mullein (of ritual tools and areas), Pine, Thyme (in baths), Vervain (of sacred spaces).

Courage Basil, Garlic, Mandrake (root), Mullein, Nettle, St John's Wort, Thyme, Wormwood, Yarrow.

Exorcism Angelica, Basil, Birch, Frankincense, Juniper, Garlic, St John's Wort.

Fertility Acorns, Geranium, Hawthorn, Mandrake, Orange (dried and powdered peel), Pine, Poppy, Sage, Sunflower (seeds), Walnut.

Friendship Lemon, Rose, Passion Flower.

Good fortune Ash (leaves), Heather, Nutmeg, Rose, Vetivert.

Happiness Anise, Catnip, Lily of the Valley, Marjoram, Saffron.

Harmony Hyacinth, Heliotrope, Lilac, Meadowsweet.

Healing Aloe, Ash (wood), Chamomile, Cinnamon, Comfrey, Eucalyptus, Fennel, Garlic, Hops, Marjoram, Mint, Nettle, Onion, Pine, Rosemary, Rowan, Saffron, Sage, Sandalwood, Thyme, Willow, Yarrow.

Hex-breaking Chilli Pepper, Galangal, Vetivert.

Love Apple, Balm of Gilead, Basil, Caraway, Catnip, Coriander, Cowslip, Dill, Dragon's Blood, Gardenia, Ginger, Ginseng, Honeysuckle, Jasmine, Lavender, Lemon, Lemon Balm, Lemon Verbena, Linden, Marigold, Marjoram, Meadowsweet, Mistletoe, Myrtle, Orange (dried and powdered peel), Orris Root, Rose, Rosemary, Valerian, Vanilla (bean in love charms, oil as an aphrodisiac), Valerian, Vervain, Violet (mixed with Lavender), Yarrow.

Luck Apple, Ash (leaves), Daisy (wear at midsummer), Hazel, Holly (for newlyweds), Ivy (for newlyweds), Mint, Rose, Rowan, Vervain, Violet (flowers).

Lust Cinnamon, Lemongrass, Nettle, Rosemary, Violet.

Meditation Chamomile, Elecampane, Frankincense, Vervain.

Mental powers Caraway, Lily of the Valley, Rosemary, Vanilla, Walnut.

Money Chamomile, Cinquefoil, Cinnamon, Clove, Comfrey, Fennel, Ginger, Mint, Poppy (seeds or the dried seedpod), Vervain.

Peace Aloe, Chamomile, Gardenia, Lavender, Myrtle, Violet.

Power Carnation, Cinnamon, Ginger, Rosemary, Rowan.

Prosperity Acorn, Almond, Ash, Basil, Benzoin, Honeysuckle.

Protection Aloe, Angelica (Root), Anise, Balm of Gilead, Basil, Bay Laurel, Betony, Caraway, Chamomile, Cinquefoil, Clove, Coriander, Dill (for children), Dragon's Blood, Fennel, Fern, Garlic, Hawthorn, Holly, Hyssop, Ivy, Lavender, Lilac, Mandrake, Marjoram,

Meadowsweet, Mistletoe, Mugwort, Mullein, Nettle, Onion, Pennyroyal (avoid when pregnant), Black Pepper, Periwinkle, Rose, Rosemary, Rowan, Rue, Sage, St John's Wort, Sandalwood, Vervain, Witch Hazel, Wormwood.

Psychic powers Ash (leaves), Bay Laurel, Bay leaves, Cinnamon, Cowslip (induces contact during sleep), Elecampane, Elder (branches used for wands), Eyebright, Hazel (wood for making all-purpose wands, forked branches for divination), Hyssop (when burnt as an incense it is possible to draw upon magical dragon energy), Lavender, Marigold (also use for prophecy), Mugwort, Nutmeg, Oak (branches for wands), Rose, Thyme, Willow (to bind together witches' brooms, forked branch for use in water witching and dowsing), Wormwood, Yarrow.

Purification Anise, Benzoin, Betony, Cinquefoil, Dragon's Blood, Fennel, Frankincense, Hyssop, Lavender, Lemon, Oak Leaves (of ritual spaces), Pine, Rosemary, Rue (of ritual spaces and tools), Sandalwood, Thyme, Valerian, Vervain.

Success Cinnamon, Ginger, Lemon Balm, Rowan.

Sleep Catnip, Hops, Lavender, Thyme, Valerian, Vervain (to prevent nightmares).

Spirituality Cinnamon, Clover (associated with the Triple Goddess), Frankincense, Myrrh, Sandalwood.

Wisdom Peach (fruit), Sage, Sunflower.

THE ELEMENTS

Just to add other factors into the equation, in most systems of magical working you will find mentioned the four (or sometimes five) Elements, often in conjunction with their directions or, as they are known in magic, quarters of the Universe or cardinal points. They are extremely powerful sources of energy and can give a tremendous boost to your spell-making.

Magical ritual calls to each Elemental kingdom and its ruler to protect each cardinal point and its properties. The four Elements are energies and manifestations of energy that make up the entire universe. They also influence our personalities and therefore what we do. Each Element has an intrinsic power and is known for having certain qualities, natures, moods and magical purposes. Each also has positive and negative traits.

The four Elements are Earth, Air, Fire and Water, and you may well find that you work best using one of them. People drawn to candle magic, for instance, are using mainly the Element of Fire, while those who work with incense are using Air, with a fair smattering of Earth in the herbs and resins.

The fifth and perhaps most important Element is that of Spirit. This is the binding principle behind everything – that which makes everything happen. Sometimes known as Aether, it is intangible. In magical working you are both its representative and its channel, so in using the other Elements you have a responsibility to act wisely and well. Now, let's take the Elements individually and consider them.

EARTH

Traditionally the direction of this Element is North. For many pagans the altar is set up facing North – that is, facing Earth – since this is usually the Element on which we rely so much and with which we are so strongly linked. Personal preference, of course, comes into play. The colour normally associated with Earth is green, and the Element is represented on the altar usually by salt or sand. Crystals, because they are totally natural substances, can also be used, although you should be careful to use these responsibly and not overuse natural resources. When invoking Earth and the powers of the North, you are looking for recovery and healing and perhaps trying to find answers to questions. They both deal with gaining knowledge, blessing, creating and shielding. Earth is feminine and is about 'having' in the sense of possessing. In the Eastern magical tradition, its colour is yellow. When working within a magical circle, this is the first corner or quarter on which you call for protection.

AIR

The direction of this Element is East and the colour usually associated with it is yellow. If you are so minded, you will follow the Celtic tradition and open your magical circle starting with the direction of this Element. Incense is often used to represent Air on the altar, since the movement of the air can be seen in the incense smoke. The Element of Air is, in fact, all movement, noise, storm and wind. When you are looking for inspiration, need new ideas or perhaps to break free from the past or undesired situations, you would use this Element. Magically, you use Air to encourage physical movement. The quality associated with it is that of thinking or the use of the intellect. In the Eastern tradition, the colour of Air is blue. When working in a magical circle, Air is the second quarter on which you call for protection.

FIRE

Fire is the Element of the South and on an altar is usually represented by a candle or a cauldron with a fire inside. Its colour is red and its associations are – because of its chaotic and erratic nature – to do with power, determination and passionate energy. You would call upon this Element for protection from evil forces, cleansing and creativity. If you do not wish to use fire itself or are not in a position where you can do so safely, you might visualize a red mist. Do be careful to maintain control, however, as this might be taken to represent anger. The quality associated with Fire is 'doing' and it is a male principle. In the Eastern tradition, the colour of Fire is also red. It is the third quarter or cardinal point on which you call for protection when working in a magical circle.

WATER

Water is the Element of the West. On the altar it is represented by a bowl of water or a goblet of wine or fruit juice. Its colour is blue and, because it represents the giving of life, it is associated with the natural Elements of sea, rain, snow and rivers. When you need cleansing, revitalizing, the removal of curses or hexes or change of any sort, you will call upon Water. It is to do with feeling, right through from the most basic passions to the most elevated forms of belief. It is predominantly feminine. In the Eastern tradition, its colour is silver. It is the fourth and final quarter that you invoke in any magical circle.

SPIRIT

When you feel you are sufficiently adept at using the other Elements, you may begin to use Spirit – the fifth Element. This has no special space but is everywhere. It should never be used negatively because, particularly when you are weak and tired, it can rebound on you. You may well find that you instinctively link strongly with the life force as Spirit, in which case you are probably succeeding in bringing all the Elements together within yourself. There is no particular colour associated with Spirit – perception is all-important. Some people see it as black, some as a kind of mother-of-pearl luminescence, and some as no colour. If you choose to represent Spirit on the altar, you may do so however you wish. You have got to use your intuition and you must have a very strong awareness of your reason for choosing that particular symbol. In the Eastern tradition, the colour is black and its essential nature is 'being'.

EVERYDAY MAGIC

The four Elements can be a way of linking your everyday self with your magical self. Each Element can be categorized by the action it heightens and the character it rules. Below is a table that should give you a speedy way of identifying what you need to use within a particular ritual to help you handle everyday problems. For instance, to overcome anger you might use the colour green in your altar dressing and candles, and the quality of analysis to help to move the energy into a different area of being. Placing a cross on the altar would help you to focus on the problem, and you might spend some time thinking through strategies for handling the situations you find yourself in.

Opposite is a technique for dealing with negative energies such as anger and resentment. It uses the Elements and their qualities in a very positive way. The circle of light links with Spirit, the dark stone represents Earth and the water acts in its cleansing capacity.

Element	Action	Character	Colour	Shape	Difficulty
Fire	Do	Pragmatism	Red	Square	Apathy
Earth	Have	Realism	Yellow	Circle	Greed
Air	Think	Analysis	Green	Cross	Anger
Water	Feel	Idealism	Blue	Waves	Lust
Spirit	Be	Synthesism	Mother-of-pearl	Star	Pride

To Disperse Negative Energy

YOU WILL NEED
A dark stone

METHOD
Visualize a circle of light around yourself.
Hold a dark stone in your hands.
Place it over your solar plexus.

Allow the negative emotion, perhaps anger and resentment, to flow into the stone.
Try to decide what colour the emotion is and identify the problem according
to the list opposite.

Raise the stone to your forehead.
Then place it over your heart.
(This helps to raise the vibration to the correct level.)

If it seems right, say:

With this stone
Negative be gone,
Let water cleanse it
Back where it belongs.

This reinforces the idea of the stone holding your anger.

Concentrate and project all your negative emotion (anger, resentment and so on)
into the stone.
Visualize it being sealed in.
With all your energy, throw it into a source of running water.

It helps if you can get up to a high place to throw your stone away, since this way
you are using Air as well.

A Love Tree Spell

This spell uses all of the Elements in a very simple fashion. As with all love spells in particular, you must take responsibility for what you do.

YOU WILL NEED
2 leaves on which you can draw
Green thread
Needle
7 coins

METHOD
On one of the leaves, draw an image of yourself.
On the other, draw a representation of your ideal love, or the ideal person you want to meet.

Using green thread, sew the two together and knot the thread tightly.

Find a tree that you like.
Within a natural crevice or hole, hide the leaf inside and secure it well.
As you are doing this, say:

Tree of Earth, Water, Air and Fire,
Grant me the love that I desire.

Bury the seven coins at the tree base.
You might like to visit the tree as often as you can, to reinforce your relationship with the Dryads and Nature Spirits.

CRYSTALS FOR RITUALS

This is a brief list of some well-known crystals that you may like to use as representative of Earth on your altar when performing rituals. Obviously you will discover for yourself certain crystals that resonate for you in your magical workings.

Agate A member of the quartz family, it is available in a range of natural and manufactured colours. It is a general healer, especially good for self-esteem.

Amethyst A crystalline type of quartz which is rich in purple. Aiding creative thinking, it is also a protector against blood diseases, grief, neuralgia and insomnia. It is said to deal with drunkenness.

Aquamarine A clear silicate, it can be greenish blue or vary to the more valuable deeper blue. Aquamarine is good for the eyes and it helps against nerve, throat, liver and stomach troubles.

Aventurine A quartz stone found in various colours, but usually green. It is helpful when dealing with skin conditions.

Bloodstone A dark green quartz flecked with red jasper. It strengthens the will to do good.

Carnelian A translucent red or orange. It makes the voice strong and is helpful when dealing with rheumatism, depression and neuralgia.

Citrine A form of crystalline quartz, it has an attractive yellow colour. 'Sherry' or 'brandy' citrine is a deep yellow orange. Wearing citrine may bring greater control over the emotions and help blood circulation.

Coral This is not an actual gemstone, but the calcareous remains of marine organisms. Colours vary, but pink to deep red are the types most often seen. Coral may help anaemia and bladder conditions.

Emerald This precious stone is a silicate. The colour is a deep dark green. It improves the intellect and memory, and it may also help with insomnia.

Garnet The name given to a group of gemstones of varying composition. Its colours range from a deep blood red through to orange and purplish red. It protects against depression and helps with self-confidence and self-esteem.

Jade Nephrite jade is a silicate having a highly prized green colour. It is beneficial in kidney complaints.

Jasper A mixed type of quartz that can occur in various colours; red jasper is common. It improves the sense of smell and helps liver, kidney and epileptic problems.

Lapis lazuli A mixture of minerals having a deep blue colour, it often contains particles of 'fool's gold'. It is an ancient stone and is useful for heart and vascular conditions.

Malachite An attractive ornamental stone, the colour is a vivid green; the best examples show banding. The copper in malachite helps with asthma.

Moonstone A silicate, this stone has a milky sheen, the best stones containing a bluish colour. Moonstone gives inspiration and enhances the emotions.

Onyx A type of agate often stained a uniform jet-black and given a high polish. Onyx aids concentration and is an important healing agent in certain ear diseases.

Opal A hydrated silica, it helps in lung conditions.

Peridot A silicate, the bottle green colour has a soft and shiny appearance. It aids digestion and improves digestive complaints.

Rock-crystal A colourless pure quartz, it is an important healing stone and helps the wearer by improving intuitive powers.

Rose quartz A translucent quartz. It enlivens the imagination and calms the emotions.

Ruby A precious stone, it is an oxide of aluminium, coloured red by the presence of chromium. It improves mental ability.

Sapphire The same composition as ruby but a rich blue colour due to traces of iron and titanium. Sapphire can also be colourless, yellow or green. The stone of friendship and love, it gives devotion, faith and imagination.

Smoky quartz An attractive crystalline which has a smoky grey to black colour. It is used to give good luck.

Tiger's eye A quartz mineral in which the crystals are needle-like and reflect the light to give the tiger's-eye effect. It is worn for clearer thinking.

Tourmaline A complex silicate, its colours range from pink through to yellow, greens and blue. It attracts inspiration, goodwill and friendship.

Turquoise An opaque stone given a blue-green colour by the presence of copper. It is a great protector and therefore a good stone to give as a gift.

THE DEITIES

The more accustomed you become to performing rituals and making spells, the more you will begin to appreciate the power of the deities and how this power was used by our forebears. While many of us probably subscribe to the belief that there is one God, we cannot help but marvel at the complexity of the energies and powers that go into making up that entity. For this reason, it is sometimes more comforting to be able to approach that complexity in the way our forefathers did – with reverence for a particular aspect. We do this when we call upon the various deities.

We have already talked of the various belief systems of polytheism, pantheism and so on earlier in the book, and now it is time to decide whether you wish to appeal to those Gods and Goddesses who so comforted and frightened our ancestors.

In a book such as this, where we have been careful to keep the perspective as wide as possible, it would be remiss not to give some information on the deities associated with the major religions, particularly when those religions are of such antiquity. Unfortunately it is possible only to give information on a very basic level. We have tried to give as much as will enable you to begin exploring for yourself the rich myriad of energies available to you.

Most religions pay due attention to the masculine and feminine polarities. If you choose to personalize those polarities, you will no doubt find comfort and nurturing in so doing. Indeed, in many ways that personalization of the energy is one of the prime functions of working with the deities. It allows us to feel close to something that is otherwise intangible; to feel that we are in touch with another dimension of being that is wiser and more powerful than ourselves.

For many people, perceiving the masculine as Lord and the Feminine as Lady is enough. Others need something more mundane and down to earth, and will attribute the masculine to the Sun and the feminine to the Moon, and by so doing allow themselves access to the rich symbolism there is in that. Yet others will want to go beyond the duality to an expression of the unity in all things and will be content to appeal to that power and that power alone.

We have tried to include a fair selection of the deities from a number of systems of belief here. Although by no means exhaustive, we hope you will find this list full enough for your requirements.

CELTIC GODS AND GODDESSES
Gaulish Gods
Belenus (also **Bel**) is the God of light and the Sun, also known as the Shining One. The most extensively worshipped Celtic God, he has particular authority for the welfare of sheep and cattle. The Feast of Beltane means 'Fire of Bel'; he was later connected with the Greek God Apollo.
Cernunnos is a God of fertility, life, animals, wealth and the

underworld. Usually shown with a stag's antlers, he carries a purse filled with coins. The horned God, he is born at the Winter Solstice, marries the Goddess of the Moon at Beltane and dies at the Summer Solstice. Worshipped all over Gaul, he is identified as Herne the Hunter in Britain. With the Goddess of the Moon he jointly rules over the cycle of life, death and reincarnation.

Ogmios is the God of scholars and eloquence. Known in Ireland as Ogma, he is a hero God who invented the runic language of the Druids, the Ogham Staves (see pages 232–43). He is shown as a bald old man dressed in a lion's skin. He is said to have gold chains hanging from his tongue which are attached to the ears of his followers to give them wisdom.

Sucellus is the guardian of forests and the God of agriculture; he also ferries the dead to the afterlife. He is often portrayed with a huge hammer and a dog by his side; in this aspect he links with the Norse Thor and the Egyptian Anubis. His consort is Nantosvelta, whose symbol is the raven, thus giving connections to the Irish Morrigan.

Taranis, whose name means 'the Thunderer', has as his symbols the wheel, representing the Wheel of Life, and the lightning flash. He is sometimes identified with the Roman God Jupiter and the Norse God Thor.

Teutates is a God of war, fertility and wealth; his name means 'the God of the tribe'. He was greatly worshipped at a time when human sacrifices were made. He was the counterpart of the Roman God Mars.

Gaulish Goddesses

Belisama is a Goddess of light and fire, forging and craft; she is the wife of Belenus. She relates to the Roman Goddess Minerva.

Epona is the Goddess of horses, mules and cavalrymen. Her cult was eventually adopted by the Roman army. She is usually shown lying on a horse, sitting side-saddle or standing surrounded by many horses. Her other symbol is that of the cornucopia – the horn of plenty – which suggests that she may also have been a fertility or corn Goddess.

Rosmerta is a Goddess of fertility and wealth. Her stick with two snakes links her to Mercury, to whom she was supposed to be married. The cornucopia – another of her symbols – identifies her as a fertility Goddess and thus connects her with Epona.

Irish Gods

Bile corresponds with the Gaulish God Belenus.

Bres is the God of fertility and agriculture. He is the son of Elatha, a prince of the Fomorians, and the Goddess Eriu.

Dagda (also **Dagde**, **DaGodevas**) is a God of the Earth and Father God, i.e. the masculine principle. A formidable warrior and skilled craftsman, he has a club that can restore life as well as kill. His symbols are a bottomless cauldron of plenty and a harp with which he rules the seasons.

Dian Cecht is a God of healing. He ruled the waters that restored life to the old and dying Gods. When Nuada lost his hand in battle, Dian Cecht made him a silver one.

Fomorians were the original occupants of Ireland, a race of demonic Gods. Defeated in battle by the Tuatha De Danann, they were given the province of Connacht in which to live and were allowed to marry some of the Tuatha De Danann. The king of the Fomorians is the one-eyed Balor.

Lugh was worshipped during the 30-day midsummer feast in Ireland. Sexual magical rites undertaken in his name ensured ripening of the crops and a prosperous harvest. He is linked with Rosmerta in Gaul and also corresponds to the Roman God Mercury, particularly in his trickster aspect. His animal totems are the raven and the lynx, representing deviousness. Lugh is the name given to the Celtic Sun God by the Irish; he was known as Lleu in Wales.

Nodens was a God of healing. His magic hounds were also believed to be able to cure the sick.

Ogma is sometimes associated with the Greek Heracles, and is usually pictured as a great warrior carrying a club. Ogmias is his Gaulish counterpart. He is the holder of all expressiveness.

Irish Goddesses

Aine is a Goddess of love and fertility; she was later known as an Irish fairy queen.

Airmid is a healing Goddess, responsible for medicinal plants. She is the keeper of the spring that brings the dead back to life.

Boann is a Goddess of bounty and fertility, whose totem was the sacred white cow. She was the wife of Nechtan, a water deity. One story is that the father of her son was Dagda. Boann and Dagda made the Sun stand still for nine months, so that their son was conceived and born on the same day; this they did in order to hide their union from Nechtan.

Brigit (also **Bridget**, **Brighid**, **Brigindo**) is the Goddess of healing and fertility, patroness of smiths, poets and doctors. Often symbolized by a white swan or a cow with red horns, she was thought to be the daughter of Dagda. Her festival is that of Imbolc, observed on 1 February. She shares attributes with the ancient Greek Triple Goddess Hecate. The pre-Christian Brigantes, from whom her name derives, honoured her as identical to Juno, the Roman Queen of Heaven.

Danu (also **Don** in Welsh) probably existed earlier as Anu, the Universal Mother. She is said to be to be the mother of Dagda, God of the Tuatha De Danann.

Morrigan was the Goddess of war and death. Married to Dagda, she is linked with negative femininity and the more fearsome characteristics of the Triple Goddess. She could transform into a crow or raven.

Sidhe were ancient hill people believed to be the spirits of the dead.

Tuatha De Danann ('People of the Goddess Danu') are the members of an ancient race who inhabited Ireland before Danu made Dagda, her son, their God. They perfected the use of magic and are credited with the possession of magical powers and great wisdom. The plough, the hazel and the Sun were sacred to them.

Welsh Gods

Amaethon is the Welsh God of agriculture.

Belatu-Cadros is a God of war and of the destruction of enemies. His name means 'fair shining one'. The Romans linked him with Mars.

Bran is a hero God and also the God of poetry and the underworld. His name means 'raven'.

Dewi The official emblem of Wales, a red dragon, is derived from the Great Red Serpent that once represented the God Dewi.

Dylan was a sea God, brother of Lleu. He is said to have slipped into the sea at birth, possibly in order to avoid the curses that their mother Arianrhod placed upon them.

Gwydion was a warrior and a magician God. He was brother to

Arianrhod. There are various stories about him, the most well known suggesting that he fathered Lleu and Dylan or that he raised and passed on his knowledge to Lleu.

Lleu (also **Lleu Llaw Gyffes**) is a God of arts and crafts and also a hero God. His name translates as 'the fair one has a skilful hand'. Brother of Dylan, he was denied a name by his mother Arianrhod, who also would not allow him to bear arms or to marry. With help from Gwydion and Math he overcame these curses, and bypassed the third when Math and Gwydion created for him a woman made of flowers, whose name was Bloduewedd. He has similarities with the Irish God Lugh.

Math was an eminent magician and lord of North Wales. He was the brother of Don, the Welsh Mother Goddess. Math could only rule when his feet were in the lap of a virgin, except when he was at war. Returning from battle, he discovered that his foot-holder (Arianrhod) had been raped by his nephews. Furious, he turned them first of all into a stag and a hind, then a boar and a sow, and then a wolf and a she-wolf.

Pwyll was Prince of Dyfed (South West Wales) who married the Goddess Rhiannon and had a son, Pryderi.

Welsh Goddesses

Arianrhod is a Moon Goddess. Her name means 'silver wheel'. She is the daughter of Don, sister of Gwydion. Given the position of foot-holder to Math, and therefore supposedly a virgin, she nevertheless gave birth to Dylan and Lleu, taking her revenge on all men (see Math) by cursing the latter. She is therefore an aspect of the Triple Goddess.

Branwen is the Goddess of love and beauty. After the death of her brother Bran, due to a war caused by her husband the Irish king Matholwch, she died of a broken heart. She is linked with the Greek Goddess Aphrodite and the Roman Goddess Venus.

Ceridwen is best known in her aspect of the 'Dark Goddess'. Her name means 'witch' or 'sorceress', and as such she was the keeper of the Cauldron of Inspiration and Knowledge. She is often described as the 'Old One' or a Hag of Creation. She is perceived as both creator and initiator. She causes things to be reborn (changed, by having been given her protection) and at the same time is in charge of the actual process of generation. She has the power of knowing what is needed, whatever the circumstances. She is also connected with wolves, and some believe that her cult dates to the Neolithic era. Ceridwen corresponds to Brigit.

Cliodhna is a Goddess of beauty. She had three magical birds who sang to the sick, sending them to sleep and curing them in the process.

Rhiannon is believed to be the Welsh counterpart of the Gaulish horse Goddess Epona and the Irish Goddess Macha. She was unjustly accused of killing her infant son and as punishment was forced to act as a beast of burden and carry visitors to the royal court. She was later vindicated.

EGYPTIAN GODS

Amun (also **Ammon**, **Amon Ra**) was a supreme God of the ancient Egyptians. His worship spread to Greece, where he was identified with Zeus, and to Rome where he was known as Jupiter Ammon. As a national God of Egypt, he was associated in a triad with Mut and Khonsu.

Anubis is the God of mummification and protector of tombs, and is often represented as having a dog's head. He is said to have weighed the souls of the dead against a feather.

Apis, a God depicted as a bull, symbolized fertility and strength in war. Apis was worshipped especially at Memphis, where he was recognized as a manifestation of Ptah, then of Ra and later of Osiris.

Atum was known as 'the complete one'. He was a great creator God thought to have been the oldest worshipped at Heliopolis, and came into being among the primeval waters of Nun. He is usually shown as a man wearing a double crown.

Bes was a protector of women during pregnancy and childbirth. Fond of parties and sensual music, he is usually shown as having short legs, an obese body and a grotesque bearded face. He is also credited with being able to dispel evil spirits.

Geb (also **Kebu**, **Seb**, **Sibu**, **Sivu**) was a God of the earth, earthquakes and fertility. His sister Nut was his counterpart as the sky Goddess.

Horus, a sky God whose symbol was the hawk, is usually depicted as a falcon-headed man. He was regarded as the protector of the monarchy and his name was often added to royal titles. He assumed various aspects; he was known to the Greeks as Harpocrates (Horus the Child) and was usually shown as a chubby infant with a finger in his mouth.

Khephra (also **Khephera**, **Khopri**) is said to have been self-created and God of the dawn Sun. His symbol was the scarab beetle. (Both the Sun and the act of self-creating are symbolized by the ball of dung which the scarab beetle rolls in front of it, and which hatches into a new beetle.)

Khonsu, whose name means 'he who crosses', was a Moon God worshipped especially at Thebes, as a member of a triad and the divine son of Amun and Mut.

Osiris, a God originally associated with fertility, was the husband of Isis and father of Horus. He is known chiefly through the story of his death at the hands of his brother Seth and his subsequent restoration by his wife Isis to a new life as ruler of the afterlife. Under Ptolemy I, his cult was combined with that of Apis to produce the cult of Serapis.

Ptah was an ancient deity of Memphis, creator of the universe, God of artisans and husband of Sekhmet. He became one of the chief deities of Egypt and was identified by the Greeks with Hephaestus.

Ra, the supreme Egyptian Sun God, was worshipped as the creator of all life and often portrayed with a falcon's head bearing the solar disc. He appears travelling in his ship with other Gods, crossing the sky by day and journeying through the underworld at the dead of night. From earliest times he was associated with the pharaoh.

Seth One of the oldest of the Egyptian deities, he is the God of chaos and evil, as well as the personification of desert drought. He is shown as a man with the head of a monster.

Thoth is the God of knowledge, law, wisdom, writing and the Moon. He is also the measurer of time and depicted either as an ibis, a man with the head of an ibis, or as a baboon.

EGYPTIAN GODDESSES

Bastet (also **Bast**) is usually shown as a woman with the head of a cat, wearing a gold earring and carrying a sistrum in her right hand. She is the Goddess of pleasure, dancing, music and joy. Cats were considered to be her sacred animal and were therefore protected.

Hathor was a sky Goddess, the patron of love and joy, represented variously as a cow with a cow's head or ears, or with a solar disk between the cow's horns. Her name means 'House of Horus'.

Isis was first a Nature Goddess, wife of Osiris and mother of Horus. Her worship spread to Western Asia, Greece and Rome, where she was identified with various local Goddesses.

Maat is the Goddess of truth, justice and cosmic order, and was the daughter of Ra. She is depicted as a young and beautiful woman, seated or standing, with a feather on her head.

Mut was the queen of all the Gods and regarded the wife of all living things. She was also the wife of Amon and mother of Khonsu. She is usually depicted with the head of a vulture. Her name means 'the mother'.

Nut, the sky Goddess, was thought to swallow the Sun at night and give birth to it in the morning. She is usually shown as a naked woman with her body arched above the earth, which she touches with her feet and hands.

Sekhmet was a fierce lion Goddess, counterpart of the gentler cat Goddess Bastet and wife of Ptah at Memphis. Her messengers were abominable creatures who could bring about diseases and other curses on mankind.

CLASSICAL GODS

Apollo (Greek), son of Zeus and Leto and brother of Artemis is presented as the ideal type of manly beauty. He is associated with the Sun and linked especially with music, poetic inspiration, archery, prophecy, medicine and pastoral life.

Asclepius (Greek), God of healing and the son of Apollo is often represented wearing a staff with a serpent coiled around it. He sometimes bears a scroll or tablet thought to represent medical learning.

Chaos (Greek) is the first created being from which came the primeval deities Gaia, Tartarus, Erebus and Nyx.

Cronus (also **Kronos**) (Greek) was the leader of the Titans. He married his sister who bore him several children who became Gods, including Zeus. He was destined to be overthrown by one of his male children and attempted to overcome this by killing them all at birth, by swallowing them. His wife Rhea defied him, hid Zeus in Crete and gave Cronus a stone wrapped in swaddling clothes to swallow instead. Zeus eventually overthrew him.

Cupid (Roman) is the God of love and was identified by the Romans with Eros. He is often pictured as a beautiful naked boy with wings, carrying a bow and arrow with which he pierces his victims.

Dionysus (Greek) Called Bacchus by the Romans, he was originally a God of the fertility of nature. Dionysus is also associated with wild and ecstatic religious rites; in later traditions he is a God of wine who loosens inhibitions and inspires creativity in music and poetry.

Erebus (Greek) is the primeval God of darkness, son of Chaos.

Helios (Greek) is the Sun personified as a God. He is generally represented as a charioteer driving daily from East to West across the sky. In Rhodes, in particular, he was the chief national God.

Hephaestus (Greek) was the God of fire (especially the smithy fire), son of Zeus and Hera, and was identified with Vulcan by Romans. He was also the God of craftsmen – he was himself a divine craftsman who was lame as a result of having interfered in a quarrel between his parents.

Hermes (Greek) is the son of Zeus and Maia, the messenger of the Gods and God of merchants, thieves and public speaking. He was usually pictured as a herald equipped for travelling with broad-brimmed hat, winged shoes and a winged rod. Identified by the Romans with Mercury, he was also associated with fertility.

Hypnos (Greek) is the God of sleep and the son of Nyx (night).

Janus (Roman) is an ancient Italian deity. He is guardian of doorways, gates and beginnings, and protector of the state in times of war. He is usually represented with two faces, so that he looks both forwards and backwards.

Jupiter (Roman) was the chief God of the Roman state and giver of victory, and was identified with Zeus. Also called Jove, he was originally a sky God associated with lightning and the thunderbolt. His wife was Juno.

Mars (Roman) was the God of war and the most important God after Jupiter. He was probably originally an agricultural God. The month of March is named after him.

Mercury (Roman) was the God of eloquence, skill, trading and thieving. He was a herald and messenger of the Gods who was identified with Hermes.

Mithras (Roman) is probably of Persian origin, a God of light, truth and honest pledges. He was the central figure of a cult popular among Roman soldiers which centred on bull sacrifice, and was also associated with merchants and the protection of warriors.

Neptune (Roman) was the God of water and the sea; he is also identified with the Greek Poseidon.

Nereus (Greek) was an old sea God, the father of the nereids. Like Proteus, he had the power of shape-shifting, or assuming various forms.

Pan (Greek) a God of flocks and herds, he is usually represented with the horns, ears and legs of a goat on a man's body. He was thought of as loving mountains, caves and lonely places, as well as playing on the pan-pipes. He is also a God of nature.

Pluto (Greek) is the God of the underworld and of transformation.

Poseidon (Greek) is the God of the sea, water, earthquakes and horses. He is often portrayed with a trident in his hand. He is identified with the Roman God Neptune.

Priapus (Greek) is a God of gardens and the patron of seafarers and shepherds. He is represented as a distorted human figure with extremely large genitals.

Proteus (Greek) was a minor sea God who had the power of prophecy but who would assume different shapes to avoid answering questions.

Saturn (Roman) is an ancient God identified with the Greek Cronus, often regarded as a God of agriculture. His festival in December, Saturnalia, eventually became one of the elements in the traditional celebrations of Christmas.

Silenus (Greek) is an ancient woodland deity, one of the sileni – a class of woodland spirits – who was entrusted with the education of Dionysus. He is shown either as stately, inspired and tuneful, or as a drunk old man.

Silvanus (Roman) is an Italian woodland deity identified with Pan. He is also worshipped in the Celtic religion.

Titans (Greek) are any of the older Gods who preceded the Olympians and were the children of Uranus (Heaven) and Gaia (Earth).

Uranus (Greek) is a personification of Heaven or the sky, the most ancient of the Greek Gods and the first ruler of the universe.

Zeus (Greek) is the supreme God. He was the protector and ruler of humankind, the dispenser of good and evil and the God of weather and atmospheric phenomena (rain, thunder, etc). He was identified with Jupiter by the Romans.

CLASSICAL GODDESSES

Achlys is the Greek Mother – the first being to exist, according to myth. She gave birth to Chaos.

Amphitrite (Greek) is a sea Goddess, wife of Poseidon and mother of Triton.

Aphrodite (Greek) was the Goddess of beauty, fertility and sexual love, identified by the Romans with Venus. She is portrayed both as the daughter of Zeus and Dione, or as being born of the sea foam. She is often connected with Phoenician Astarte and Babylonian Ishtar.

Arachne (Greek) was a spider Goddess. Originally a mortal, she was a talented weaver who challenged Athene to compete with her. The contest was held and her work was faultless apart from the subject matter which showed some Gods, particularly Zeus (Athene's father), in an unflattering light. Athene was greatly displeased and in retribution turned Arachne into a spider.

Artemis (Greek) is a huntress Goddess, often depicted with a bow and arrows. She is associated with birth, fertility and abundance. She was identified with the Roman Goddess Diana and with Selene.

Athene (Greek) is identified with the Roman Minerva and often symbolized as an epitome of wisdom and strategy; she is also called Pallas. Statues show her as female but fully armed; the owl is regularly associated with her.

Aurora (Roman) is the Goddess of the dawn, corresponding to the Greek Eos.

Bona Dea (Roman) was an Earth Goddess of fertility. Her name means 'good Goddess'. Worshipped by women only, no men were allowed present during her rites. The Romans would even cover up statues of the male Gods when her rite was performed.

Ceres (Roman), the corn Goddess, is commonly identified by the Romans with Demeter.

Circe (Greek) is the Goddess of Aeaea, a mythic island in the north Adriatic. Her name means 'she-falcon'. Her sacred tree is a willow.

Cybele (Greek) is a Goddess of caverns and the primitive Earth. Also known as a bee Goddess, she ruled over wild beasts.

Demeter (Greek) is a corn and barley Goddess and also Goddess of the Earth in its productive state. She is mother of Persephone. She is identified with Ceres and Cybele; her symbol is an ear of corn.

Diana (Roman) is an early Goddess identified with Artemis; she is associated with hunting, virginity and the Moon.

Eos (Greek) was the Goddess of the dawn, corresponding to the Roman Goddess Aurora.

The Fates (Greek and Roman) are the three Goddesses (also called the Moirai and the Parcae) who presided over the birth and life of humans. Each person was thought of as a spindle around which the three Fates (Clotho, Lachesis and Atropos) would spin the thread of human destiny. They also have power over other Gods.

Flora (Roman) is the Goddess of flowering plants.

The Furies (Greek) are the spirits of punishment, often represented as three Goddesses (Alecto, Megaera and Tisiphone) with hair made from snakes. They implemented the curses pronounced upon criminals, tortured the guilty with stings of conscience and inflicted famines and plagues.

The Graces (Greek) are beautiful Goddesses, usually three (Aglaia, Thalia and Euphrosyne), daughters of Zeus, personifying charm, grace and beauty which they grant as physical, intellectual, creative and moral qualities.

Hecate (Greek) is the Goddess of dark places, often associated with ghosts and sorcery, and worshipped with offerings at crossroads. Identified as queen of the witches in the modern day, she is frequently identified with Artemis and Selene; her name means 'the distant one'.

Hera (Greek) was worshipped as the queen of heaven and a marriage Goddess. The Romans identified her with Juno.

Hestia (Greek) is a Goddess of hearth and fire, much like Brigit. She was believed to preside at all sacrificial altar fires, and prayers were offered to her before and after meals. In Rome, Hestia was worshipped as Vesta. Her fire was attended by six virgin priestesses known as vestal virgins.

Iris (Greek) was the Goddess of the rainbow. She also acted as messenger of the Gods.

Juno (Roman) was originally an ancient Mother Goddess and became the most important Goddess of the Roman state. She was the wife of Jupiter.

Minerva (Roman) is the Goddess of handicrafts, commonly worshipped and associated with Athene. Because of this association, she came to be regarded as the Goddess of war.

Muses (Greek and Roman) are the Goddesses who presided over the arts and sciences. Customarily nine in number (Calliope, Clio, Erato, Euterpe, Melpomene, Polyhymnia, Terpsichore, Thalia and Urania), their functions and names vary considerably between different sources.

Nemesis (Greek) is a Goddess usually portrayed as the agent of divine punishment for wrongdoing or presumption. She is often little more than the personification of retribution.

Nike (Greek) is the Goddess of victory who challenged her suitors to outrun her.

Persephone (Greek) was called Proserpina by the Romans. Hades, king of the underworld, wanted her as his wife. Her mother, Demeter, disagreed. Hades tracked Persephone down, carried her off and made her queen of the underworld. Unable to find her, Demeter began to pine, and famine began to spreadaround the world. She eventually found her with Hades, but because Persephone had eaten of the pomegranate (Hades' fruit), it was agreed that she would spend six months on Earth and six months in the underworld. From a magical perspective, the story symbolizes the return of fertility to the Earth.

Selene (Greek), Goddess of the Moon, is identified with Artemis.

Tethys (Greek) is a Goddess of the sea, daughter of Uranus (Heaven) and Gaia (Earth).

Themis (Greek) was the daughter of Uranus (Heaven) and Gaia (Earth). She was the personification of order and justice, who convened the assembly of the Gods.

Venus (Roman), the Goddess of beauty, is identified with Aphrodite. She was a spirit of kitchen gardens in earlier times.

Vesta (Roman), the Goddess of the hearth and household, was considered important enough to have her own handmaidens, the vestal virgins.

NORSE GODS AND GODDESSES

Deities in Scandinavia were originally of two sorts: Aesir and Vanir. The latter were largely nature deities rather than fertility Gods and Goddesses, and were incorporated into the former after warring with them.

The Scandinavian Creation myth is that the Gods Odin, Vili and Ve (Odin's brothers) were walking by the sea when they found two trees out of which they fashioned the parents of the human race, giving them spirit, life, wit, feeling, form and the five senses. They then retired to Asgard where they dwelt in a great house or hall called Gladsheim. Valhall in Gladsheim was Odin's place of the warriors, while the 'world tree' (a universal column sustaining everything) called Yggdrasil was one version of the tree of life. It is sometimes thought to be the sacred ash tree.

Norse Gods

Balder, whose name means 'bright', was the son of Odin and Frigg. The wisest of the Gods, his judgements were final. He was killed by Loki who gave him mistletoe, the only plant that had not agreed to protect him.

Frey is the God of Yule traditionally born on the Winter Solstice, usually 21 December. He is a God of peace and plenty who brings fertility and prosperity. His effigy was paraded by the people on a wagon throughout the land in the dead of winter. His father was Njord.

Loki is the personification of malicious mischief. Probably initially a fire God, he is supposed to bring the Gods great hardship but also to be able to relieve this. He is somewhat capricious and not to be trusted. He contrived the death of Balder and was punished by being bound to a rock.

Njord rules the winds and quietens both the sea and fire. He is appealed to when undertaking a journey and when hunting. He is worshipped by seafarers. He is also the God of wealth and is often coupled in toasts with his son, Frey.

Odin (also **Woden**) is said to have sacrificed an eye to drink from the Fount of Wisdom. His eye became hidden in the well that watered the Tree of Wisdom and Understanding. Odin was also a magician and wise one. He learned the secrets of the Runes by hanging himself from the ash tree Yggdrasil for nine nights. He was a shape-shifter and was known as Father of the Gods. Wednesday (Odin's Day) was named after him.

Thor is the Thunderer who wields his divine hammer – he was the strongest of the Gods. His chariot racing across the sky is said to generate thunder, though other stories suggest this is done when he blows into his beard. He is also a fertility God and goes to war against giants, monsters, trolls and dwarves. Thursday (Thor's Day) was named after him.

Tyr is the God of battle, identified with Mars, after whom Tuesday is named.

Norse Goddesses
Freya, the daughter of Njord, is the Goddess of love, beauty and sexuality. Her sacred animal is the cat and she wears a feather dress when flying. She is said to choose the souls of those who have fallen in battle to take them to Valhalla (Odin's heaven). She is particularly skilled in magic.

Frigg is Odin's wife and the foremost of the Asynjur (Goddesses). She is the patroness of the household and of married women. She was, and is, invoked by the childless. Also mother of the Aesir, she gives her name to Friday. She was inadvertently instrumental in Balder's death – all things took oaths not to hurt him, except mistletoe which was considered by Frigg to be too young.

Idunn was the partner of Bragi, the God of poetry. She possessed the apples of immortality which rejuvenated the Gods when they grew old. They therefore depended upon her and her goodwill for the continuation of life. (Scandinavian Gods were not immortal.)

Norns were the three virgin Goddesses of destiny (Urd or Urder, Verdandi and Skuld). They sit by the well of fate at the base of the ash tree Yggdrasil and spin the web of fate.

Ostara's symbols are the egg and the hare. She is a Goddess of fertility who is celebrated at the time of the spring equinox. She was known by the Saxons as Eostre, the Goddess of spring, from whom we have derived the word Easter.

Skadi was the consort of Njord and is said to have preferred to live in the mountains rather than by the sea. She is the Goddess of death, independence and hunting.

MISCELLANEOUS

There are some Gods and Goddesses who do not fit into any of the usual classifications. They can be used as a starting point for further research into other cultures or as personifications of qualities.

Astarte (Phoenician) is a Goddess of fertility and sexual love; she later became identified with the Egyptian Goddess Isis and the Greek Aphrodite, among others.

Chac (Aztec and Mayan), a rain and vegetation God, and the lord of thunder, lightning, wind and fertility.

Enki (Sumerian) is a God of the underworld and water.

Huehueteotl (Aztec), a fire God, is also patron of warriors and kings. Associated with creation, he is often depicted as a crouched old man with a bowl of burning incense on his head.

Ishtar (Babylonian) is a Goddess whose name and functions correspond to those of Astarte.

Kinich Ahau (also **Ah Xoc Kin**) (Mayan), the Sun God, is usually shown with jaguar features, wearing the symbol of Kin (the Mayan day). As Ah Xoc Kin, he was associated with music and poetry.

Marduk (Babylonian), the chief God of Babylon, became the lord of the Gods of heaven and earth after conquering Tiamat, the monster of primeval chaos.

Quetzalcoatl (Aztec) is an ancient deity and greatly revered; he is also believed to have been the creator God and is identified with the planet Venus. He is also associated with breath, wind, rain and sea breezes.

Shamash (Sumerian) is a Sun God and giver of laws.

Tammuz (Babylonian), lover of the Goddess Ishtar, corresponds to the Greek Adonis. He became the personification of the seasonal death and rebirth of crops.

Tezcatlipoca (Aztec) is an all-powerful God who can see everything that happens in the world, as it is reflected in his mirror. He is associated with night, the jaguar, sorcery, natural forces, human strength, weakness, wealth, happiness and sorrow.

Tonantzin (Aztec) is a Goddess of fertility.

The Power of the Feminine

Here is an example of a modern ritual that calls upon the power of Freya, the Goddess of Love. It is best done at the time of a full Moon when you can use it to re-empower yourself. Freya and the Disir, in particular, are helpful when you need a more personalized power. The Disir were a group of nine powerful feminine supernatural beings (possibly priestesses) in Scandinavian mythology who wore black or white cloaks according to the individual rituals, and carried swords. They were concerned with divination and the dispensing of karmic justice, in which they were merciless. The Disir had the power to bind or release, using the power of the Runes.

YOU WILL NEED
Staff
Sword or dagger (your athame)
Hooded cloak or wrap (black or white)
A mask (if you wish)
Jasmine or lotus incense
Powerful instrumental music

METHOD
Light the incense.
Play the music.
Put on the cloak with the hood pulled up and the mask, if using.
(This represents the mystery of the feminine.)

Take the staff in one hand and the sword or dagger in the other.
Stand in the centre of your sacred space.
Tap the staff firmly on the ground nine times and say:

Freya, leader of the Disir,
Come to my assistance now.
As fades my power,
I would make it strong

Raise your sword and say:

Hear my call,
I am your child, mighty Freya.
No one shall belittle me,

No one takes my power.
Turn towards the East, raise your sword and say:

Take notice, creatures of Air
I reclaim my power.

Turn towards the South, raise your sword and say:

Take notice, creatures of Fire
I reclaim my power.

Face the West, raise your sword and say:

Take notice, creatures of Water
I reclaim my power.

Finally, turn towards the North, raise your sword and say:

Take notice, creatures of Earth
I reclaim my power.

I ask the protection of Freya and the Disir.
I reclaim my power.

Tap the floor nine times with the staff.
Say nine times:

Freya protects.
I claim my power.

Stand quietly while you visualize yourself becoming suffused with brilliant white light. See this light expanding until it fills your sacred space, then moves out even further. Sense this light enter your body and mind, making them stronger and more powerful.
Later, if you wish, you may dedicate a talisman to Freya.

MOON PHASES, MAGICAL DAYS AND PLANETARY HOURS

A working magician, witch or spell-worker needs to know that each day has particular relevance and is dedicated to one of seven of the planets, starting with the Sun. By consulting the lists for each day, you should be able to choose the best day for the most auspicious working of spells and enchantments. It is amazing how quickly you will begin to remember which days are for which purpose.

It is suggested that you look carefully at all aspects of your spell, and decide what is the primary purpose and what the secondary. For instance, you might have an appointment with your solicitor to sign a contract to buy a house. You might choose to do a magical working on Sunday, which is good for law, Wednesday for legal appointments or Thursday for material wealth. It will depend on what your personal priority is; you must learn to trust your own intuition. If you wish to follow the colour correspondences, you may also wish to have candles, altar coverings or your own personal robes suitable for the day concerned.

You have a great deal of choice as to the actual timing of your spell or magical working. First, take the most important aspect of the purpose of your working and check through the days. Find the most appropriate day and decide whether it is possible for you to do your working on this day. Usually, you will find that you have a choice of times in which to work correctly, but if this is not the case, either wait until the next available correct day and time or choose a different planetary influence to help you in your task.

MOON PHASES

First, it is a good idea to look at the best Moon phase for your workings, since each has particular qualities:

• The New Moon is a time for going deep within and re-establishing your links with the spiritual side of yourself.
• The First Quarter Moon is a time for initiating or planning a project or giving you clarity.
• The Last Quarter Moon is a period for considering your achievements, taking time to make the most of your experiences and mourning your losses to let them go.
• The Full Moon is a time for going out into the world, connecting with other people and expressing yourself creatively.

The Moon passes through your astrological Sun sign once

during every lunar cycle. At this time there is often a feeling of considerable power, as though everything has dropped into place. The emotional side of you, which is after all ruled by the Moon, is seemingly protected by the outer you and operates very successfully. Affirmations and spells initiated on the day the Moon is in your Sun sign are usually granted. There is often a time during each lunar cycle when you are very sensitive and aware of your feelings. A little research will probably show that this shift of energy occurs when the Moon in the heavens moves through the sign that it was in when you were born.

The New Moon is a seed point – a time for going deep within yourself and re-establishing your links with the spiritual side of yourself. When the Moon is new in your birth sign, it is a good time to set goals or aspirations for the coming year. This placing happens some time around your birthday, so it is often worthwhile to think of your own personal commitment to yourself and what you really want. You might care to carry out a ritual of rededication to your life's path. You might consider the following words:

Where East is East, I call upon the powers of Air to gust through the old and usher in the new.

Where South is South, I call upon the Inferno to blacken and make ash of guilt and regrets, to burn into my heart and soul to fire new growth.

Where West is West, I call upon the powers of Water to wash over pessimism and make pure my yearnings.

Where North is North, I call upon the powers of Earth. May my darkness be buried in you whilst your strength renews and shows the way ahead.

The Full Moon in your sign is a time for going out into the world, connecting with other people and expressing yourself creatively. It is most likely to be the time for a party, which is fortunate since the movement of the planets dictates that it is usually halfway between birthdays. It marks a stage in the year where you can look both forward and back.

The Moon will also pass through each of its phases in your sign during the year. The First Quarter Moon in your Sun sign would be a good time for initiating or planning a project, or casting a spell to give you clarity. The Last Quarter Moon is a period for considering your achievements, taking time to make the most of your experiences and mourning your losses with the idea of being able to let them go.

MAGICAL DAYS

Just as each God had responsibility for certain actions, their various days are best for magical workings. These 'best days' are as follows:

Sunday *(Sun – yellow, gold, orange)*: advancement, ambition, authority figures, buying, career, children, civic services, crops, drama, fairs, fun, goals, God, health, law, men's mysteries, personal finances, promotion, selling, speculating, success, totem animals, volunteers.

Monday *(Moon – white, silver, grey, pearl)*: all things pertaining to water and bodies of water, antiques, archetypes, astrology, children, dreams/astral travel, domestic concerns, emotions, fluids, household activities, imagination, initiation, magic, new-age pursuits, psychic pursuits, psychology, reincarnation, religion, shape-shifting experience, short trips, spirituality, the public, totem animals, trip-planning, women, women's mysteries.

Tuesday *(Mars – red, pink, orange)*: action, aggression, beginnings, business, buying and selling animals, combat, confrontation, courage, cutting actions, dynamism, gardening, guns, hunting, mechanical things, movement, muscular activity, partnerships, passion, physical energy, police, repair, sex, soldiers, sports, strife, surgery, tools, woodworking.

Wednesday *(Mercury – purple, magenta, silver)*: accounting, advertising, astrology, clerks, communication, computers, correspondence, critics, editing, editors, education, healing, hiring employees, intelligence, journalists, kin, languages, learning, legal appointments, memory, merchants, messages, music, neighbours, phone calls, placing ads, siblings, signing contracts, students, visiting friends, visual arts, wisdom, writing.

Thursday *(Jupiter – blue, metallic colours)*: broadcasting, business, charity, college, correspondence courses, doctors, education, expansion, forecasting, foreign interests, gambling, growth, guardians, horses, logic, long-distance travel, luck, material wealth, merchants, philosophy, political power, psychologists, publicity, publishing, reading, religion, researching, self-improvement, social matters, sports, studying the law.

Friday *(Venus – green, pink, white)*: affection, alliances, architects, artistic ability, artists, beauticians, beauty, chiropractors, cosmetics, courtship, dancers, dating, decorating homes, designers, engineers, entertainers, fashion, friendships, gardening, gifts, grace, growth, harmony, household improvements, income, luxury, marriage, music, painting partners, planning parties, poetry, relationships, romantic love, shopping, social activity, soulmates.

Saturday *(Saturn – black, grey, red, white)*: binding, bones, civil servants, criminals, death, debts, dentists, discovery, endurance, farm workers, financing, hard work, housing, joint money matters, justice, karma, the laws of society, limits, manifestation, maths, murderers, neutralization, obstacles, plumbing, protection, reality, relations with older people, sacrifice, separation, stalkers, structure, teeth, tests, transformation, wills.

PLANETARY HOURS

Each hour of the day and night is also matched to a planetary influence. Planetary hours can be very useful, especially if you can't make it to the right Moon phase or even the right day. You can wait for both the appropriate day and planetary hour, if you wish. Planetary hours are divided into two parts: sunrise to sunset, and sunset to sunrise.

Because the Sun and only six planets are used as correspondences, you have a chance to use those influences either during the day or the hours of darkness. Planetary hours are always calculated with reference to the rising Sun, so each time you wish to use a planetary hour, you must first know precisely when the Sun rises where you are living.

How to discover the planetary hour

• Decide on which influence you would like most for your magical working.

• Consult the Magical Days list above to decide which planet is most appropriate.

• Find out at what time the Sun rises in your area – it changes slightly from day to day.

• Look at the two Planetary Hours charts below and choose one. Your choice will depend on whether you prefer working during the day or after sunset. On the relevant chart, find the day and hour you wish to use. If the matter is urgent, choose today's day.

Charts of Planetary Hours
Hours of the Day

Hour	Sun	Mon	Tue	Wed	Thur	Fri	Sat
1	Sun	Moon	Mars	Mercury	Jupiter	Venus	Saturn
2	Venus	Saturn	Sun	Moon	Mars	Mercury	Jupiter
3	Mercury	Jupiter	Venus	Saturn	Sun	Moon	Mars
4	Moon	Mars	Mercury	Jupiter	Venus	Saturn	Sun
5	Saturn	Sun	Moon	Mars	Mercury	Jupiter	Venus
6	Jupiter	Venus	Saturn	Sun	Moon	Mars	Mercury
7	Mars	Mercury	Jupiter	Venus	Saturn	Sun	Moon
8	Sun	Moon	Mars	Mercury	Jupiter	Venus	Saturn
9	Venus	Saturn	Sun	Moon	Mars	Mercury	Jupiter
10	Mercury	Jupiter	Venus	Saturn	Sun	Moon	Mars
11	Moon	Mars	Mercury	Jupiter	Venus	Saturn	Sun
12	Saturn	Sun	Moon	Mars	Mercury	Jupiter	Venus

Hours of the Night

Hour	Sun	Mon	Tue	Wed	Thur	Fri	Sat
1	Jupiter	Venus	Saturn	Sun	Moon	Mars	Mercury
2	Mars	Mercury	Jupiter	Venus	Saturn	Sun	Moon
3	Sun	Moon	Mars	Mercury	Jupiter	Venus	Saturn
4	Venus	Saturn	Sun	Moon	Mars	Mercury	Jupiter
5	Mercury	Jupiter	Venus	Saturn	Sun	Moon	Mars
6	Moon	Mars	Mercury	Jupiter	Venus	Saturn	Sun
7	Saturn	Sun	Moon	Mars	Mercury	Jupiter	Venus
8	Jupiter	Venus	Saturn	Sun	Moon	Mars	Mercury
9	Mars	Mercury	Jupiter	Venus	Saturn	Sun	Moon
10	Sun	Moon	Mars	Mercury	Jupiter	Venus	Saturn
11	Venus	Saturn	Sun	Moon	Mars	Mercury	Jupiter
12	Mercury	Jupiter	Venus	Saturn	Sun	Moon	Mars

THE WHEEL OF THE YEAR

Let us now take a look at the cycle known as the Wheel of the Year. For pagans, this consists of eight Sabbats (celebrations of belief). All are solar in nature, commemorate the stages of the relationship between the Sun God and Mother Earth, and mark the passing of the year with natural milestones such as planting and harvest. Some pagans would define the Sabbats as major and minor. The major – and best loved ones – are Samhain, Imbolc, Beltane and Lughnasadh. The minor ones are Yule (Winter Solstice), Ostara (Spring Equinox), Litha (Summer Solstice) and Mabon (Autumn Equinox). This subdivision is by no means made by all pagans, many of whom feel that the Sabbats are of equal significance.

It should be noted that these seasonal celebrations are celebrated in reverse in the southern hemisphere.

All eight celebrations have particular rituals associated with them and can be celebrated in as simple or complex a manner as you please. It is a time to honour the life force, however one perceives it, and to give thanks both for and to it.

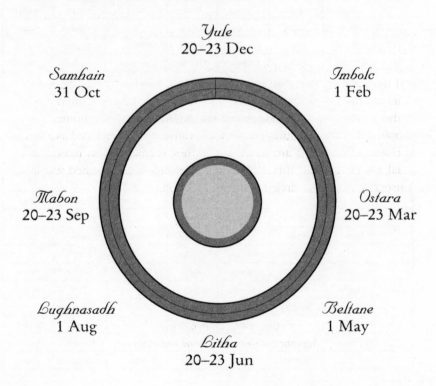

Yule
20–23 Dec

Samhain
31 Oct

Imbolc
1 Feb

Mabon
20–23 Sep

Ostara
20–23 Mar

Lughnasadh
1 Aug

Beltane
1 May

Litha
20–23 Jun

Many of these seasonal celebrations have been appropriated by the Christian religion; we see this particularly at Candlemas, which was originally Imbolc, Easter which was the celebration of Ostara and Christmas which, of course, is the Yule festival. Many of the customs that survive today have their origins in the seasonal festivals. Those around Yule have survived almost intact.

THE MAJOR SABBATS

Below you will find appropriate rituals for all eight Sabbats, though for ease of understanding you may wish to familiarize yourself with the major festivals first before progressing to the equinoxes and solstices; we have therefore divided them into Major and Minor. In our perusal of the festivals we start with the festival of Samhain, often considered to be the Witches' New Year, celebrated on 31 October.

Samhain — 31 October

Samhain is the third and final harvest. The dark winter half of the year commences on this Sabbat. Traditionally, the door between the physical realm and that of spirit is open. Many of the customs that made Samhain a celebration of this in former times have survived in Halloween games. At this time, the Dark Mother and Dark Father, symbolized by the Crone and her aged consort, are paid due respect. Food offerings are left on altars and doorsteps for the wandering spirits, and a candle is often placed in the window to help the spirits and ancestors to come home. Many people did not travel during Samhain because it was perceived as a time of chaos when things are often not as they seem. For this reason, any ritual associated with this Sabbat should always be performed within a consecrated and cast circle for your protection.

YOU WILL NEED

Your wand

Cauldron

A black candle

Plate of bread and salt

An apple

Oak leaves or an oak twig

Appropriate herbs (e.g. sage and allspice)

METHOD
Cast your circle (see pages 41–3).
Hold the wand in your power hand.
Tap the cauldron five times and say:

I ask for your blessing Dark Mother and Father of Darkness,
As the veil between two worlds thins.
I greet my ancestors and loved ones who have gone before me.
May only those who wish me well enter within this circle.

Touch the wand to the plate of bread and salt, the herbs and the apple. Say:

Welcome all ancestors to share this feast with me.
The bread, salt and apple are here prepared as a suitable feast, thus representing the
fruits of the Earth.
Acknowledging the presence of the Gods, we remember that death is a moment in the
ever-turning Wheel of Life.

Now take some of the bread, dip it in the salt and herbs and eat it.
If there are any leftovers, leave them outside as an offering to the spirits.

Light the black candle in the cauldron and say:

We greet all those gone before us who are free of Earth's ties.

Spend a few moments thinking of your loved ones, then say:

I thank you for your presence here tonight.

Cut the apple across its width to reveal the pattern of the seeds and say:

This apple symbolizes the three aspects of Maid, Mother, Crone, birth, life and death.
There is no fear, for tonight we understand the cycle and acknowledge it in its fullness.

Eat some of the apple and say:

We love, we honour and we bless.
So be it.

Share the remainder of the apple by putting it outside for the birds and animals.
Close your circle in your own way.

Imbolc — 2 February

Imbolc, the festival of the Maiden, marks the centre point of the dark half of the year. It is the time for blessing the seeds and consecrating agricultural tools. At Imbolc, the Crone of winter transmutes into the young Maid of spring. As the world prepares for growth and renewal, all maiden Goddesses, but particularly Brigit, are honoured. Since Brigit is the guardian of the sacred flame, candles are lit and placed in windows.

On Imbolc in Ireland they make Bride's Cross. Brigit's cross, to give it another name, is sometimes three-legged – a triskele – signifying the fact that she is a Triple Goddess. Sometimes it is an equal-armed cross woven from reeds. Brigit is also invoked in the blessings of sacramental candles for the church; this harks back to the time when candles were made during Imbolc. Her mantle is hung outside the door.

YOU WILL NEED
White candles for the altar
A white candle and holder for each room in your home
Reed cross
Corn dolly (if liked)
A piece of white cloth (to represent Brigit's mantle)
Incense such as jasmine, wisteria, cinnamon or violet

METHOD
Light the altar candles and the incense.
Invoke Brigit using words such as:

Lady of Light,
Maiden and Goddess,
Bless us with your presence here tonight.

Wrap the corn doll in the white cloth and say:

As you offered your mantle for sanctuary for the babe,
So we signify this tonight.
As bride we honour you also.

Place the doll on the altar.

Now, taking your candle for the room you are in, light it from the altar candle which, for you, represents the Goddess.

Place the new candle carefully in the window.
Spend a few moments with the candle thinking of Brigit's power.
Then say:

As this flame burns, so let it signify the eternal flame sacred to Brigit.

Repeat this for each room of your home, lighting a new candle in turn.

Return to your altar and lift up the cross and say:

Protect us now as the light brightens.
We honour your symbol.

Now place the cross on your front door so you are protected.

Beltane – 1 May

At this time, the coronation of the Sun God Bel (see page 111) is celebrated with a feast. The feasts held at Beltane (which means 'Fire of Bel') were occasions of unabashed sexuality and promiscuity, when the custom was that trial marriages of a year and a day could be undertaken and couples would spend the entire night in the woods. Even married couples felt free to behave without restraint and fear of censure. The maypole was a symbol of this rampant sexuality, and the weaving of the ribbons as people danced represented the sacred marriage of the God and Goddess. Any ritual performed at Beltane takes on the symbolism of a marriage feast and all the merry-making that goes with it.

YOU WILL NEED
A white ribbon
A red ribbon
Flowers, preferably white ones with five petals
Your cauldron (you can fill the cauldron with flowers if you wish)
A white altar cloth and usual tools – you will need to include the pentacle
(see pages 39 and 45) for this ritual

METHOD
Face East and kneel before the altar (you can wear a flower garland, if you wish).
Put the ribbons on the pentacle with the end of the white ribbon covering the end
of the red one and say:

Oh my Father and Mother Goddess, it is the time of union.
Through your happy joining, so shall happiness spread to all.
Through your abundance, so shall nature be abundant.

Start to plait the ribbons, thus creating a simple maypole symbol.
Concentrate hard and say:

Praise to you ancient God and Goddess.
You are our creators and from your union shall all beings rise and awaken.
Sacred art thou.

Afterwards, do what you want with the ribbons, perhaps hanging them by your mirror as a reminder of the union of masculine and feminine, positive and negative, and follow up the ritual with some sort of spring blessing or activity such as a walk in the woods to gather fresh twigs for your altar.

Lughnasadh – 2 August

The first of the three harvest Sabbaths is called Lughnasadh; this is known as Lammas in Scotland and is celebrated on or around 1 August. The word 'Lughnasadh' means the funeral games of Lugh, the Irish Sun God, who hosted them in honour of Tailte, his foster-mother. As autumn begins, the nights grow longer and the Sun rises farther towards the South, Lugh allegorically is dying and loses some of his strength. Lughnasadh originally coincided with the first reapings of the harvest, giving seeds and fruit for our use as well as ensuring future crops, since the first seeds are the best for replanting.

YOU WILL NEED
Barley, oats and fruit
Corn doll, if one has been made (this remains on your altar and represents Tailte)
Cider and bread for the feast
A red altar cloth
Orange candles
Sandalwood or rose incense

METHOD
Cast your protective circle.
Light the incense and candles.

Hold some of the grain in your hand.
Face East and say:

Reaping! Reaping! It is the time of harvest reaping!
Nature's burgeoning glory sacrificed as is the God for our continuance.
We too must make way, must make surrender in our lives.
Now the Goddess enters crone-hood
We ask for her secrets and magic
That we may use them for the Greater Good.

Rub the grain heads together with your fingers.
Allow the grains to fall on to the altar (signifying grain threshing).
Take a piece of fruit.
Taste it, revel in its juices and say:

I am one with the fruits of the harvest.
Its energies are my energies.
Show me the path to goodness and light.

Hail Moon Goddess! Hail worldly Mother! Hail Sun Lord!
I bow to your greatness and the wealth you have afforded me.
No ills or misfortunes shall come of my hand unto others.

Finish off the fruit.
Follow up with your own magic if you like – perhaps a healing spell.

Afterwards, have a simple feast of berries, bread and other ripened fruits.
Walk through fields and orchards or spend time alongside natural sources of
water, reflecting on the bounty and love of the Gods of nature.

OTHER TRADITIONS

Other celebrations developed within the pagan tradition
give slightly different emphases to those shown in the Wheel
of the Year. In countries where light was at a premium, the
solstices often took on great significance, and the Sun played
a prominent role in them. Today's practitioners of magic can
please themselves as to which traditions they choose to follow.
We now show how the Celtic year and the Norse celebrations
were managed.

THE CELTIC YEAR

The Celtic year was divided into four segments and this, more than anything, gives the modern-day practitioner a real sense of how the periods in between the major festivals were and can be handled. There was always good reason for marking the solstices, and each one had its own rituals associated with it. The rituals we give below are perhaps more appropriate in modern times.

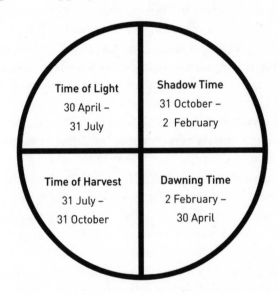

Shadow Time (31 October–2 February) This marks the beginning of the Celtic winter at Samhain on 31 October and the beginning of the New Year. At this time, cattle were brought down from the hills and the family ghosts were welcomed. The Sun would be encouraged to shine on the Winter Solstice (21 December) by the burning of oak or pine logs. The season would end when the first ewe's milk was available and was marked by the festival of Imbolc on 1 February. Everyone looked towards the future but also back to the history of past family members as well as to issues that might affect the family.

Dawning Time (2 February–30 April) This runs from Imbolc to Beltane (1 May). Its important time is when hens begin to lay again around the Spring Equinox; the first of these eggs are offered to the Goddess Ostara. The Easter bunny is a rather tame modern-day substitute for the March hare, which was sacred to the Goddess.

This is a good time to start anew, to encourage new projects and to move house. The day before Beltane (30 April) marks the beginning of the Celtic summer, when young couples would cavort in the fields and have sex to encourage the crops to grow.

Time of Light (30 April–31 July) This runs from Beltane to Lughnasadh (1 August) and includes the Summer Solstice (20–23 June), when huge 'Sun wheels' were rolled down the hills and 'bone fires' (which literally burned bones) were used to mark the event. The corn God was sacrificed at this time with a view to ensuring a good harvest. This is a good time for prophetic dreams and to focus on new relationships. Using what you have had in the past in order to maximize the future should be considered, as should children and new love interests.

Time of Harvest (31 July–31 October) This period runs from Lughnasadh to Samhain and contains the Autumn Equinox, which runs from 20 to 23 September. The harvest feast at this time pre-dates the Christian harvest festival. It formed a sympathetic magical ritual designed to guarantee that there would be enough food during the winter, by displaying and consuming the finest of the harvest. It is a time for consideration of matters concerning money and to think of the older members of the family. The year should be reassessed and goods should be stored for the winter. What happens now could well influence what happens in the next year.

THE NORSE YEAR

Various traditions within Asatru, which follows Norse belief, celebrate their festivals in ways similar to the Celts. Their seasonal days of celebration are:

Summer Finding, which is held at the time of the Spring Equinox, around 20 March. Dedicated to Ostara, this particular celebration uses a green and yellow theme, spring flowers and herb incense.

Winter Finding is held at the time of the Autumn Equinox, around 21 September. Acorns, pomegranates and pine cones might be used as ritual enhancements, and the colourings are the rich golden hues of autumn.

Midsummer is held at the time of the Summer Solstice, around 21 June. Celebrations using the fruits of summer have significance. Lavender and chamomile, along with other dried herbs, work well.

Yule starts at the time of the Winter Solstice, around 21 December, on the Mother Night of Yule. It lasts for approximately 12 days and is the most important day of the Norse year. Yuletide is primarily a fire festival, with the Yule log being the focus of sympathetic magic. The Yule log of the Norsemen was Ash, said to be the world tree or Norse Yggdrasil.

THE MINOR SABBATS

The following rituals are considered by some to be minor festivals. In fact, as you will see, they have significance for many people.

Yule – 23 December

Yule is a celebration of rebirth and the renewing of the old. It is the start of longer, lighter days as the Lord of the Sun arises from the Goddess. At this time, you might want to decorate your home with evergreens, although mistletoe, which is sacred to both Druids and the Scandinavians, is still banned from churches as being unholy; the Scandinavians acknowledged it as being unruly.

There are two aspects of light that are worth mentioning in connection with this festival, both from differing cultures. Candles played their part in the pagan festival of Midwinter as sympathetic magic to ensure the return of the Sun. Earlier still, the Egyptians had for centuries annually watched and waited for the star Sirius to appear in the sky, for this announced the birth of Osiris as Horus from the womb of Isis – yet another birth story.

The Yule log symbolizes the idea of the continuation of light. The ritual here honours that tradition.

YOU WILL NEED
Yule log
Saved piece of the previous year's Yule log, if possible
2 white candles for your altar
A black candle (to represent the God from Samhain)
Red candles
Green candles
A green altar cloth
Evergreen tree
A wreath (symbolic of the yearly wheel and of the Goddess)

METHOD
Cast your circle.
Place the Yule log at the rear of the altar.
Bring the God candle to the front of the altar and say:

Here this candle symbolizes the Sun God.
Its final flicker His passing, and here its flame once again lights His return.

Take one of the white (altar) candles and light the God candle.
Turn to the Yule log on which you have placed a piece of last year's Yule log, taking
the altar candle with you (it is a nice touch to place the coloured candles actually
on the Yule log).

Light the red candle and say:

Blessed be the nubile Goddess.
May this world be forever young in her presence.

Light the green candle and say:

Blessed be the maternal Goddess, fresh and rosy with babe.
And so shall all that springs from her be strong, adventurous and bountiful.

Light the third candle and say:

Blessed be the deep-rooted Goddess, wise, powerful and temperate,
the she-keeper of magic and the ever-turning wheel.

Having lit the candles on the Yule log, put the altar candle in its place.
Ensure that the old piece of Yule log is alight.
Return to the front of the altar, face towards the East and say:

Tonight the Lord of the Sun is born again.
The Goddess and the God are together in harmony.
The Sun reaffirms as the wheel is a-turning once again.
We praise the Goddess and the newly born God, our Father and Mother.

Now perform any seasonal activities you have in mind whilst burning the Yule log
(preferably inside). Singing and dancing, decorating the tree and drinking a glass
of wine are just a few seasonal pastimes.

Afterwards, close the circle as normal.

Ostara – 21 March

This springtime festival celebrates new life and fresh beginnings. Decorated eggs celebrate the life-renewing qualities of the Goddess, and did so long before the custom was adopted by the Christians. As life quickens within her, the Goddess manifests her beauty in flowers, herbs and the pastel colours of spring. The cycle of the year acknowledges the process of constant renewal and the God worships this. Most cultures acknowledge the freshness of spring with some kind of flower festival and the planting of grain. This ritual can be performed either during the day if you appreciate the light, or at night when you honour the Moon.

YOU WILL NEED
Fresh flowers
Jasmine or rose incense
Green and yellow candles, if liked (otherwise use a single white candle)
Bowl of water
A single white flower

METHOD
Float your single white flower in the bowl, contemplating its beauty.
Light the candle(s), thinking all the while of the regenerative power of nature.
Light the incense, thinking of the perfumes generated by the Goddess.
Sit or stand, and quietly consider the cycle of nature and Mother Earth's great power.

Stand up with your feet about 18 inches (45cm) apart.
Reach towards the centre of the Earth through the soles of your feet.
Feel your 'roots' sinking deep down into the Earth, from which you can draw energy.

Feel the energy being fed back to you, rising up through you towards the light.
Reach your arms upward towards the light.
Feel its energies moving downwards through you.
Let those energies mingle with those of the Earth.
Allow the new energies to swirl around and through you, cleansing, healing and balancing, and say:

Ostara, lady of flowers and strong new life,
Be born anew in me tonight.

Ground yourself by running your hands over your body from head to toe.
Sit quietly and contemplate how you will use your new energy.

Return your energy to your solar plexus and leave your sacred space.

Litha – 21 June (Summer Solstice)

Also known as Alban Heruin by the Druids, this is the longest day of the year – a day on which both light and life are plentiful. As Lord of the Forests, the Sun God is at his strongest on this day. Known at this time as the Green Man, he is often seen seated on a throne; he is acknowledged in early churches in the guise of the Green Man, as a face surrounded by foliage. Midsummer Night's Eve is important for many people because of the folk customs still associated with it. Modern Wiccans sometimes mistakenly refer to this time as Beltane – Beltane is actually the word for the May festival, which has its own rituals.

This ritual is also a celebration of the Goddess. She is now with child, and nature reflects this with the fruitfulness of the harvest. Now is when energy overflows; needless to say, this is a fine time for magical and purifying rites.

YOU WILL NEED
Summer herbs such as lavender and wisteria
Greenery and flowers
Water
White pouch with a red tie
A white altar cloth
2 white candles
A red candle (to represent the Sun God)
A green candle (to represent the Earth Goddess)
Cauldron

METHOD
Fill the pouch with the herbs.
As you fill it, think of all your negativities and difficulties being placed in the bag along with the herbs.

Light the white candles.

Place the cauldron in the middle of your altar and say:

Now at Midsummer, at Litha, the time of light,
I acknowledge the turning wheel for,
As from today, the light begins to fade.

Light the green Goddess candle on the left of the cauldron.
Place the water in front of the candle and say:

Lady of Power, I ask your blessing.

Light the red God candle to the right of the cauldron and say:

God of fertility and fruitfulness, I ask your blessing.

Pick up the herb pouch and hold it up while saying:

Lord of the Sun, burn away the negative.
Purify me through your powerful light.

Ignite your pouch using the flame from the red candle.
Drop the pouch into the cauldron and say:

Great Goddess and God, on this enchanted night I pray for your guidance in
self-understanding and worldly perception.
Afford me delight and happiness, and ward off any danger brought by my own doing.

As the pouch burns, it clears away all your negativity.
When it has burnt out, signify your acceptance by pouring a little of the water into
the cauldron where it is mixed with the ashes.

Spend a little time contemplating the gifts of the God and Goddess.

Finally, dispose of the water and ashes by pouring them on to the bare earth.

Leave the red and green candles to burn out.

Mabon – 21 September (Autumn Equinox)

Mabon is when day and night are divided equally. Thanks are given to the sunlight and respects are paid to the approaching dark. A fundamental time of balance, it is when to complete old business as we prepare for rest, relaxation, reflection and the winding down of the year at Samhain.

YOU WILL NEED
Your usual ritual tools
Cauldron
A yellow candle
A green candle
Strong-smelling incense such as pine or sage

METHOD
Cast your circle as usual.
Acknowledge the Elements, then say:

This, now a time of thanksgiving,
The Triple Goddess draws near.
Light and dark stand equal
And we rest.
The harvest is complete.

Light the coloured candles from the altar candles.
Moving clockwise, carefully carry the coloured candles around your sacred space.
Starting at the East, at each Element direction pause and say:

Bless now my harvest, guardians of the Elements.

Place the candles in holders on the altar.
Tap the cauldron three times with your wand and say:

Death, life – both are balanced,
Negativity, positivity are accepted as equal.
I am now complete.
May the Gods and Goddesses guide me now.

Close the circle.
Now is the time for divination, for guidance and wisdom.
Meditation at this time is useful.

MOON RITUALS

In the rituals concerning the Wheel of the Year we have honoured the Goddess in her guise as Mother Earth, but she can also be honoured as the Moon Goddess or the Triple Goddess. In this aspect she reflects the phases of the Moon as Maid, Mother and Crone. Many will want to honour her frequently. For this reason, we include rituals that honour these phases. We start with the Goddess resplendent in all her power.

The second of these rituals is for self-initiation and might be used by the solitary practitioner. You are presenting yourself for approval to powers and energies that will help you along your path to self-improvement.

Simple Full Moon Ritual

This ritual can be performed indoors as well as outside. Try to have a representation of the full Moon floating in the water – it can be made of white paper – or use a white flower, so long as you cannot see its reflection.

YOU WILL NEED
Bowl of water
A white paper Moon or flower

METHOD
Raise the bowl towards the Moon in the sky and say:

Hail to thee, white swan on the river.
Present life, tide-turner,
Moving through the streams of life, all hail.
Mother of old and new days,
To you, through you, this night we cling to your aura.
Pure reflection, total in belief, touched by your presence,
I am in your power and wisdom.
Praise your power, your peace, my power, my peace.
I am strong. I praise. I bless.

Replace the bowl on the altar.
Stand for a few moments appreciating the power of the Moon.

Self-initiation Ritual

A self-initiation ritual is a very spiritual act and is best done at the time of a Full Moon.

YOU WILL NEED
Your usual ritual tools (see pages 44–6)
Salt
A bell or rattle
Frankincense oil
Jewellery (perhaps to represent your deity)

METHOD
Meditate without interruption for at least an hour.
Cast your circle and acknowledge the four directions (see pages 94–5).
Then face towards the East, raise your arms in greeting and say:

Where magic dwells and two worlds meet,
I stand at the door to part the veil,
Protected and powerful, my circle around me.

Stand with your feet together and your arms outstretched, and say:

Hear my call, O Great One.
I call upon thee and the Ancient Gods.
I desire to walk the hidden paths of old,
To stand within the temple of learning and receive instruction.
I await the call to enter and be initiated.
Only the Great Goddess and her consort can grant that boon.

Put a pinch of salt on your tongue and say:

Mortal I am, loved and cared for by the Goddess and her consort.
Let her be the judge of my actions now and in the future.

Put the frankincense oil on the pentacle.
Kneel before the altar and say:

May the Lord and Lady hear my words!
I hereby dedicate my life to the Old Gods and the Old Ways.
Let them instruct me from henceforth.

Stand up, pick up the bell and face the North.
Acknowledge the guardians of that direction, ring the bell three times and say:

Behold, O guardian of the North.
I am a child of the Lord and Lady.

Follow this by acknowledging each direction in turn.

Return to the altar.
Take the oil and, with a drop on the forefinger of your power hand, lightly anoint
your throat and, if you honour the Greek Gods and Goddesses, say:

May the Goddess Hera seal my lips amongst those who do not believe.

Anoint your heart area and say:

May the God Apollo teach me to know truth.

Anoint the palms of your hands and say:

May the Goddess Artemis guide my hands.

Anoint your feet and say:

May the Goddess Hecate direct me in my journeying.
Bless me, Gods and Goddesses both.

Stand in silence to receive the blessing.
Wait until you sense an acknowledgement in the atmosphere around you.

To dedicate your jewellery, lay it on the pentacle or sacred cloth and say:

Through the power of the God and Goddess is this [jewellery] blessed.
A key to magical power from other realms and ancient knowledge.

Hold the jewellery up and say:

In the name of the Goddess and her consort,
In this jewellery I pledge my power.

Close the circle as usual.

Dark Moon Ritual

The Dark Moon was considered to be the time when the Moon turned her face away from the world. The Ancients accepted this as a time of power, not a lack of energy, and understood that it gave potency to women and all they represented. One such icon is the Egyptian Goddess Hathor, known as the Lady of the Sycamore, Queen of Heaven, Queen of the West (or the dead) and House of the Womb of Horus. The mirror, tambourine and sistrum, in which she is said to have embedded herself in order to drive away evil spirits, are sacred to her. She is a protector of women and motherhood. She also has power over love, pleasure, flowers, the sky and the Moon, as well as more mundane things such as prosperity.

In this ritual, you put yourself in the position of acknowledging the presence of the power that was perceived as Hathor, and which is still perceived today as a potent force.

YOU WILL NEED
An ankh (Egyptian Cross of Life, see pages 198 and 201)
Suitable incense such as lotus

METHOD
Cast your circle of protection in your usual way, acknowledging the four cardinal points as you wish.

Say aloud, or silently communicate, these words:

Hail, Hathor, Queen of the West,
I request your presence here.

Remain quiet for a few moments, until you can sense what seems to be a presence with you. (Remember, this is a subjective experience and no one can tell you what it will feel like.)

Bow your head for a few moments to acknowledge the power and energy.
Now is the time to be spontaneous as you meet the Goddess –
do what feels right for you.
You may wish to signify opening a veil between this plane of existence and that of the Goddess or stepping forward to meet her.

Project thoughts or words of welcome to Hathor and recognize that you are to learn from the experience.

Taking the ankh in your hands, hold it to your heart.
This helps you to make the loving connection necessary in this ritual.

FACE EAST:
Hold the ankh up high and say:

Great Hathor, I listen for your words of power.

TURN TO THE SOUTH:
Hold the ankh up high and say:

Great Hathor, I seek your guidance in action.

TURN TO THE WEST:
Hold up the ankh and say:

Great Hathor, I ask for your nurturing.

FINALLY, TURN TO THE NORTH:
Hold up the ankh and say:

Great Hathor, I welcome your grounding.
Let now our magic begin!

Return to the altar.
Lay aside the ankh and say:

O Great Hathor, I listen and absorb your proffered gifts,
Words of power, knowledge and wisdom.

Now you must signify that you are returning to your own world.
Place your power hand on the altar and say:

Now I return to this world of mine and the tasks therein.
Praise be to Hathor.

Depending on how you were moved to welcome her, close the veil between the
planes of existence or step back from the altar.

Close your circle of protection as usual.

5

FORMS
OF MAGIC

It is worthwhile stressing that the Moon Goddess in her triplicate form of Maid, Mother and Crone has always been worshipped as a deity. Many cultures give credence to the Triple Goddess, recognizing that the Moon in her phases personifies femininity. The various forms of magic that we look at next all owe a degree of allegiance to the Moon Goddess in her various guises.

CANDLE MAGIC

In learning how to dress and charge candles (see pages 98–9), you have already familiarized yourself with the basic elements of candle magic. There are three magical principles at work here: concentration, visualization and willpower. The simple act of preparing the candle for burning means that even before you start, you are already linking with the Element of Fire and all its power.

The candles used in spell-making and magic should be unused – that is, virgin. Vibrations in candles that have been used for another purpose will distort the effectiveness of your spell and indeed may cause harm to the spell undertaken. The size and shape of the candles is not important, though most practitioners prefer to use high-quality candles that have colour running all the way through as opposed to dipped candles. Beeswax candles are best because they are wholly natural, if a little more expensive. Paraffin wax is perfectly adequate, particularly when the candle is properly prepared and if you use candles fairly frequently. The actual burning of the candle is the most important aspect, so make sure the wick is a good one. You do not necessarily need large candles in order to succeed in your spell-making, particularly as it is unwise to leave candles burning for too long unattended. A properly charged small candle will be just as effective as a larger one.

Positive Candle Magic

The simplest form of candle magic is demonstrated in To Disengage Gently (pages 81–2), where something is burnt in the candle flame and then the ashes disposed of. This method of using the candle flame can also be used in a more positive fashion.

YOU WILL NEED
A white dressed candle
Paper

METHOD
Light the candle.
Write down the intention of the ritual you are performing on
a clean piece of paper.
You could use symbols to represent your needs using perhaps the
Runic, Ogham or Egyptian alphabet.

As you write it down, visualize your desire, whatever it may be, coming true.
Feel what it would really be like to be offered a new job, imagine your manager
telling you that your salary has been increased or see yourself with a better job,
salary and improved love life.

Carefully fold up the paper on which you have written the intention.
Fold the paper into half, quarters and then eighths, all the while
thinking of your aim.
Place the corner of the folded paper in the candle flame until it catches light,
always concentrating on what it is you want to have happen.

You may wish to bury the ashes later in order for the spell to have its full effect.

KNOT MAGIC

Although not well known, knot magic has a venerable history. In Mesopotamia it was carried out in various ways which are not so different from those used today. It seems that a number of knots (usually odd numbers) were tied in a cord. For instance, to get rid of a problem for an individual, the magician would tie knots in a cord to represent the problem. He would then recite or chant an incantation or spell, or would take his magical words from a well-known myth. At the same time, he would undo the knots, thus releasing the person from the hold the problem had over them. Sometimes, in order to ensure that the difficulty was got rid of completely and permanently, the cord would be burned afterwards. This method was used for exorcism, dispelling negativity or for healing.

In certain situations, the magician would recite a curse while concentrating on the source of the problem and knotting it into the cord. Afterwards, the knotted cord would be buried, the belief being that this ensured it remained active. Alternatively, the sufferer's head, hands or feet would be bound and the cords cut away to signify freedom. Usually a black or white cord (or sometimes both) made from the hair of a sheep or goat was used, though a red cord was also used.

Preparing Your Cord

YOU WILL NEED
Three lengths of cord, each 9 feet (3m) long (preferably natural such as silk or wool), in colours that are significant to you

METHOD
Start braiding the lengths of material together.
As you do so, think of three becoming one.

Concentrate all your energies into what you are doing.
(Remember, when performing these actions, you are making the braid an extension of yourself.)

If you wish, you can make a mental link with your favourite deities and ask them to bless your work.

When you have finished, tie a knot in both ends to prevent it unravelling.

Consecrate the finished article by placing it on your altar (if you use one) or holding it in your hands.

Make three anticlockwise circles above the cord with your power hand.
Say words such as:

I hereby cleanse and purify you. I send away any defilement that may lie within.

Visualize the cord surrounded by a bright light.
Imagine it shining brightly, then let the image fade away.

Now make three clockwise circles above the cord and say words such as:

I bless and consecrate you for the purpose of [name your purpose].

Once again, see the cord surrounded by bright light.
Hold the image for as long as you can, then let it fade.

When not in use, keep the cord protected, for instance by wrapping it
in a clean cloth.

To Cure Sickness

Knot magic can be good for getting rid of illnesses; here is an example of
a ritual that will help to do this. It works on the principle of binding the
illness into the cord, so it is a form of sympathetic magic combined with
positive thought.

YOU WILL NEED
8-inch (20cm) length of cord

METHOD
Mark the cord six times so that you have seven equal lengths.
Make sure you are well grounded.

Repeat the following six times and tie a knot each time:

Sickness, no one bids you stay.
It's time for you to fade away.
Through these knots I bid you leave,
By these words which I do weave.

Put the cord in a container of salt (this represents burying in the Earth).

Create a seal for the container with the above incantation written on a
piece of paper.
Then dispose of the container appropriately, perhaps in running water.

The number six has particular relevance here because it is widely accepted as the
number of the Sun, which is restorative and regenerative.

To Clear Evil Intent

This next incantation banishes hexes (an evil influence put upon you by
someone else) and curses. Knot magic, because it binds the other person,
has long been used for the purposes of undoing such acts. It is said that,
if someone has used knot magic against you, if you can find the original
cord used and undo the knots (clear the curse), you can be free of it. This
is one of the few times when it is considered correct to turn something
back on its originator, a kind of instant retribution. If you cannot find
the original binding cord, the following will suffice since it represents the
original burying of the bottle which is part of casting a hex.

YOU WILL NEED
A length of string
Bottle

METHOD
Bury the string.
After three days, dig it up.
Put the bottle on the floor or ground and say:

A curse on me you buried deep
To make me sick, you evil creep.
I place a knot into this twine
And so your work was worked in vain.

Shatter the bottle and undo the knot at the same time; the original curse
is now invalid.

The curse is transferred by the power of your spell to the cord, which is then
disposed of, preferably by burning. The assumption is that your magic is stronger
than the person who has wished you ill.

Tying a Knot for Love

Now, for something perhaps more light-hearted, we turn to love. This is a knot spell for helping you to find your true love.

YOU WILL NEED
Three lengths of cord or string of various pleasing pastel colours,
perhaps pink, red and green

METHOD
Braid the cords very tightly together, all the time concentrating on what you want.

Firmly tie a knot near one end of the braid, thinking of your need of love.

Tie another knot, and then another, until you have tied seven knots,
equally spaced apart.

Wear or carry the cord with you until you find your true love.

After that, keep the cord in a safe place or give it to one of the Elements – you
could burn and scatter the ashes in the ocean or a stream.

CRYSTAL MAGIC
Crystals are such an integral part of spell-working that it is worthwhile taking the time to learn as much as you can about them, so that you can use them in whatever way is appropriate for you. You might, for instance, like to place a large crystal of, say, rock quartz on your altar as representative of the Earth Element and all its goodness. On the other hand, you may wish to wear a 'charged' crystal (a crystal that has had extra energy added to it) to protect you.

FINDING YOUR CRYSTAL
• Stand in front of a group of crystals.
• Close your eyes.
• Open your eyes quickly and pick up the first crystal you see or the one that attracts you in any way.
• When holding a particular crystal, you may find that your hands tingle. This usually means it is for you.

160

CLEANSING A CRYSTAL

When you acquire a new crystal, you should first of all cleanse it and then dedicate it for the purpose intended. This can be done simply by holding the crystal while consciously thinking that it will be used only for good, or during a meditation. You could also call upon your deities, if you wish, using your own ritual. There are many different ways of cleansing crystals. Below are several of the more practical approaches.

• Take the crystal to the sea, clean it in sea water, and allow the water to wash over it. The crystal should then be left in the Sun or in Moonlight, whichever pleases you most, where it can 'energize'.
• If you cannot use sea water, soak the crystal in salt water for anything from one to seven days – you will know instinctively how long is needed. Use the proportions of approximately three tablespoons of salt to a cup of water (the water must cover the stones); put the salt water in a glass container with the crystals and leave in a sunny or moonlit place.
• Bury the crystal in commercial sea salt for at least seven and up to 24 hours (overnight is good), then rinse it with pure water and 'energize' it in the Sun as before.
• If you have a sacred space out in the open, bury the crystal for 24 hours, and as you bury it, ask that it may be cleansed ready for your work. Don't forget to mark the spot where it is buried.
• Smudge the crystal thoroughly with, for example, a sage smudge stick or favourite incense. That is, allow the crystal to be engulfed in the smoke from the incense until such time as it feels clear.
• Put the crystal in the middle of a large group of crystals or on top of another mineral (one that is a specific energizer, such as rock crystal) for 12 to 24 hours.
• Clean the crystal in flowing spring, lake, river or tap water, and then energize it by leaving it in the Sun. It is important to think of the crystal being cleansed by the movement of the water.

PROGRAMMING A CRYSTAL

Crystals are prepared for programming by charging them. Programming a crystal aligns the energy of the crystal to the intent. Below are three of the most common ways of programming.

• Place the crystal on a large crystal cluster dedicated to the specific purpose for which it is required.
• Place the crystal in the centre of a circle of other crystals whose ends are pointing towards the centre and the new crystal.
• Put the crystal in Sun and/or Moonlight, stating the specific intent connected with the crystal.

HERBS, PLANTS AND TREES FOR MAGICAL WORKING

Earlier, in the section on Ritual Herbs, we gave a list of the various uses for herbs and also a concise alphabetical list so that you could make the correct choices when setting up your rituals and spells. Here, we expand on that list, giving the gender of the plant, which planet it is ruled by and its Element. This is because, as you become more knowledgeable, you will want to be more specific in your choices. You will very quickly learn which herbs and plants are the right ones for you.

A–Z OF MAGICAL PLANTS

Aloe is feminine and ruled by the Moon. Its Element is Water. Its magical properties are protection, success and peace. Aloe has always been known for its healing qualities, for treating wounds and maintaining healthy skin. It helps to combat a variety of bacteria that commonly cause infections in skin wounds.

Amaranth (**Cockscomb**) is feminine and ruled by Saturn. Its Element is Fire. When used magically, it is said to repair a broken heart, so therefore would be useful in certain love spells and rituals. Formerly it was reputed to bestow invisibility.

Angelica is a masculine plant ruled by Venus. Its Element is Fire. It is particularly useful when dealing with protection and exorcism; the root can be carried as an amulet with the dried leaves being burnt during exorcism rituals.

Anise is masculine and ruled by the Moon or Jupiter. Its Element is Air. Its magical properties are useful in protection and purification spells. It brings awareness and joy.

Apple is feminine and ruled by Venus. Its Element is Water. It is used most effectively in the making of magical wands, in love spells and good-luck charms.

Ash is masculine and ruled by the Sun. Its Element is Water. Its uses are protective and it is often chosen as a material for making brooms for cleansing and wands for healing. If the leaves are put underneath a pillow, they will help to induce intuitive dreams. The leaves bring luck and good fortune when carried in a pocket or bag worn around the neck.

Balm of Gilead is feminine and ruled by Saturn. Its Element is Water. The buds are carried to ease a broken heart and can be added to love and protection charms and spells.

Basil, one of the most masculine of plants, is ruled by Mars and has Fire as its Element. It is protective, good for love and, if carried in your wallet or purse, is said to promote wealth. It is also useful for healing relationships and for assuring genuineness in a partner.

Bay laurel is a masculine plant ruled by the Sun and the Element of Fire. It promotes wisdom and is also a protector, bringing to the fore the ability to develop psychic powers. It ejects negative energy.

Benzoin is a masculine plant that the Sun rules along with the Element of Air. A good purifier and preservative, it is used widely in purification incenses.

Betony is masculine and is ruled by Jupiter and the Element of Fire. Its magical properties are protection and purification. It can be added to incense for this purpose or stuffed in a pillow to prevent nightmares.

Caraway is a masculine plant ruled by the planet of Mercury. Its Element is Air. Its magical properties are protection and passion. When added to love sachets and charms, it attracts a lover in the more physical aspect.

Carnation is masculine and is ruled by the Sun. Its Element is Fire. Traditionally, it was worn by witches for protection during times of persecution. It adds energy and power when used as an incense during a ritual.

Catnip is feminine and is ruled by Venus. Its Element is Water. Its magical properties are connected with cat magic, familiars, joy, friendship and love. As an incense, it may be used to consecrate magical tools.

Chamomile is masculine and is ruled by the Sun or Venus. Its Element is Water. Its magical properties show that it is good as a meditation incense, for centring and creating an atmosphere of peace. Sprinkle it in your home for protection, healing and money. Plant chamomile in your garden to be the guardian of the land, and you will have certain success. It is an excellent calming herb.

Celandine is masculine and is ruled by the Sun. Its Element is Fire. When worn as an amulet, it helps the wearer to escape unfair imprisonment and entrapment. It alleviates depression.

Cinnamon is masculine and is ruled by the Sun. Its Element is Fire. Its magical properties are used to help in spiritual quests, augmenting power, love, success, psychic work, healing and cleansing. It is used in incense for healing, clairvoyance and high spiritual vibrations; it is also reputed to be a male aphrodisiac. Use it in prosperity charms. It is an excellent aromatic and makes a good anointing oil for any magical working.

Cinquefoil is masculine and is ruled by Jupiter. Its Element is Earth. Hang it around your doors and windows to protect you from evil. It is used in spells and charms for prosperity, purification and protection.

Clove is masculine and is ruled by the Sun. Its Element is Fire. Wear it in an amulet or charm to dispel negativity and bind those who speak ill of you. Cloves strung on a red thread can be worn as a protective charm. It helps with money matters, visions, cleansing and purification.

Clover is masculine and is ruled by Mercury; it is also associated with the Triple Goddess. Its Element is Air. Use it in rituals for beauty, youth, healing injuries and curing madness. A four-leaved clover is said to enable one to see fairies and is considered a general good-luck charm.

Comfrey is a feminine plant and is ruled by Saturn. Its Element is Water. It is useful for travel, casting spells for money and healing. It also honours the Crone aspect of the Goddess.

Coriander is masculine and is ruled by Mars and the Element Fire. It is a protector of the home and is useful in the promotion of peace. It encourages longevity and is helpful in love spells.

Cowslip is feminine, ruled by Venus with its Element Water. Said to bring luck in love, it also induces contact with departed loved ones during dreams. A woman who washes her face with milk infused with cowslip will draw her beloved closer to her.

Cypress is masculine and is ruled by Saturn and its Element is

Earth. It is connected with death. Often used to consecrate ritual tools, cypress also has preservative qualities.

Daisy is feminine and is ruled by Venus and the Element Water. If you decorate your house with it on Midsummer's Eve, it will bring happiness into the home. Daisies are also worn at Midsummer for luck and blessings. Long ago, young maidens would weave daisy chains and wear them in their hair to attract their beloved.

Dandelion is masculine plant and is ruled by Jupiter and the Element Air. It is useful for divination and communication.

Dill is masculine and is ruled by Mercury. Its Element is Fire. It is useful in love charms. Dill may also be hung in children's rooms to protect them against evil spirits and bad dreams.

Dragon's blood is masculine and is ruled by Mars with the Element Fire. A type of palm, it is widely included in love, protection and purification spells, usually in the form of a resin. It is carried for good luck; a piece of the plant kept under the bed is said to cure impotency. Dragon's blood increases the potency of other incense.

Elder is a feminine plant ruled by Venus and the Element Air. Its branches are widely used for magical wands and it is considered bad luck to burn elder wood. Leaves hung around the doors and windows are said to ward off evil.

Elecampane is a masculine plant ruled by Mercury and the Element Earth. It is a good aid in meditation and for requesting the presence of spirits.

Eucalyptus is feminine and is ruled by the Moon and the Element Air. It is used in healing rituals and in charms and amulets. If the leaves are put around a blue candle and burnt, this is good for increasing healing energies.

Eyebright is masculine and is ruled by the Sun. Its Element is Air. This plant is said to induce clairvoyant visions and psychic dreams if you anoint your eyelids daily with an infusion of leaves.

Fennel is masculine and is ruled by Mercury. Its Element is Fire. Including the seeds in money charms is said to bring prosperity and ward off evil spirits. The plant itself is used for purification and protection.

Fern is feminine and is ruled by Saturn and the Element Earth. This plant is a powerful protector, and if grown near your home it will ward off negativity.

165

Frankincense is a masculine herb that is under the rulership of the Sun and therefore the Element of Fire. A purifier of ritual spaces, it is probably the most powerful aid to meditation there is.

Gardenia is feminine and is ruled by the Moon with its Element Water. Used extensively in Moon incense, it attracts good spirits to rituals and enhances the love vibration.

Garlic is a masculine herb ruled by the planet Mars and consequently the Element Fire. It protects and is a useful healer and promoter of courage.

Ginger is a masculine herb ruled by Mars and Fire. It encourages power and success, especially in love and financial dealings. It is also a good base for spells because it enhances the vibration.

Ginseng is masculine, ruled by the Sun with the Element Fire. It aids love and lust and is useful in enhancing beauty. It is also a good reliever of stress.

Hawthorn is masculine, ruled by Mars and the Element Fire. It is used in protective sachets. It can enforce celibacy and chastity, and is said to promote happiness in marriage or other relationships.

Hazel is masculine and ruled by the Sun and the Element Air. It is a very good wood for magical wands and is the only wood that should be used for divining. It also promotes good luck, particularly when it is bound by red and gold thread.

Holly is masculine and is ruled by Mars and its Element Fire. When planted around the home, it protects against evil. Holly Water is said to protect babies, and when thrown at wild animals it calms them down. The leaves and berries can be carried as an amulet by a man to heighten his masculinity and virility, enabling him to attract a lover.

Honeysuckle is feminine and is ruled by Jupiter and its Element Earth. Planted outside the home, it brings good luck. It is also used in prosperity spells and love charms, and to heighten psychic ability.

Hops, a masculine plant ruled by Mars and the Element Water, is best used in healing and for aiding sleep.

Hyssop is masculine. Its ruler is Jupiter and its Element Fire. The plant was widely used during the Middle Ages for purification, cleansing and consecration rituals. Use it in purification baths and for protective and banishing spells. Hyssop works best in the form of an essential oil in incense.

Ivy is a masculine plant, ruled by Saturn and its Element Water. It protects the houses it grows on from evil and harm. In the old traditions, ivy and holly were given to newlyweds as good-luck charms.

Jasmine is feminine and is ruled by Jupiter and the Element Earth. It attracts men and has been used throughout history by women for this purpose.

Juniper is a masculine plant, ruled by the Sun and its Element Fire. It gives protection against accidents, harm and theft. Once they have been dried and worn as a charm, the berries are used to attract lovers. Juniper also breaks hexes and curses.

Lavender is a masculine plant ruled by Mercury and the Element Air. It is one of the most useful herbs and can be used for healing, promoting good wishes and sleep; it can also be used to attract men.

Lemon balm is feminine and is ruled by the Moon or Neptune and the Element Water. It is a strong aphrodisiac and promotes fertility, but is also an antidepressant that is especially useful at the end of a relationship.

Lemon verbena is feminine, ruled by Venus and the Element Air. It is used in love charms to promote youth, beauty and attractiveness. Wear it around your neck or place it under a pillow to prevent bad dreams. It helps to heal wounds.

Lilac is a feminine plant that is ruled by the planet Venus and the Element Air. It is a good protector that also banishes evil and can be used for exorcism rituals.

Linden is feminine and is ruled by Jupiter and its Element Water. It is said to be the tree of immortality and is associated with conjugal love or attraction and longevity. It is supposed to help in preventing intoxication.

Lovage is masculine, ruled by the Sun. Its Element is Water. The dried and powdered root should be added to cleansing and purification baths to release negativity. Carry it to attract love and attention. Also carry it when meeting new people.

Mandrake is a masculine plant ruled by Mercury and the Element Earth. It is very useful in incense for increasing the sex drive (both male and female) and is best used prior to the Full Moon.

Marigold is masculine and ruled by the Sun with its Element Fire. Prophecy, legal matters, the psychic, seeing magical creatures, love, divination dreams, business or legal affairs and renewing personal energy are all assisted by marigold. It is good for finding someone who has done you wrong. It is sometimes added to love sachets. It should be gathered at noon.

Marjoram is masculine and is ruled by Mercury with the Element Air. It protects against evil and aids love and healing; it is also helpful for those who are grieving.

Meadowsweet is feminine, its planet is Jupiter and it is ruled by Water. It is a sacred herb of the Druids and gives protection against evil influences; it also promotes love, balance and harmony. Place meadowsweet on your altar when making love charms and conducting love spells to increase their potency. It can be worn at Lammas to join with the Goddess.

Mint (**Spearmint** and **Peppermint**) A masculine plant that is ruled by Mercury or Venus and has the Element Air. It promotes healing, the ability to gain money and is useful for successful travel. Known to be a digestive, it also calms the emotions.

Mugwort A feminine plant that is ruled by Venus and the Element Air. It is widely used by witches and promotes psychic ability and gives prophetic dreams. It is very good for astral projection.

Mullein A masculine plant, it is ruled by Saturn and has the Element of Fire. It is used for courage and protection from wild animals and evil spirits. It is also used for cleansing and purifying ritual tools and altars, as well as the cleansing of psychic places and sacred spaces before and after working there. It guards against nightmares and can be substituted for graveyard dust.

Myrrh A feminine plant that is ruled by the Moon or Jupiter and Water. It is purifying and protective and is especially useful when used with frankincense.

Myrtle is feminine, ruled by Venus and its Element is Water. Myrtle was sacred to the Roman Goddess Venus (see page 123) and has been used in love charms and spells throughout history. It should be grown indoors for good luck. Carry or wear myrtle leaves to attract love; charms made of the wood have special magical properties. Wear fresh myrtle leaves while making love charms, potions or during rituals for love, and include it in them. Myrtle tea drunk every three days maintains youthfulness.

Nettle is a masculine plant ruled by Mars its Element is Fire. It is a guard against danger and promotes courage.

Nutmeg This plant is feminine, ruled by Jupiter and its Element is Air. It helps to develop clairvoyance and psychic powers. When used with green candles, it aids prosperity. It is also said to help teething.

Oak This plant is masculine and is ruled by the Sun and the Element of Fire. It is often used by witches and used in power wands. It also protects against evil spirits and can be used to promote a better sex life.

Orange Feminine, this plant is ruled by Jupiter and the Element of Water. It can be used as a love charm, whilst in the Orient it is used for good luck.

Orris root A feminine plant, orris root is ruled by Venus and has the Element of Water. The powder is used as a love drawing powder and to increase sexual appeal. Used in charms, amulets, sachets, incenses and baths, it will also protect you. Hung on a cord, it can act as a pendulum.

Parsley A masculine herb that is ruled by Mercury and Air. It wards off evil and is a useful aid to those who drink too much. Parsley may be used in purification baths and as a way to stop misfortune.

Patchouli A feminine plant which is ruled by Saturn, its Element is Earth. This plant is aphrodisiac and an attractant of lovers for either sex. It is sometimes used in fertility talismans and can be substituted for graveyard dust. Use it with green candles to ensure prosperity. Sprinkle it on money to spread your wealth.

Pennyroyal A masculine plant which is ruled by Mars, its Element is Fire. It is used for protection, and, because it prevents weariness during long journeys, it is often carried on ships. Also an insect deterrent, it should be avoided while pregnant.

Pepper (**black**) A masculine plant which is ruled by Mars with its Element of Fire, it can be used in protective charms against the evil eye. Mixed with salt, it dispels evil, which may be why it is used on food.

Pimpernel A masculine plant which is ruled by Mercury and has the Element of Air. You should wear it to keep people from deceiving you. It wards off illness and stops accidents. The juice is used to purify and empower ritual weapons.

Pine This plant is masculine and ruled by Mars, and has the Element of Air. It helps you to focus, and if burnt, it will help to cleanse the atmosphere where this is done. Its sawdust is often used as a base for incense, particularly in workings associated with money.

Poppy is feminine, ruled by the Moon and has the Element of Water. It is said that you can eat poppy seeds as a fertility charm; they can also be used in love sachets. Also carry the seeds or dried seedpod as a prosperity charm.

Rose A feminine plant that is ruled by Venus and the Element of Water. It is perhaps the most widely used plant in love and good-luck workings. Roses are also added to 'fast-luck' mixtures designed to make things happen quickly. It is also a good calmer when situations become difficult.

Rosemary A masculine plant that is ruled by the Sun and the Element of Fire. It improves memory and sleep; it is an excellent purifier. It should be used to cleanse your hands before performing magic or rituals. It should be hung in doorways to prevent thieves.

Rowan This is a masculine plant which is ruled by the Sun and the Element of Fire. Rowan wood is used for divining rods and wands; its leaves and bark are used in divination rituals. It is also used for protection, good luck and healing. Two twigs tied together to form a cross make a protective device.

Rue This plant is masculine, ruled by the Sun and the Element of Fire. Protective when hung at a door, it can break hexes by sending the negativity back from whence it came. It is good for clarity of mind, clearing the mind of emotional clutter and purification of ritual spaces and tools.

Saffron This is masculine, ruled by the Sun and the Element of Fire. It was used in rituals to honour the Goddess of the Moon, Ashtoreth. It dispels melancholy and restores sexual prowess in men. It is used to cleanse the hands in healing processes and is also used in prosperity incenses.

Sage This plant is masculine, ruled by either Jupiter or Venus and the Element of Air. It promotes financial gain and good wishes, while it is also a good healer and protector.

St John's wort A masculine plant which is ruled by the Sun and the Element of Fire. This protects against bad dreams and encourages the willpower to do something difficult.

Sandalwood This is feminine, ruled by the Moon and its Element is Air. It has high spiritual vibrations so should be mixed with frankincense and burned at the time of the Full Moon. Anything visualized at this time is said to come true. It also clears negativity, so is good for purification, protection and healing workings.

Sunflower This plant is masculine and is ruled by the Sun and the Element of Fire. It is extremely useful, as the seeds aid fertility while the plant allows you to discover the truth if you sleep with it under your bed. It is said to guard the garden against marauders and pests.

Thyme A feminine herb that is ruled by the planet Venus and the Element of Water. It is a good guardian against negative energy and an extremely good cleanser if combined with marjoram. It helps to develop psychic powers and is said to make women irresistible.

Valerian This plant is feminine and ruled by Venus and the Element of Water. One of the best sleep enhancers available, it also promotes love and rids your house of evil. It is said to protect against lightning.

Vanilla This plant is feminine, ruled by Venus and its Element is Water. The bean is used in love charms, while the oil is worn as an aphrodisiac. Mix it with sugar to make love infusions.

Vervain This herb is feminine and is ruled by Venus with the Element of Earth. Good for the ritual cleansing of sacred spaces, magical cleansing baths and purification incenses, it should be hung over the bed to prevent nightmares. Vervain is also excellent for use in prosperity charms and spells, as it brings good luck and inspiration. It should be picked before Sunrise. While it is said to control sexual urges (supposedly for seven years), it is also used in love and protection charms, presumably to ensure fidelity.

Violet This plant is feminine, ruled by Venus and its Element is Water. It brings changes in luck or fortune. Mix it with lavender for a powerful love charm. A violet and lavender compress will help in eliminating headaches. The flowers are carried as a good-luck charm. The scent will soothe, clear the mind and relax the wearer.

Walnut This is masculine, ruled by the Sun and the Element is Fire. Carry the nut as a charm to promote fertility and strengthen the heart. It attracts lightning.

Willow This tree is feminine and ruled by the Moon. The Element is Water. Willow wands can be used for healing, and willow is at its strongest at the New Moon. It guards against evil and this is the wood where the expression 'knock on wood' comes from.

Witch hazel is masculine, ruled by the Sun with the Element of Fire. The wood is used to make divining rods. It gives protection, promotes chastity and heals the heart. It cools all the passions.

Wormwood is masculine, ruled by Mars with the Element of Air. It is poisonous but sometimes burned in smudge sticks (see page 176) to gain protection from wandering spirits. It is said that it enables the dead to be released from this plane so they may find peace. It is also used in divinatory and clairvoyance incenses, initiation rites and tests of courage. Mixed with sandalwood, it summons spirits.

Yarrow This herb is feminine and ruled by Venus. Its Element is Water. There is evidence that yarrow was often a component in incense used for incantations. It is a powerful incense additive for divination and love spells, too. It exorcises evil, dispelling negativity, yet also enhances psychic ability and divination. Yarrow tea drunk prior to divination will enhance powers of perception; a touch of peppermint enhances the action of this brew and always helps it to work better. The plant is also used in courage, love and marriage charms.

Yucca is masculine, ruled by Mars and its Element is Fire. It is said to help with shape-shifting (becoming something else). If a strand of a leaf is tied around one's head and then an animal is visualized, the wearer 'becomes' (takes on the qualities of) that animal. Yucca is used to purify the body before performing magic. To get rid of illness, bathe at least twice using suds from the boiled plant juices. A cross formed from yucca leaves is said to protect the hearth, the centre of the home.

PRACTICAL USES FOR HERBS

Herbs have always had extremely practical uses in addition to magical properties. Traditionally, women who had learned their craft as witches had also learned about the healing properties of the herbs they used. This aspect of a witch's abilities falls into the category of folk medicine, but it also entailed the women linking in with an ancient tradition by which a deity was assigned to each herb. Sometimes witches earned a reputation for being able to achieve miracles, but when something went wrong they would be blamed for it or accused of putting the evil eye on people they did not like. Notwithstanding that they had done their best with the resources they had, these women were both revered and feared. Often the women would add other strange ingredients to their lotions and potions. In Scotland as late as 1865, there is gruesome evidence that the ashes from a human skull were much sought after as an ingredient in a cure for epilepsy. In this particular case, the powder was required to be added to a mixture administered to a girl suffering from fits.

Today, many ingredients similar to those used by our ancestors are available to us for healing purposes. Unlike the healers of old, we can avail ourselves of scientific information to ensure that we use specific herbs appropriately. Below are some traditional recipes that have proved their worth. Often it is the synergy (combined influence) of the herbs that makes them so effective. Just as essential oils derived from plants can be combined, so also can the herbs themselves in order to achieve a particular end.

Acid Indigestion

Warm a cup of milk and steep four eucalyptus leaves in it.
Drink this to ease discomfort.

Athlete's Foot

Besides keeping your feet dry and powdered with orris root, try a vinegar rinse of one cup of water and one teaspoon cider vinegar to which one tablespoon of thyme and red clover have been added.
Soak for 15 minutes daily.

Bee/Wasp Stings

A drop of myrrh juice on the sting will help draw out the poison.

Bruises

Take one pint of almond oil and one pound each of balm of Gilead and St John's wort, which you should bruise by pounding in a pestle and mortar.
Warm together over a low flame.
When the oil has taken all the colour out of the buds, cool and strain the liquid.
Then apply as needed to the bruised area.

Burns

A poultice made from wheat flour, molasses and baking soda will relieve a burn and often hasten the healing process.

Chancre Sore

Soak a handful of sorrel in warm water until soft.
Strained and drunk as a tea, this will help clear the sore up.

Chapped Skin

To one ounce of melted wax, add four ounces of glycerine and four to five drops of oil of roses or rejuvenating oil. Warm until well mixed and apply as needed.

Coughs

In three pints of boiling water, place a large quantity of peppermint leaves, five fluid ounces of rum, three fluid ounces of lemon juice, one ounce of cinnamon bark and one ounce of comfrey root. Blend well, allow to cool, then strain.
Add eight ounces of sugar and two fluid ounces of honey.
Bring the entire mixture to a rolling boil.
Cool and store in an airtight container

Dandruff

Take one measure each of violet leaves, peppermint, nettle, red clover, witch hazel and rosemary. Mix them together. Before shampooing, warm a quarter measure of the dried herbs in two measures of water and use as a rinse.

Earache

Mix ten drops each of anise oil, sweet almond oil and onion juice. Add a pinch of pepper. Dampen a small ball of cotton wool with the mixture and place in the affected ear. Wrap your head in a warm towel and lie on your side for 15–20 minutes with your head tilted to retain the drops.

Eye Rinse

In half a pint of water, warm one ounce of elder flowers and half a teaspoon of salt. Strain and use as needed to refresh eyes or relieve itching.

Fever

Infuse the peel of two oranges and one lemon in whisky.
Take two teaspoons after each meal.

Heartburn

Add two teaspoons each of cinnamon, lavender flowers, baking soda,
peppermint leaves and half a teaspoon of ground ginger to four ounces
of water and allow to steep.
Strain and drink warm after meals.

Itching

Bloodroot pulverized and steeped in apple vinegar until well incorporated, then
added to lotions made from aloe, coconut oil and/or cocoa butter will ease itching.

Urticaria

Infuse one pint of black alder bark in one quart of water and one cup of olive oil.
Wash the affected area frequently.
A viable and easier alternative is to make a poultice of clay mud.

Sleeplessness

Equal quantities of the stalks and leaves of valerian, catnip and peppermint made
into a tea will ensure better sleep.

Sore Throat

Tea made from sage leaves and mixed with honey and lemon will ease
a sore throat.

Stomach Ache

A tea of equal quantities of mint, strawberry leaf, catnip and blackberry mixed
with one tablespoon of brandy should ease the stomach.

An alternative is ground brown rice steeped in warm water for 15 minutes.
Add sugar and nutmeg to taste.
Add to boiled milk and drink.

Toothache

Mix oils of peppermint and clove.
You can then mix this with a teaspoon of rum, if liked.
Apply directly to the tooth.

Wound Infections

Add two sliced onions and two ounces each of beeswax, honey and elder leaves to
ten ounces of petroleum jelly.
Warm over a low flame for about 30 minutes.
Strain and apply to the wound with a clean dressing.

SMUDGE STICKS

Anyone who works with herbs knows that they can work on very subtle levels, particularly on the spiritual. 'Smudging' is traditionally a Native American spiritual practice which is used to clear an atmosphere of spiritual contamination and negativity. Smudge sticks are long bundles of sweet-smelling plant substance which are wound tightly, then lit at one end until they catch fire. They are then blown out so they continue to glow as they release the smoke.

There are many good commercial types of smudge stick available, but you may like to make your own. The leaves and soft stalks are the parts of the plants used. Here are some examples.

Cedar Some so-called cedars are actually members of the juniper family. Many types of cedar needles are used for smudge sticks.

Sage There are many types of sage; *Salvia apiana* and *Salvia columbariae* are two of the best known. Most grow very tall and have long lives. Sage brush is not a part of the sage family – it belongs to the wormwood clan, although this, too, is used for 'smudging'.

Sweet grass Sometimes called vanilla grass, this is a tall green grass that turns yellow when dried. The aroma of sweet grass is more pungent when the plant is dried.

Wormwood In the Native American culture, *Artemisia spinescens* is occasionally used for smudge sticks. Artemesias, sometimes called sage, belong to the wormwood family; they have no connection to the sage that grows in Europe.

Making a smudge stick

The first thing to remember when you are making your own smudge sticks is that, as with any spiritual intent, be sure to wash and cleanse yourself – deliberately getting rid of any negative energy in the process – before you begin. There are also a few other guidelines you'll need to follow.

• Before picking the plant matter, honour the plant and ask its permission to take a branch or stem for your spiritual intent. Respect the plant and let it continue to give of its life.
• When picking stems, make sure they are long enough to be bound together.
• Use any of the herbs mentioned earlier or use pine or cypress, if your location allows. You do not have to use plants and herbs that are in your immediate vicinity – but if you have grown the plants yourself, this will give you tremendous satisfaction.
• If you want to, add essential oils, but use them sparingly and try to choose one that will enhance the purpose of, or add an extra quality to, your bundle.

Smudge stick techniques

Arrange a small handful of leaves and stems fairly symmetrically into a bundle; don't use too many. Put the stems in a rubber band to keep the pieces together while you tie the bundle, removing it when you have finished. Take a long piece of thick cotton twine and place the bundle top (the thicker end) in the middle of it. Using the two ends of the cotton, bind the bundle together tightly in a criss-cross fashion, starting at the top and finishing at the bottom part of the stems. Some leaves or twigs may protrude, which is why you need a receptacle to catch falling ashes. Take your time over this – the more secure you make the bundle, the better it will burn. Bind the end of your bundle securely with the twine and perhaps make a dedication to your purpose. You will now have a cone-shaped bundle. Let it dry out thoroughly before burning it, because it won't burn properly unless the plant matter is dry.

To use the herb bundle, light the thicker top end and then blow out the flame out so that it smoulders. Some bits may drop out of the bundle, so have a bowl or receptacle handy to catch them.

Smudge sticks are moved to where the fragrant smoke is needed. In rituals, you would use the cardinal points. Walk around slowly, wafting the smoke into the corners of the room as you do so. (You may have to keep blowing on the lit end to keep it burning. As you blow, remember that you are using the principle of Air.) You can also direct the smoke with either hand, the small branch of a plant, or even a special crystal or stone. Amber can also be used – especially appropriate as it is a resin from a plant. This action should get rid of any negative vibrations at the same time as energizing the protective frequencies.

If you want to 'smudge' a friend (or yourself), waft the smoke all around the body, starting at the head and gradually moving down to the feet. Move in a clockwise direction because this creates positivity. You can direct the smoke with your hand or a feather, or whatever feels good for you. A seashell is a good idea since it represents the Goddess. You can also chant or sing at this time. Whatever you do, do it with a pure mind and spirit – do whatever is right for you. When you have finished, keep the bundle safe until it has extinguished itself and then open a window to clear the space.

Decorative bundles

If you don't intend to burn the bundle, there are many other possibilities open to you. Bundles can be bound with colour, feeling and meaning. Oils will add energy and aroma. You can use flowers such as rose, marigold or lavender. You can use spices and fruits, as well as fragrant wood, minerals, crystals or resins. Depending on how you plan to display the bundle, you can use pretty much anything that has meaning and fragrance.

INCENSE

As well as making use of herbs as plants, decorations and for healing, their most important use in magic was – and still is – in incense. Incense symbolizes the Element Air and the spiritual realms, and has been part of ritual use by occultists and priests alike for thousands of years. Granular incense, with its basis of resins and gums, is nowadays usually preferred for magical workings or ritual worship. It has a magic all of its own. For this reason, a good incense burner will be one of your most important tools. You should choose this carefully, and not just for its aesthetic sense, because it is vital that the incense is allowed to burn properly.

Since time immemorial, people have burned sweet-smelling woods, herbs and resins to perfume, cleanse and clarify the atmosphere in which they exist. During outdoor rituals, special woods and herbs with magical qualities would be thrown on to bonfires or into altar cauldrons. In the home, open-hearth fires could be used to give off perfumed smoke which sweetened or freshened the air. The word 'perfume' means 'through smoke'.

Initially, resins and gums were used most successfully, so in areas where resinous trees grew, these were used to honour the gods. Egypt became especially renowned for its high standard of blending and the use of ritual incense. There was a particular class of incense – which is still available today – called Khyphi. It required magical techniques and the finest ingredients for its manufacture. Some incenses were mind-altering and could produce trance-like states.

Nowadays, incense is most often encountered in the form of joss-sticks, which were introduced in the West in the 1960s by travellers to India who brought them back with them. For short rituals, these work very well, though they are not to everyone's taste. Dhoop, or incense cones, as they are known, are another way of using the same material.

By far the best method is to burn the granular type on a charcoal disc. In this method, the charcoal disc is lit and placed in a fireproof receptacle. The incense is then piled on to the concave surface and allowed to do its work. After use, the charcoal discs remain very hot. You should dispose of them very carefully, dousing them with water and ensuring they are no longer 'alive', and thus potentially harmful. You might like to bury what remains of the incense as an offering to the Earth.

Many of the herbs we have already encountered are suitable for incense, if you wish to make your own. You should choose your correspondences carefully, according to your spell or ritual. You will soon find out through experimentation what works for you. You can also use essential oils as part of your incense-making.

When blending your own granular incense, it is important to use a pestle and mortar to grind and mix all the ingredients together properly. You may wish to consecrate your pestle and mortar first.

Granular incense usually consists of a base of incense gums to which are added the woods and herbs of choice before the mixture is blended using fragrant oils.

Blending granular incense

• When blending, first grind the gum resins (such as gum Arabic or benzoin) until the granules are like granulated sugar.

• Then add the woods, herbs and spices, all of which should have been finely ground and thoroughly blended together.

• Add the essential oils a drop at a time and mix well. Quantities will depend on your own personal preference and what is available. The blending of the incense is an important part of the process, both from the perspective of the synergy of the ingredients and the personal energy you add to the incense.

• At this point, you might like to dedicate the incense to the purpose intended, saying perhaps simply, 'I dedicate this incense to be used in [name ritual]'.

• Place the incense mixture in a strong polythene bag (so that it retains its pungency), then put it into a clean jar with a screw-top lid.

• Do not use for at least 24 hours, to enable the perfumes and qualities to blend properly.

• Label the jar, noting the ingredients and the date of the blend. Also note the intention or purpose for which the incense is made.

• Make incense in small quantities so it does not lose its potency.

THE PROPERTIES OF OILS

At various points in this book, we have spoken of the many oils that can be utilized as adjuncts to the various types of magic. They are an easy way of using plants in magical workings, particularly when space is at a premium. Below are some oils that we think should be part of every magical practitioner's way of working. All of them are simple to acquire and, if stored according to directions, will last for some time, even though the initial expense may seem to be prohibitive. (If you want to delve further into the art of using essential oils, there are many good reference books available.)

Cinnamon (*Cinnamomum zeylanicum*), with its warm vibration, brings into our hearts love from higher realms, if only we allow it.

The warm glow of cinnamon exudes right through space and time, transforming sadness into happiness. Cinnamon was used in China in 2700 BC, and was known to the Egyptians by 1500 BC.

Clary sage *(Salvia sclarea)* has benefits for both our physical and mental aspects, teaching us to be content with what we have. It brings prosperity of the spirit and the realization that most problems arise in our imagination. This herb lifts the spirit and links with eternal wisdom.

Frankincense *(Boswellia carterii)* holds some of the wisdom of the universe, both spiritual and meditative. Able to cleanse the most negative of influences, it operates as a spiritual prop in a wide range of circumstances. It works far beyond the auric field, affecting the very subtle realms of energy and adapting the spiritual state. Frankincense is sometimes called olibanum.

Geranium *(Pelargonium graveolens)* resonates with Mother Earth and all that is feminine. It typifies the archetypal energy of Goddess culture. Its energy is transformational and as such it must always be used with respect. It comforts, opens our hearts and heals pain.

Jasmine *(Jasminum officinale)* provides us with our personal sanctuary and allows us access to a greater understanding of the spirit. It is said that jasmine brings the angelic kingdom within our reach, thus allowing us to be the best we can. It gives understanding and acceptance of the true meaning of spirituality.

Lavender *(Lavandula angustifolia)* is caring and nurturing. By allowing the heavenly energies close to the physical, it brings about healing and thus signifies the protective love of Mother Earth. Gentle and relaxing, it changes our perception to enable us to make progress. Lavender will not allow negative emotion to remain present within the aura for long.

Myrrh *(Commiphora myrrha)* signifies the pathway of the soul, allowing us to let go when the time is right. Wounds of body, mind and spirit are healed by myrrh, and it brings realization that we no longer need to carry our burdens, releasing them from deep within. If combined with other oils, it enhances – and is enhanced – by them.

Neroli *(Citrus aurantium)* is one of the most precious essential oils, its vibration being one of the highest. It is pure spirit and is loving and peaceful. It brings self-recognition and respite because it allows development of a new perspective, allowing us to cast off the bonds of old ways of relating and to develop unconditional love. In magical working, it allows one to be a pure channel.

Nutmeg (*Myristica fragrans*) helps us to reconnect with the higher realms of spirit and to experience again a sense of spiritual wonderment. When the spirit is affected by disappointment, spiritual pain and displacement, nutmeg works to bring hopes, dreams and prayers back into focus. At one time, nutmeg was given to people who were thought to be possessed by spirits.

Rose absolute (*Rosa centifolia*) In India the 'Great Mother' was known as the 'Holy Rose', and this personification reveals just how profound the effects of this perfume are when used magically. Said to be the perfume of the guardians or messengers who guide us in times of need, it is a soul fragrance which allows us to access the Divine mysteries. It is associated with the true needs of the human heart.

Rosemary (*Rosmarinus officinalis*) reminds us of our purpose and our own spiritual journey. It opens the human spirit to understanding and wisdom, and encourages confidence and clarity of purpose. It cleanses the aura and enables us to assist others in their search for spirituality.

Sandalwood (*Santalum album*) acts as a bridge between heaven and Earth and allows us to make contact with Divine beings. It enables us to be calm enough to hear the music of the spheres and beings us into balance with the cosmos. It clarifies our strength of conviction.

Ylang-ylang (*Cananga odorata*) gives a new appreciation of the sensual side of our being. It balances the spirit so that we can be open to pleasures of the physical realm while still appreciating spiritual passions. It brings a sense of completion to the tasks that belong to the physical realm. Used magically, it achieves a balanced manifestation.

ESSENTIAL OIL BLENDS

The following blends can be used for anointing candles and blessing objects, as well as for personal use. When you combine oils, they should be shaken together well and left for at least an hour so that the synergy begins to work. Synergy takes place when the subtle vibrations of the oils blend to create a further vibration – the energy of the oils is therefore enhanced. Because the main interest of many readers is in relationships and security, we give below some oil blends that deal with these areas of life.

If you are intending to use any of these blends as massage oils, remember to use a carrier oil such as almond or grapeseed. Neat essential oils should, as a rule, never be used on the skin or ingested.

Romance Magnet Oil

2 drops ylang-ylang oil
2 drops sandalwood oil
2 drops clary sage oil

To attract love, rub romance magnet oil on to a pink candle and then burn it for three hours a day, every day, until the person makes an advance. The candle should be snuffed rather than blown out.

Lover's Oil

5 drops rosewood oil
5 drops rosemary oil
3 drops tangerine oil
3 drops lemon oil

Lover's oil may be used to enhance a relationship in all sorts of ways. Consecrate a candle with lover's oil and light it half an hour before your date arrives.

Marriage Oil

2 drops frankincense oil
3 drops cypress oil
2 drops sandalwood oil

This combination of oils is used to reinforce a marriage relationship, whether the union is good or not.
It may also be used to steer a relationship towards marriage.
Simply burn a pink or lilac-coloured candle anointed with marriage oil when you and your partner are together.

Desire Oil

3 drops lavender oil
3 drops orange oil
1 drop lemon oil

Desire oil is meant to entice another person to want you. If someone already does but needs a little pushing, a red, orange, pink, blue or white candle should be anointed and lit when the two of you are together. If you love someone and they are showing no response, speak their name as you light a candle blessed with desire oil. Allow the candles to burn for two hours before you snuff them out.

Dream Potion

10 drops jasmine oil
10 drops nutmeg oil
3 drops clary sage oil

This oil can be used to enhance the atmosphere of the bedroom before sleep. It is best burnt in an aromatherapy lamp rather being used as a body oil.

To Strengthen an Existing Relationship

10 drops rose oil
10 drops sandalwood oil
5 drops lavender oil

This oil can be used as a perfume or to scent the atmosphere.

Aphrodisiac Oils

Use this mixture as a perfume or added to two ounces of unscented massage oil (such as grapeseed or almond oil), and have fun!

10 drops ylang-ylang oil
2 drops cinnamon oil
5 drops sweet orange oil
3 drops jasmine oil

Alternatively, 10 drops each of patchouli, sandalwood and ylang-ylang oil is also a fairly potent mixture as an aphrodisiac.

Sacred Space Blend

20 drops juniper berry oil

10 drops frankincense oil

10 drops sandalwood oil

5 drops rosemary oil

2 drops nutmeg oil

This is a good blend to use when you need to create a sacred space or magical circle. Burnt in an aromatherapy lamp, it clears and enhances the atmosphere.

Goddess Oil Blend

10 drops neroli oil

5 drops nutmeg oil

10 drops sandalwood oil

10 drops jasmine oil

When you invoke the Goddess, this oil is wonderful for allowing your vibration to meet with hers.

Prosperity Blend

Equal parts of patchouli and basil oil

This combination creates the right vibration for prosperity of all sorts (not necessarily financial).

Protection Blend

10 drops juniper oil

5 drops vetiver oil

5 drops basil oil

2 drops clove oil

Should you feel that you are in need of protection, this oil can be burnt in an aromatherapy burner or sprinkled on a tissue and placed on a warm radiator.

USING ESSENTIAL OILS IN THE AURIC FIELD

As they begin working magically, almost every practitioner will find that they become more sensitive to the vibrations of the everyday world. A crowded train, for instance, when you are bombarded by the various vibrations of your fellow travellers, can be very difficult to handle. This difficulty arises because your own particular 'forcefield', called the aura – which you carry with you always – begins to vibrate at a different level than the one to which you are accustomed and do not notice on an everyday level.

If you begin to do a great deal of magical work, you must learn to protect yourself, perhaps from onslaughts of negativity or subtle vibrations over which others have no control. Always remember that you have at your disposal the means for control, and it should become a regular part of your routine to enhance your own aura and to protect that of others. Essential oils can help you to do this. You may find that you need to be more specific in your use of oils and expand beyond the basic list given on pages 180–2.

METHODS OF USING OILS FOR PROTECTIVE PURPOSES

Method 1

Put just one drop of your chosen pure essential oil in the centre of your palm and rub your hands together. In this instance, the oil is used neat. Holding your hands about 4 inches (10cm) away from your body, smooth around the outside of this space, starting from the top of your head down to your feet and then back up again. Make sure you have covered every part that you can reach of this very subtle body. This is also known as protecting your aura.

Method 2

Use your chosen oils in a spray or diffuser, spraying around your body and over the top of your head, ensuring that you cover the whole area. Prepare your oils in advance, combining them as necessary. Leave them for a week in a quiet, dark place away from electrical equipment. On the eighth day, use a new fragrance sprayer, preferably a glass bottle; add about an ounce of the purest water available and the essential oils, and shake the sprayer vigorously.

Energizing oils

The following are energizing oils (the proportions used can be to your own personal preference):

Basil
Coriander
Eucalyptus
Fir
Lemon
Peppermint
Spruce

Harmonizing oils

The oils in this next group are used for establishing harmony, both in the person who uses them and in the atmosphere:

Clary sage
Fennel
Geranium
Ginger
Juniper
Lavender
Mandarin
Orange
Petitgrain

Here is a selection of recipes based on all these oils.

Cleansing blend

This blend cleanses the aura, as suggested above, and gives an idea of the correct proportions to use.

Pine   4 drops
Lemon   3 drops
Basil   3 drops
Fir needle   5 drops
Spruce   5 drops

Aura harmonization
The blend below is particularly useful when you wish to cleanse and harmonize your aura.

Geranium	4 drops
Juniper	2 drops
Orange	6 drops
Fennel	1 drop
Petitgrain	6 drops

Connecting with the essential
The oils below will help you to make a connection with your spiritual self, the essential you.

Frankincense
Rose
Neroli
Linden blossom
Jasmine

Linking blend
Here is a blend which helps to form the link between your spiritual self and your ordinary, everyday self.

Galbanum	1 drop
Frankincense	4 drops
Jasmine	2 drops
Neroli	7 drops
Rose	7 drops

THE SIGNIFICANCES OF COLOUR

We have previously spoken of the spiritual centres (chakras). Within the auric field, these centres give off vibrations that can be seen clairvoyantly as tones and colours. These colours reflect the mental, physical, and spiritual elements of a person.

Below is a brief list of the significance of colour. You can see that you can use this list to co-ordinate your candles, altar dressings, robes and so on, if you wish. For instance, if you were trying to create a new business, you might use orange in your rituals.

Red relates to the physical realm. It can represent pain associated with the body. It also suggests passion – not just anger, but positive passion as well.

Orange centres around creativity and excellent imagination; it also relates to feelings in relationships.

Yellow inspires rational thought and strong will. It is also an emotional colour in the sense that it represents your relationship with the outer self and the world in which you live.

Green is harmony, symbolizing balance and self-knowledge, i.e. knowing what one is capable of.

Blue is peace, strength, calmness, recognition of the real self and the ability to express wisdom.

Purple is the connection with true creativity, of the mystic and spirituality. It also relates to one's proper place within the overall scheme of things.

White is spirituality, transformation and transmutation.

6

CHARMS, AMULETS AND TALISMANS

Originally the word 'charm' referred to the action of enchantment. A series of words would be sung or spoken with the objective of causing something to happen which was out of the normal. Later the words would be spoken or chanted over an object with the purpose of having the object itself play a part in achieving the desired result. A good example of this is the enchanted apple that the wicked stepmother used to bring Snow White under her power. Later, 'charm' came to mean the actual object itself, as well as the words of power. Nowadays, it is used more familiarly in the former sense than the latter, and not many people will use spoken or sung charms. Nevertheless, for it to be a magical charm or, more correctly, a charm with magical powers, it must have been enchanted.

The difference between charms, amulets and talismans is perhaps best understood if we look at them in the following way. The Words of Power – *hekau* from the Egyptian – constitute the starter motor that charges up the engine, which has an inherent power of its own – the amulet – and only when the car – the talisman – receives the correct power, both from the Gods (planetary power) and the Words of Power, can it travel to its destination. This is the use of Universal power or magic.

In terms of magical workings, the words of power awaken the inherent powers of the amulet, which can then be worn by its owner. The amulet becomes a constant reminder of the potential energy available and also the need for protection from some of those energies. It is sometimes marked with a symbol that gives information as to which powers are being called upon. You will find information on some suitable symbols in the sections on the Runes and the Ogham Staves (see pages 217–44). Before that, we also give you information on symbolism, which can be used either in enchanting charms, creating amulets or fashioning talismans.

The power utilized in respect of a talisman comes from beyond the object, from cosmic forces. With a talisman fashioned at the right time to tap into the greater cosmic energies, the symbols become more complex in order to protect the information hidden within it, which makes it pertinent for only one purpose and often only one person. The talisman is a personal key to the correct energy and power. We shall go into this in more detail later.

CHARMS

Any magical words, phrases, chants and incantations recited for protection against, for instance, disease or to ward off evil are technically known as charms. As we have seen, charms are popularly regarded as objects that have been blessed and charged with magical energy or enchanted. Often they are small representations of articles that have a symbolic meaning, such as a horseshoe or a four-leaf clover. This practice of miniaturization dates back to Egyptian times when funerary goods were buried with the corpse, representing what was needed in the afterlife.

Charms, spoken and otherwise, are still found in folk magic, and are often silently recited as a formula, mantra or prayer. Technically, when charms are inscribed on paper, parchment or other material, then they became amulets. Charms which involved prescribed actions – such as spitting or turning around three times clockwise – were often used in agricultural communities to protect against a poor harvest.

Corn dollies and the more recent kitchen witches are both examples of poppets, which can be enchanted to use as tangible charms to invoke prosperity. There is a belief that the scarecrow was an effigy of the fertility God and was designed to protect the crop from malevolent spirits, as well as marauding birds.

Magical words or charms are always extremely powerful, particularly when their significance is known to some people and not others. The word *abracadabra* demonstrates this very well. Regarded today as a pantomime joke, the word dates from antiquity and was a chanted vibration which was designed to open doors that had been closed with magic.

During the medieval period, when doctors were few and far between, witches were revered as healers. Many used charms to effect changes, and there was a general ignorance as to how the witch actually created a healing environment. The Church approved of the use of prayers and the Scriptures as cures and protection against evil, but it also disapproved of the use of them without what was accepted as the correct training and knowledge. There was thus a great deal of ambivalence towards those who blurred the boundaries between religion and magic.

The Church did encourage the use of many holy charms such as rosaries and holy relics, however, though it was not until the 17th century that rosaries were blessed by priests as amulets, offering protection against fire, tempest, fever and evil spirits. In one case during the 17th century, holy words were used as charms when a Nottingham sorcerer sold copies of St. John's Gospel to break a witch's spell. He also prescribed the recitation of five Paternosters, five Aves and One Creed, assuming that Christian prayer and recognizable Holy Words were specific charms against witchcraft, which used other forms of Words of Power.

Charms were often verses that were spoken or sung and were usually very simple, just stating the intent. Such verses were often used to protect against witchcraft and indeed were used by witches themselves to protect against hexes and bad thought. The following 19th-century English charm is one such example.

He who forges images, he who bewitches
The malevolent aspect, the evil eye
The malevolent lip, the finest sorcery,
Spirit of the Heaven, conjure it!
Spirit of the Earth, conjure it!

Witches also had their own good-luck charms:

The fire bites, the fire bites;
Hog's-turd over it, Hog's-turd over it, Hog's-turd over it;
The Father with thee, the Son with me,
The Holy Ghost between us both.

After reciting the verse, the witch spat once over each shoulder and three times forwards. This is interesting since it mixes Christian thought – in the acknowledgement of the Trinity – with superstition, in the spitting (perhaps in the face of the Devil).

The term 'charm' – now considered obsolete in its sense of spoken verse – has been replaced by words like 'chant' and 'incantation', and yet charms and incantations may still be recited when participating in magic-related activities such as gathering medicinal herbs or consecrating objects. They are also used in Shamanic cultures to conjure spirits, destroy ènemies, create talismans and exorcise disease.

Nowadays, the charm is more usually seen as a blessed object worn much like an amulet. (A list of objects used in this fashion is shown on pages 200–15.)

CHANTS

Chanting is an ancient and universal practice that is still in use today in meditation and ritual ceremonies. As we have seen, to enchant something or someone was initially to surround them with sound. Accepted as a way of altering the consciousness and raising psychic power or energy, chanting is believed to form a connection with the Divine. It is even today done to the accompaniment of drumming, hand-clapping, rattles and other musical instruments, such activity providing the emotional lift that brings about an increase in psychic power, often to the point of ecstasy.

In groups, chanting can be very effective and beautiful. Gregorian chant is a well-known example of this within the Western Christian religion; less well known are forms such as Gallican, Mozarabic and Ambrosian; there are also other Eastern Christian forms such as Greek and Russian Orthodox. In the Jewish religion, biblical and holy texts form the basis of the chant, whilst Buddhism and Hinduism also have their own traditional chants which are fast becoming accepted within the Western world. Practitioners of Yoga, for instance, will use the very powerful 'Om' or 'Aum' accepted as the vibration of Creation. Followers of Islam chant the 99 'Beautiful Names' of Allah. Hebrew mystics and magicians use the secret names of God, such as Yahweh, Adonai and Elohim. Native Americans also observe chanting in preparation for many activities and ceremonies. Chants, or mantras, are also greatly venerated in other Shamanic societies.

In ancient Greece, female sorcerers and seers are said to have howled their chants, believing that this created the powerful vibrations to augment the power of their words. Medieval sorcerers and magicians sang their chants in forceful voices in order to raise power. This practice pre-dated the raising of highly focused energy developed by modern-day magicians and witches. These latter use as their mantras the names of the Goddess and the horned God, as well as other deities. Chants are also done for magical purposes to achieve an altered state of consciousness and create psychic energy. Below is one such chant, which should be repeated nine times.

Eko, Eko Azarak
Eko, Eko Zomelak
Eko, Eko Cernunnos
Eko, Eko Ardia

Chants may also consist of rhymes, alliterative phrases and charms that are created or taken from other sources such as books or poetry. In some traditions, it is believed that a chant used as a tool for healing should not be used more than three times lest the chanter become infected by the very condition they are attempting to cure.

Charming Technique

When next you give a present, consider 'charming' the object to enhance its power, thus creating a highly significant gift containing your own personal vibration. You might like to use the following technique for this.

YOU WILL NEED
A charm in the form of a heart (gold for male, silver for female)

METHOD
Hold the object in your power hand.
Use a form of words that can be recited in a sing-song manner, such as the ones
that call upon the Gods and Goddesses.
(You might use the names of your own favourite deities.)
Feel the energy building up in you and allow it to flow into the object.
Let it bring, for instance, health, wealth and happiness.

When you feel that the object is completely charged, you might 'seal' it
with the words:

Health I bring you,
Happiness too,
Wealth herein,
And all for you.

It would be possible to charm any good-luck symbol in the same way, such as the commercial 'charms' for suspending on a bracelet or pendant. You might, for instance, use a small church as a wedding gift, or a key for someone coming of age.

You will need to cleanse the purchased object in much the same way as you did with your crystals and consecrated altar objects. Everything should be washed in (sea) salted water or left in the Sun before it is given. Obviously you must use your own discretion, since some metals will discolour in salt water. You could, under those circumstances, use a clean cloth that has been soaked in salt water. When the object has been cleaned, it should be rinsed quickly in cold water and wiped with a second cloth that you have dedicated for the purpose. The charm should be charged and given on the day that is appropriate for the way it is to be used. (See Magical Days and Planetary Hours on pages 131–3.)

Some research of your own will give you ideas as to the spoken charms you might like to use. Your own carefully thought-out words will have more impact.

AMULETS

Amulets are always present, no matter how civilized a culture may be; their use has received a considerable boost with the interest that has developed in magical practices. This usage seems to be universal, stemming as it does from the human need for protection from what is perceived as evil or not easily understood. Amulets also fulfil a very basic need for some sort of connection to the Earth and its gifts. Most children, for instance, will find or be given a 'lucky stone' or object which is cherished for many years without them being quite aware of the significance of something that might be considered an amulet.

The design, shape and understanding of amulets has undoubtedly changed through the centuries, but their purpose remains the same. The term 'amulet' is derived from either the Latin word *amuletum*, a word of unknown origin probably meaning 'to baffle' or 'do away with', or the old Latin term *amoletum*, which signifies a means of defence. In earlier times, three types of amulets were recognized: objects for protection against trouble and adversity; those which drove away evil influences both medically and from a mental perspective; and those which contained substances such as herbs and oils used as medicine. These latter were often worn next to the skin in order to release their inherent properties.

All ancient cultures attached great importance to the use of amulets. The Egyptians employed them almost universally. One of the most notable amulets of ancient Egypt is the Eye of Horus, also called the *udjat* or *wedjat*, the all-seeing eye (see illustration overleaf). Others are the scarab and the ankh, or Egyptian Cross of Life, both of which are also illustrated on the next page.

The Eye of Horus ensured universal protection – see page 205.

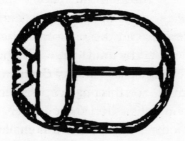

The scarab signified resurrection after death and protection against evil magic – see pages 212–13.

Ankhs, with their closed top, symbolized everlasting life and regeneration – see page 201.

Seals in the form of small cylinders were used as amulets by both the Assyrians and the Babylonians. These often contained semiprecious and precious stones. Each stone possessed its own unique magical powers. A list of such properties, according to modern-day belief, is given on pages 260–6 so that the reader can carry on the tradition. Various animal-shaped amulets, such as the ram for masculinity and the bull for virility and strength, have also been found, and again we have provided information for modern-day use.

The Hebrews wore crescent Moons to ward off the evil eye, and often attached bells to their garments to ward off evil spirits. This is an interesting use of vibration or sound as protection, since the sound of the bell was thought to scare off the demons. This usage – similar to the enchantment in a spoken charm – is also seen in Eastern religions in the use of wind chimes and prayer bells. Cylinder seals used by the Hebrews often contained written prayers, spells and the magical name of God in various forms.

The Arabs, too, carried on this practice, using the more important characteristics of God, e.g. 'God the provider' or 'God the just'. They would also wear small pouches containing grave dust as protection. In Africa, the fetish, often fashioned from feathers and shells, afforded the people protection. Beads were largely used in this way, particularly when fashioned from natural objects.

In the 17th to 19th centuries, such methods became popular when protection against witchcraft was perceived to be necessary. Interestingly, the books of magical instructions called Grimoires, which were used by magical practitioners, were also thought to afford their owners a degree of protection.

The Tetragrammaton, the four letters of the Hebrew personal name for God, YHWH and pronounced Yahweh – or, in English, Jehovah – is believed to be very powerful in magical workings and has been fashioned into amulets by using different spellings. It was believed to help magicians in conjuring up demons and give them protection from negative spirits – nowadays, it is an invocation.

Amulets are also representative of the inherent powers of things – thus, an object fashioned in the shape of something else is a manifestation of the latter's power. In Shamanistic societies, totems and sacred objects are not just specific animals but are representations of mystical powers, and if we can put ourselves in touch with them, they can be sources of sensible advice and ways of living our lives.

Animals are often considered to be messengers of the Great Spirit and are on Earth to teach us simplicity. Today, many witches, who in previous times often had a cat as a familiar, are tending to adopt Shamanistic practices and so other animals such as bears, deer, eagles and fish can also perform the function of acting as familiars or power animals; they provide us with access to the animal kingdom and let us tap into their inherent power. It is worthwhile recognizing, however, that power animals are not only mammals. Insects and reptiles, for example, are some of the oldest sources of magical power known to humanity.

One way of finding your own power animal is to pay attention to your everyday waking life. Allow yourself to feel the power of the animal (the inner) and develop your own ritual, or outer way, of calling on its power. The power of the animal is more important than the actual animal itself.

OBJECTS FOR USE AS AMULETS

Below are some definitions of objects that might be used as amulets and as representations of power in modern-day talismans. Talismans form keys to the higher magical realms. In the sense that small articles may also be used as charms, it is worth remembering that charms have had words of power spoken or sung over them, whereas amulets have an intrinsic power of their own. These articles may therefore be used as charms, amulets or in talismanic work. It depends upon your preparation of them for use. Do not be afraid to experiment and find out what suits you best. Remember that natural objects, such as stones or pieces of tree branch, can also be amulets. When they look like something else, such as the head of an animal, they can have added potency. This is why we are so fascinated by misshapen vegetables and fruit. It may just be that the object is under the influence of a greater power and therefore magical!

Acorn An acorn symbolizes new beginnings and rebirth, and also strength of purpose. An acorn anointed with musk oil and carried in your purse, pocket or charm bag will help to attract the opposite sex. To increase your income, anoint an acorn with 3 drops of pine oil when the Moon is waxing and then bury it in your garden as close as possible to the front door of your house.

Amaranth is a symbol of immortality, faith and fidelity. It is sacred to the Moon and her Goddesses, and is used for enhancement of fidelity and psychic perception.

Anchor Represents stability, hope and salvation. It favours all matters to do with the sea and protects against physical harm.

Ankh (**Crux Ansata**), the Egyptian Cross of Life, is the key to spiritual wisdom and the hidden mysteries. Representing the life force and creative energy, it is a strongly protective symbol. It brings about health and abundance and, through knowledge, gives power over the temporal (physical) realm.

Ant An amulet in the form of an ant will help the wearer to be industrious and hard-working. Placed on the altar, it will attract career opportunities.

Antelope The head of the antelope or ibex is one of earliest known amulets, dating to 4500 BC. It was first associated with speed, then with evil as the God Seth. It is regenerative in its powers and also signifies overcoming – transcending – death and its associated fears.

Antlers (**Horns**) Most cultures pay deference to the power of the antler, which suggests power over the forces of nature. They are sacred to the horned God Pan and represent fruitfulness.

Anvil This represents physical strength, the primal force of Nature as it manifests Earth and matter. In that sense, it suggests the feminine principle and the forging of partnerships and links. It has a connection with all Thunder Gods.

Arrowhead Carry an arrowhead for protection against enemies, bad luck, hexes, jealousy, evil spirits and all negative forces. Place one over your front door (or under the mat) to prevent burglars.

Asp The asp was an Egyptian symbol of royalty. It carries the same symbolism as the snake from a Shamanistic point of view, particularly favouring those seeking personal advancement. It also gives help and protection from those in authority.

Axe has a meaning similar to that of an arrowhead. It represented the Chief, God or Divine Being and had significance as the double-headed axe, which was said to represent the spiritual journey, in common with the double-headed hammer. It signifies power of all sorts. In the last few hundred years, it has been replaced as a symbol of power by the sword.

Badger The badger's courage is commemorated in the wearing of this amulet. It also represents the balance of negativity and positivity, and the idea of living successfully in the underworld.

Bamboo This is a Buddhist emblem symbol representing truth, integrity and lasting friendship. Its aspect of wisdom means that it symbolizes a healthy old age and would be a good amulet to use for businesses that have been in existence for some time.

Bat This creature signifies long life. In Chinese folklore, five bats represent the 'five blessings': Wealth, Health, Love of Virtue, Old Age and Natural Death. It is especially beneficial to educational matters, since it symbolizes arcane knowledge. It is said to bring good fortune.

Beads These are magically significant whether they are made from crystals or ordinary materials such as wood. In African magic, beads were invested with supernatural meaning owing to the high regard that primitive Africans had for their overlords – the Carthaginians – and their Gods. Necklaces and pendants even today are worn as amulets, and prayer beads and rosaries also make use of beads.

Bear The bear is reputedly the guardian of the world and symbolizes inner knowing and healing, as well as the watcher. Such an amulet calls on the protection of the energy of the bear clan.

Bee The bee represents immortality and the soul. It is a messenger of the Gods and, as an amulet, brings wealth through inspiration and intuition.

Bells symbolize the angelic forces and are used to frighten off the Devil and evil spirits. They were put on anything that needed safeguarding (horses, babies, etc) to give them protection against evil actions or thoughts. They can also represent the four Elements and the cycles of the seasons, which is why they are rung at rituals.

Birds symbolize humans' quest for their utmost potential and the Unconscious. As an amulet, it protects the wearer on long journeys and ensures safe travel.

Buckles, **Belts** or **Girdles** were often associated with Isis or Venus (see pages 118 and 123) and as such, offered Divine protection. Symbolizing personal fulfilment, these articles also represent physical wellbeing and moral strength and were often used as ties for other protective objects. It is for this reason that the girdle is so important in magical workings such as knot magic.

Buddha's footprints This is an Indian amulet said to signify the eight emblems of Buddha: the Wheel of Law (cause and effect), the Golden Fish, (first incarnation of Vishnu), the Lucky Diagram, (long life), the Lotus (good luck), the Conch Shell (wealth), the Umbrella (majesty), the Vase and the Trumpet of Victory.

Buffalo The buffalo possesses great strength and also represents the Great Spirit. Sometimes taken also to represent death, this protects the wearer from harm.

Bull To increase fertility in women and virility in men, wear a bull-shaped amulet or place one under the bed before making love. This also commemorates overcoming the lower urges.

Butterfly This is a widely accepted symbol of the psyche and the soul. It signifies the continuous cycle of life, death and resurrection. It suggests joy, laughter and pleasure.

Caduceus This is a powerful image in health matters and is an almost universal symbol for medicine and communication. Representing the wand or staff of Mercury or Hermes, messenger of the Gods (see page 119), it promotes knowledge and understanding. On a slightly more mundane level, it represents commercial success and safe travel.

Castle Symbolizing self-knowledge, spiritual enlightenment and esoteric wisdom, the castle is a strongly protective image. It suggests the doorway to knowledge and power.

Cats A black cat crossing your path is said to be lucky. In Egypt, cats were under the protection of the Cat Goddess Bastet (see page 117), and hence they are now seen as witches' familiars. As amulets, they seek the protection of the Lunar Goddess in her many forms. They are often worn as small charms on bracelets. In China, they are portents of misfortune, poverty and ill-health.

Corn or **Wheatears/Sheaves** This representation of Mother Nature signifies abundance, fertility and wealth. Symbolizing the harvest, corn makes a connection with Demeter (see page 122) and other corn Goddesses.

Cosmic egg This combines two very potent symbols: a serpent entwined around an egg. It stands for the cycle of birth, life, death and rebirth. As a health and fertility symbol, it is strongly protective.

Cow The cow represents the Mother forms of the deities whose qualities are nurturing and caring. In Egypt, amulets with cows' heads were almost certainly dedicated to Hathor.

Cowrie shell Because of its shape, which is similar to the cornucopia or horn of plenty, this represents prosperity. In Egypt it was thought to represent the female genitalia; when worn on a woman's girdle, it was said to afford her protection. In Polynesian societies it was considered a valid form of exchange token.

Crescent There is a strong connection between the Crescent and the Moon. As an amulet, the Crescent is said to bring success in love and promote good motherhood. The crescent points should always be turned to the right. Any amulet or charm connected to the Moon puts the wearer under the protection of the Goddess and also puts them in touch with their feminine, emotional side.

Crocodile Wearing this symbol as an amulet is a protection against the powers of the negative. First seen in Egypt, it protected against being eaten by the reptile, since, if this happened, the dead person could not go on to the afterlife because the parts of their being would be scattered. It is a general symbol of rebirth in many cultures.

Cross This is a protective device against all forms of evil, especially the Devil. It is found in many forms, such as the Egyptian ankh (see pages 198 and 201) or the equal-armed Maltese cross. The cross is thought to restore good health and is probably the symbol most often worn universally. Esoterically, it stands for the union of opposites: spirit and matter, positive and negative, male and female, sacred and secular, and also for the coming together of all planes of existence. It is much used in talismanic work to represent balance and manifestation in the physical world.

Crow This signifies justice and fair dealing, and in some cultures the creation of negativity. Using this symbol either as an amulet or in talismanic work gives you access to these qualities.

Crown The crown represents victorious strength and marks authority and rulership. As a symbol, it signifies the recognition and reward which success brings.

Cupid An amulet or charm in this form represents love and, as Cupid is the counterpart of Eros, is used in love charms. It also suggests the breaking of a taboo.

Deer This embodies compassion and grace. Wearing a brooch or having a representation of the deer in the home calls on the powers of Gods such as Herne the Hunter or Cernunnos.

Dog Loyalty and guardianship are qualities inherent in the dog, particularly the domestic variety. Wearing this amulet signifies protection.

Dolphin Wise and happy, the dolphin suggests the exploration of deep emotion and psychic abilities. It has come to be accepted as initiator of new power and therefore guardian of the human race. It also represents safety in travelling.

Dove The dove is the soul, the life spirit and transfiguration. The symbol of the turtle dove protects the wearer against death, fire and lightning. Associated with Mother Goddesses, it brings peace and tranquillity into your home or workplace. It also signifies communication and love.

Dragon By tradition, the dragon symbolizes royalty and riches. Knowing the answer to many universal riddles, it is a symbol of heaven, the Sun and the essence of Nature. The qualities of fire are called upon by the wearing of a dragon symbol. It is a protection against ill-fortune. In Chinese lore, the dragon represents luck, material gain and wealth.

Dragonfly This suggests imagination and breaks through illusions, thus gaining power and understanding through any dreams you may have.

Eagle The eagle signifies expectation of power, high ideals and spiritual philosophy. It signifies the teaching of higher spiritual aspirations. In China and Japan it symbolizes aggression, fearlessness and courage. It also means good fortune and the highest of Gods. It is the father-principle and the solar emblem of all sky Gods.

Eye of Horus Also known as the *udjat* or 'all-seeing eye', this is an ancient symbol used as an amulet for wisdom, prosperity, spiritual protection, good health, the increasing of clairvoyant powers and protection against thieves. Following on from this symbolism, any eye suggests the Sun, stability and purpose. It is one of the most powerful charms there is.

Falcon This is another amulet linked with Horus (see pages 116–17), and is meant to represent the protection of the God. Falcon-headed Gods were important deities in Egypt.

Fan In Eastern tradition, the fan represents protection and safety, so makes a pleasant love charm. It is a lunar symbol depicting life unfolding.

Feather This is the symbol of the wind and the soul's journey to other realms. It is truth, knowledge and power, and is a general omen of good fortune. It is said to help with games of skill rather than strength.

Fingers Two fingers held across the palm is a symbol of protection and assistance in Egyptian lore. Such a charm represents security. Fingers in talismanic work represent direction.

Fish Used by most religions to represent the deity, a fish often signifies the universal mother, fertility and procreation. It stands for the psyche, intuition and the unconscious. The fish also symbolizes gracefulness and going with the flow. The carp represents expansion, particularly from the Chinese meaning. In Europe, however (following Celtic tradition), the carp and the salmon are often interchangeable. Wealth, abundance and general prosperity are a more general meaning.

Fleur-de-lys This is a stylized lotus or lily which signifies health, wealth and happiness. It is a representation of the Trinity – even perhaps the Triple Goddess – and is also the flower of light, life and love.

Flowers These are manifestations of developing life and nature, and represent spring and beauty. They often signify the successful completion of a contract, either personal or connected to business.

Fly In Egypt, this may have been used as a protective device. Fly amulets were found with the head of a falcon, the crescent Moon, a uraeus (see page 215) and an *udjat* eye (see pages 198 and 205), which would suggest that protection was expected on all levels of existence.

Four-leaf clover Good fortune is said to smile on you if you carry a four-leaf clover, or if you wear a pin, ring or pendant shaped like one. The four-leaf clover (a highly magical plant and a powerful amulet of Irish origin) is believed to be the most powerful of all natural amulets. The first leaf signifies fame, the second wealth, the third faithful love, and the fourth health.

Fox An amulet in the shape of a fox symbolizes elusiveness, agility, cleverness and sometimes deviousness. You might wear this, for instance, if you had to be particularly sharp at a business meeting.

Frog It is said that to promote friendship or reconcile enemies you should engrave the image of a frog on a piece of beryl and carry it near your heart or wear it as a necklace. A frog amulet is also good for increasing fertility and virility. It is a lunar symbol. In Egypt, the four male creator Gods all had frogs' heads. They were a symbol of regeneration and perhaps a symbol of Hecate (see page 122) in her animal form. This type of amulet was replaced by scarab amulets. The frog is a symbol of life and the creator, potential life, health and strength.

Fruit (general) This tends to represent Nature's harvest and earthly fulfilment. It can also suggest worldly desires, reward for past labours and, by association with the idea of the cycle of life, immortality.

Garlic One of the oldest and most famous of natural protection amulets, garlic has been used throughout the world in a variety of ways. Witches and Shamans use it as a carrier for healing energies.

Gods/Goddesses An amulet or a representation of any of the Gods and Goddesses, particularly when worn as a bracelet, brooch or necklace, immediately puts the wearer under the protection of that deity.

Grapes signify the wine of life, fertility and sacrifice, thus giving the attributes of youthfulness and vigour. At the other end of the spectrum, the association is with wisdom and truth, hospitality and peace and prosperity.

Grasshopper The symbolism of the grasshopper is favourable to agricultural matters, in the sense of abundance and fullness. Signifying riches and wealth, this image probably supersedes the dragonfly, in the sense that the grasshopper is more grounded.

Gryphon/Griffin This is a strongly protective symbol representing moral fortitude and physical strength. A hybrid solar symbol incorporating the characteristics of the lion and the eagle, it can be used most potently in talismans.

Hammer This representation of the formative, masculine principle is particularly powerful in techniques of manifestation (having something happen). It signifies victory over one's enemies or obstacles, and is especially beneficial for business or career ambitions. Esoterically, it is an attribute of all Thunder Gods. The double-headed hammer is said to stand for the labyrinth and for justice and vengeance in equal measure.

Hands Always important as symbols, hands represent friendship, love and trust. The various types of hands worn as amulets are as follows: the Hand of God represents Divine power; the Hand of Fate suggests destiny; the Hand of Fatima gives Divine protection. Any of them avert evil and provide security.

Hare With a strong connection to the Moon in her form as Mother, the hare stands for regeneration, fertility and rebirth. In Egypt latterly, amulets of the hare were always fashioned from green stone. The rabbit, since the dawn of Christianity, has taken on much of the symbolism of the hare (see Ostara Ritual on pages 145–6). The energy of the hare is said to favour new enterprises.

Hawk Similar to the falcon in its symbolism, the hawk signifies all-seeing, perception and observation. A hawk amulet would be worn for protection and to give focus to one's life.

Heart In Egypt, the heart was said to represent the soul. It also more universally represents the seat of love and therefore devotion. Tradition in amuletic and charm lore used to dictate that a heart should only be fashioned in gold, though this is now changing and many other materials are used. A silver heart given by a woman would acknowledge her own femininity.

Hedgehog This symbolizes regeneration (after hibernation or a period of stasis). The hedgehog is said to be protective and is also said to conquer death. We still see the protective element depicted today in garden ornaments.

Heron The image of the heron is similar to that of the ibis (see below), and suggests intuition and organization.

Hippopotamus As an amulet, this warns off bad temper and also stands for regeneration. The hippopotamus Goddesses in Egypt were symbols of female fertility.

Horse The image of a horse symbolizes freedom, stability and courage. It would also bring you under the sway of Epona, the horse Goddess.

Horseshoe The horseshoe is a well-known good-luck symbol in many parts of the world. It is often taken to represent the Moon in her crescent form. According to superstition, you should nail an iron horseshoe with the convex side up for protection against sorcery and bad luck. For good luck, nail it over your door with the convex side pointing down. Wear any type of horseshoe-shaped jewellery or carry a miniature horseshoe charm in a charm bag to promote fertility.

Hummingbird This signifies pleasure but also symbolizes the fierce warrior. It can alternatively suggest a spiritual vibration, since the bird achieves stillness by fast movement, thus giving the idea of dynamic stillness.

Ibis The ibis represents spiritual aspiration and the soul. Always a very important bird to the Egyptians, it was sacred to their God Thoth (see page 117). It is said to heighten psychic perception and also gives a degree of protection on the physical level.

Indian head The symbol of the Indian head is considered by many to be the most powerful of amulets. It can also be used as a good-luck charm when gambling.

Jaguar Symbolizing the wisdom of the Shaman and focused power, an amulet or charm in this form would both protect and encourage.

Keys symbolize health, wealth and love. As they both open and close, they also signify birth and death, beginnings and endings, as well as new opportunities. A key can represent initiation and wisdom. To give them away is a token of surrender. An amulet or charm in this form often stands for life itself. Crossed keys suggest power over heaven and earth.

Knot The knot in the form of the Egyptian figure of eight (known as *tjes*) was supposed to protect the soul from dismemberment in the other world. The intricate Gordian knot was designed to protect the kingdom of Phrygia from fragmentation. The Celtic knot is a protective device when worn as an amulet. The Lover's knot represents perfect union.

Ladder In Egypt, a ladder was a symbol of Horus, linking with heaven and bringing help when needed. The ladder also represents authority, ambition and career opportunities. When you wear an amulet incorporating this symbol, the various options available to you are made obvious often through fresh insight or what may seem like extraordinary means.

Ladybird This is supposed to represent the Virgin Mary. Because of this association, killing a ladybird will bring you bad luck. Wearing a ladybird as a brooch or pendant puts you under Mary's protection and brings good fortune and money.

Lantern/Lamp The lantern or lamp is symbolic of the Divine Light and spiritual power. It signifies guidance and protection of the highest order, often that which is generated by faith.

Laurel wreath This represents worldly success and achievement and a degree of public recognition. From an esoteric viewpoint, it is a triumph of life over death and also represents immortality. Used as an amulet or inscribed on a talisman, it opens the way to the right framework for success.

Leaf Signifying growth, the symbol of the leaf concerns rejuvenation, hope and a revival of energy. Sometimes it can represent recovery from illness and it can also denote prosperity in business.

Lion The lion symbolizes nobility and is a symbol of the Sun. It protects through courage, and as an amulet it represents the courage of conviction. It is the fiery principle and sometimes represents the spark of life.

Lizard An amulet in the form of a lizard is said to give vision in the sense of far-sightedness and the ability to create an acceptable future. It also has connections with the crocodile.

Lotus/Lily The lotus is a very powerful symbol representing serenity and that which is manifested from purity. The lily often represents perfection and freedom from worry. Symbolizing a change of state, it can be taken as a symbol of death.

Lynx The lynx is the keeper of confidential information and symbolizes perspicacity. As an amulet, it represents a type of instinctive wisdom.

Mistletoe Revered by the Druids as the Golden Bough, mistletoe is considered to be unholy by the Christian Churches. It represents the feminine principle, but perhaps in its more capricious sense. Mistletoe is also said to establish and maintain family unity.

Mouse The mouse represents innocence, faith and trust. Worn as an amulet, it reminds the wearer of the necessity of an eye for detail.

Mushroom The mushroom stands for hidden wisdom and mystic power. It is said to be ruled by the Moon and brings business success and domestic happiness.

Ouroboros This universal symbol of a serpent or dragon biting its own tail represents the totality of life, the cycle of continuous energy. Containing integration, disintegration and reabsorption, opposing principles are balanced and held at a tension that promises perfection. It therefore represents life itself.

Owl To increase knowledge, wear an owl-shaped amulet made of gold, silver or copper. The symbol of the owl (sacred to the Greek Goddess Athene, see page 121) also brings good luck. The owl is said to work with the psychological Shadow, bringing knowledge from hidden places. It also represents wisdom in the sense of knowledge of the Mysteries.

Oyster shell In Egypt, the oyster shell as an amulet meant 'sound, whole and healthy'. It was supposed to protect the wearer from harm, although Hypatia, the Greek philosopher and mathematician, is said to have been murdered by a Christian mob who skinned her alive using oyster shells. Oyster shells today tend more to represent the Moon, because of the association with mother-of-pearl and its luminescence.

Palm branch This is representative of the triumph of good over evil, and is a solar emblem. It promises victory and acclaim, more usually by hard work than by sheer luck. It is often taken to represent just rewards.

Panther Representative of the feminine, this is a protective device which brings one under the sway of cat Goddesses such as Bastet (see page 117). As an amulet, it is a reminder of the power, speed and grace of the animal.

Peacock The peacock is a solar emblem and suggests long life and enduring love. It also symbolizes incorruptibility, immortality and resurrection. Because of the 'eyes' in its tail feathers, it is said to link with Horus and the Egyptian pantheon of Gods.

Phoenix The symbol of the phoenix as a bird of transformation and regeneration is well known. It represents the continuity of life and the overcoming of obstacles. Ruled by the Element of Fire (since it is from Fire that it regenerates), it also signifies opportunities and benefits. As a solar symbol, it also represents renewed youthfulness.

Pine cone This is an emblem of Cybele, the Greek Goddess of plenty (see page 122). With its many seeds, the pine cone signifies abundance, health, wealth and power. Worn as an amulet or kept within the home, it is said that you will never lack the good things of life. Miniaturized as a charm, it still has the same significance.

Pineapple A symbol of fertility also having a connection to the Mother Goddess, the pineapple represents good fortune and fruitfulness.

Puma Said to be the Shaman's companion on journeys to other worlds, the puma is the spirit of grace and inherent power. While the animal is elusive, it is also protective within spiritual journeys and it personifies these characteristics as an amulet.

Pyramid Crystals shaped like pyramids possess the power to balance emotional qualities and are said to bring wisdom. It is thought that wearing an amulet in the shape of a pyramid improves concentration and increases or re-energizes psychic powers. As an amulet, it also attracts good luck.

Rainbow Through its symbolism as the bridge between the physical and the spiritual, the rainbow implies raised consciousness. Representing the seven spiritual centres (chakras) in the body, it also signifies transfiguration and transmutation. On a more mundane level, it indicates success, achievement and rewarding journeys.

Ram/Sheep The ram or sheep is a symbol of masculinity and also of fertility. In Egypt, the ram's head signified power. Nowadays, as an amulet, the ram suggests the astrological sign of Aries.

Raven The raven represents inner journeys and dreams. Messenger and watcher for the Gods, it also represents mystery, though sometimes in the form of the Trickster. It is sacred to Morrigan (see page 114), among others, so wearing a raven amulet gives protection by this capricious Celtic Goddess.

Rice Grains of rice are representative of fertility and essential nourishment. Rice finds its place in the contents of witches' bottles as amulets and also in some prosperity spells (see page 87). It also represents domestic happiness. Other grains may also be used for the same purpose, thus linking with the corn Goddesses.

Rose/Rosette The rose or rosette with four petals signifies femininity and also earthly passions. It was a symbol for the cross (see page 204) and signifies completion and perfection. This is seen in the symbol used by the Rosicrucians. Roses and rosebuds are often used in love spells.

Scarab beetle One of the most famous of all Egyptian amulets, the sacred scarab is an emblem of the Great Creator of the Universe. It is a symbol of perpetual renewal of life and is sacred to the God

Khephra (see page 117). It stands for health, strength and virility. Wear scarab beetle jewellery for good luck and protection against all evil forces.

Scorpion The wearing of an amulet in this form was a protection against the sting of the scorpion. Much of the sacred imagery was later transferred to the scarab.

Seashells are a symbol of femininity and all the Goddesses, particularly the Mother Goddesses. Signifying birth and regeneration, they can be worn as jewellery, placed on altars or kept about the person as a sign of allegiance. They represent prosperity and marital bliss.

Ship/Boat As the nurturing aspect of the mother principle, the ship or boat has a connection with the Mother Goddesses. Also, in ancient belief, it suggests the Sun God as he plies his boat across the sky. It has therefore come to represent passage between the various planes of existence. More recently, it has come to mean commercial success and personal progress.

Skull To help break the chains of any addiction, wear a gold skull-shaped charm necklace as a magical amulet. It is said that if you rub the skull three times a day, while focusing your eyes upon it and thinking about the misery that your addiction brings, you may be cured.

Snake The snake has always stood for transformation and arcane knowledge because of its ability to shed its skin. As an amulet, it reminds us of the necessity for constant change and transformation. In Egypt it was thought to protect the wearer against venomous snakes. As the uraeus (see page 215), it was supposed to protect the dead.

Spider As a representative of Fate and the weaver of destiny, an amulet in the form of a spider reminds the wearer of the intricacy with which life is formed. A lunar symbol of eternal transmutation, it is also representative of the fragility in each of us. It signifies business expertise, insight and astuteness, and also unexpected luck concerning money.

Stag This signifies the masculine power of regeneration. Like the deer, it symbolizes all that is natural – it is the giver of spiritual gifts, beauty and mystical signs. It puts us under the protection of the Nature Gods such as Pan.

Stork/Crane As the herald of spring and new life, it becomes obvious why the stork has become the symbol for new babies. In its other meaning, it signifies a long and fruitful life. In some cultures, it is said to protect households.

Sun Carry a gold charm shaped like the Sun in a gold or yellow coloured velvet charm bag if you wish to acquire wealth, good health, success and/or fame. This is also an effective amulet to use if you feel that others have been causing you unnecessary problems.

Swan The symbol of the swan is traditionally said to be a guide into dreamtime, giving access to the hidden parts of us that are enclosed in the unconscious. It also suggests dignity and majestic power. As an amulet, it calls upon the energy and power that is our birthright.

Sword The sword represents justice and authority. It is a powerful protection against all forms of harm and also suggests courage and strength. It stands for the masculine principle and therefore for assertiveness arising from belief. It is of assistance in all commercial undertakings.

Thunderbolt The thunderbolt traditionally represents celestial fire and creative energy. It is sacred to all sky Gods such as Thor, and as a symbol it is good when aggression is needed. It is said to bring success over business rivals, so as an amulet it is worth having when such a vibration is needed.

Torch/Flame This is the spark of life and has similar connotations to the lantern or lamp (see earlier). It often represents spiritual illumination and truth. It is obviously a fire symbol and speaks of prosperity and fertility, though perhaps more on a spiritual level than a material one.

Tree This is a universal symbol depicting the interrelationship between the spiritual and physical planes and sometimes the Underworld. It is the world axis and links with Yggdrasil, the Tree of Life and the Tree of Knowledge. It is the process of birth, death and rebirth. On the material plane, it is success, personal advancement and domestic happiness.

Tulip bulb Carry a tulip bulb as a natural amulet to bring love into your life. It is said that you should wear one around your neck or sleep with one under your pillow at night to attract a new lover.

Turtle/Tortoise Said to be a representation of the three planes of existence – the spiritual (upper shell), the mental (body) and the physical (lower shell) – it is a powerful symbol. For spiritual protection, particularly against psychic attack, stimulation of creativity and strengthening of divinatory powers, wear a gold turtle-shaped charm or amulet. This also ensures longevity, good fortune and compassion towards others. The turtle also signifies shyness, and in Egypt was used as a protective device against evil.

Unicorn The unicorn is an ancient symbol of chastity and protection, and its fabled horn was said to be used in medieval times as an amulet to detect poisons in the food or drink of kings, queens, popes and other eminent clergy and nobility. A lunar emblem, it is said that it can only be seen by virgins and is protective of their virtue.

Uraeus The uraeus or cobra head is an Egyptian symbol which wards off evil influences and guards against harm. It represents the all-seeing eye of God and the powers of life and death. It ties in with the symbolism of the snake (see page 213).

Vulture An amulet in the form of a vulture would afford protection by Wadjet, an Egyptian Goddess. In ancient Egypt, the vulture is usually seen side by side with the cobra or uraeus. Together, they are a symbol of sovereignty.

Wolf A potent power animal, the wolf stands for Earth wisdom, knowledge and protection. As 'Leader of the Way', the wolf has some significance, and its image when used as an amulet gives a degree of protection.

Yin Yang Both an ancient and a modern symbol, the Yin Yang is the embodiment and unification of all opposites. Rather than just representing the feminine and the masculine, it also represents dynamic and passive energy. It is a Chinese cosmic symbol.

SYMBOLISM AND CORRESPONDENCES

Amulets are defined as protective devices worn around the body, or sometimes placed next to other objects, to protect them from various evils. As we have seen, they were common in all societies and all periods of antiquity. Almost anything could act as an amulet: a piece of cord knotted around the wrist, a crystal carried in a small bag around the neck (we have already seen some of the qualities of crystals on pages 108–10), or a piece of iron tied to one's bed. This type of amulet could be fashioned at home and probably relied a great deal on folk magic for its efficacy. The use of such amulets called for no special education or technical skills.

Amulets are often hard to identify. When we come across a decorated ring, for example, how – without knowledge of the particular magic which might have been used or some kind of clairvoyant ability – can we tell whether it was an amulet or just a piece of jewellery? Not everyone would have known about the subtle vibrations inherent in a magical amulet. Many of the Egyptian artefacts now believed to have been worn as amulets may well have simply been a fashionable piece of jewellery. For example, a scarab beetle inscribed on the bottom with the Eye of Horus would almost inevitably be an amulet, whereas an ordinary scarab might not.

Many ancient amulets range from the unrefined to the beautiful, but some are too elaborate to have been made by mere amateurs. In their content, they show that their manufacturers must have had at least some access to the technical expertise of a magical practitioner and a degree of familiarity with the images, methods and symbolism of the 'international' magic of late antiquity, which we acknowledged earlier in the book. Below, for instance – referring back to crystals which may be worn as amulets – are some correspondences which might be given to a jeweller to bring the wearer under the protection of the seven planets known at the time. Each planet rules particular crystals and metals, and combining them makes a very powerful magical device. Incidentally, should you wish to experiment, these correspondences are still valid today.

We shall consider later how these correspondences might be used in the fashioning of talismans. Personal jewellery is a very valid way of unobtrusively using amuletic knowledge.

Planetary jewellery

Sun   Diamond or topaz set in gold

Moon   Pearl, crystal or quartz set in silver

Mercury	Opal or agate set with quicksilver
Venus	Emerald or turquoise set in copper
Mars	Ruby or any red stone set in iron
Jupiter	Sapphire, amethyst or cornelian set in tin
Saturn	Onyx or sapphire set in lead (this should not be worn next to the skin)

VIKING RUNES AND OGHAM STAVES

Representations of ideas and concepts pre-date the use of alphabets, and these representations were often two-dimensional. In the Norse and Celtic traditions, we find much more extensive use of this two-dimensional representation. Instead of objects or drawings in the shape of animals, there are simple lines symbolizing animals and known objects inscribed on natural materials. The symbolism used would have been recognized by the people of the time. Nowadays, we have access to a much more extensive 'library' of images that may be used in the actual fashioning of amulets, as opposed to the use of naturally formed materials.

Inscriptions such as the Runes and the Ogham Staves hold great mystery for us, enhancing their suitability for use as amulets, and in the hidden languages used in talismans (see page 244). The Runes are Nordic, whereas the Ogham Staves belong to the Celtic tradition. We begin with the Runes.

THE ORIGINS OF THE RUNES

No one knows exactly how old the Runes are. Symbols similar to Runes appear as cave markings as early as the late Bronze Age in 1300 BC; they are mentioned in the Bible, but their use in ritual and as an oracle for consultation certainly pre-dates their use as a written language. Runic forms of inscription were evident – and seem to have been in use for some time – before the advent of written language inscriptions. They were representations of matters that were important to the people and, like many of these systems, often had relevance on more than one level of existence. An inscription could represent an animal, for instance, and could also stand for the qualities of that animal applied in certain situations. In this way, they approach the concept of sympathetic magic.

The word *runa* means 'mystery' or 'secret proceeding', and it seems likely that only the elders of the community and those who acted in a priestly capacity knew the true esoteric meaning of an inscription. To the ordinary person, they were simply a means of divination. The early Runemasters and Runemistresses developed a system of symbols composed of vertical and angled straight lines from their existing fund of mystic or religious symbols, which would endure when cut into wood or could be easily inscribed on to other natural materials. The 24 symbols became known as the *Futhark* or *Futhork* alphabet after the names of the first 6 Runes (*Fehu, Uruz, Thurisaz, Ansuz, Raidho, Kenaz*), and it is these 24 symbols – plus a blank Rune representing Destiny – which now comprise the modern-day Rune set. Ancient Pagan or Anglo-Saxon Runes are the same 24 basic Runes with some variations in their form due to usage over the centuries.

As with the Ogham Staves, which we shall deal with shortly, Runes were no doubt initially cut in wood and probably later inscribed on stone. The straight lines could easily be cut across the grain in wood, and short upward or downward lines would survive when cut with the grain, which is why there are no curved lines in this system. The Runes were a potent tool and source of learning which can still be applied today.

Runes can be worn as amulets, used as objects of power on your altar or as meditative aids. We suggest you experiment and spend time with the representations until you find one or more that suit you in your workings. We have not used the divinatory meanings here, only the basic interpretations, although you may wish to follow other lines of enquiry.

There are three 'Aettir' or sets of Runes, each bearing the name of the god corresponding to the first Rune within its family:
• The Aett or Set of Freya, Goddess of Fertility and Love.
• The Aett or Set of Hagalaz or Heimdall, Watcher of the Gods.
• The Aett or Set of Tiwaz, God of Justice, Law and Reason.

THE AETT OR SET OF FREYA, GODDESS OF FERTILITY AND LOVE

Fehu (Cattle)

This is the Rune of wealth and the price we have to pay for what we want – whether that is through action or inaction. The basic meaning of Fehu is wealth, which could be measured in the number of cattle owned. Hence, the image of cattle equates with wealth. The word 'fee' comes from this term. As an amulet, this Rune reminds us of the intrinsic wealth we have, but also of the price we must pay, whether that is through action or inaction.

Uruz (Aurochs)

This is the Rune of strength, courage and overcoming obstacles. The Norse and Icelandic Rune poems talk of privation for the herdsmen and tempering by ordeal. The aurochs was an enormous ox-like beast. Its horns were worn on Viking helmets, transferring by sympathetic magic the strength of the creature to the warriors. The image of harsh reality and obstacles to be overcome by strength and endurance lives on in the poems of the North. Many of the Runes use symbolism of the extreme conditions in which the Vikings lived. The aurochs was very much part of this environment. When we wear this as an amulet, we too become conscious of the power of the aurochs.

Thurisaz (Thorn)

This is the Rune of protection, challenges, secrecy and conflicts. The thorn tree, which can offer protection from intruders, is associated with this image. Frost giants or 'rime-thurses' who fought the Gods maintained the cosmic balance by representing the ancient rule before the Aesir (see page 23) came into being. Thurisaz is also associated with Thor (see page 125), who sought to protect the realm of the Gods from the frost giants. Thurisaz is therefore a Rune of challenge for those who want to make changes or go against long-held tradition. This becomes an amulet of protection and also of challenge.

Ansuz (A God)

This is the Father Rune, the Rune of Odin, the All-Father. It is also the Rune of inspiration. Odin wanted the gift of divine utterance (wisdom) for which he needed the mead of poetry, and there was a harsh price to pay. The power of these Runes is in the struggle to reconcile opposites, not in the battle between good and evil, when good always wins. This Rune acknowledges humanity's own weaknesses and journey towards a greater understanding. Wise words and the way we speak them can be of paramount importance. As an amulet, this Rune represents wisdom and right speech.

Raidho (Riding)

This is the Rune of travel and journeys, and specifically those that are long and hazardous. It uses the symbolism of the wheel – the Sun wheel as it passes through the skies. Also suggested is the wheel on the wagon of the old fertility Gods on their journey through the year. The Raidho Rune suggests an impetus so powerful that change is inevitable. Action and uncertainty are sometimes necessary if we are to progress; preparation for any journey is always important. Symbolizing this journey, Raidho reminds us to be aware of our actions.

Kenaz (Torch)

This Rune symbolizes the inner voice, inner strength, guidance and illumination. Kenaz is one of the Fire Runes. A torch was made from pine dipped in resin, which was then used to light both grand castle and hovel alike. All-purpose, it was used to kindle the 'Need' fire which was lit at times of celebration (see page 223). The cleansing aspect of fire is important, and the aspect of eradication is an important one when this Rune is worn as an amulet. The fire within maintains clarity without.

Gebo (Gift)

Gebo is the Rune of giving and generosity, and it is also the Rune of mutuality. All issues relating to exchange – both giving and receiving – are signified in this Rune. (In the Norse traditions, a gift always required one in return, so giving must be done with thought.) Gebo can also indicate a gift or talent received from one in authority, so when worn as an amulet it reminds us of the inherent knowledge available to us.

Wunjo (Joy)

This is the Rune that represents success, recognition and personal happiness, but this is happiness through one's own efforts and success through determination rather than as a gift from others. Traditionally, those who have been through hardship can sometimes appreciate life's gifts better and learn to take happiness as it comes. For the Vikings, happiness meant shelter, food and warmth; there is a practicality about this Rune when worn as an amulet. Joy can be built from those three things.

THE AETT OR SET OF HAGALAZ OR HEIMDALL, WATCHER OF THE GODS

Hagalaz (Hail)

This is known as the Mother Rune, and in the *Futhark* (Rune alphabet) it occupies the position of the sacred number 9. As the six-pointed star, Hagalaz had a geometric shape found in the composition of many natural life forms, mirrored in fractals today. Hagalaz is regarded as the 'cosmic seed'; ice was involved in creation along with fire. The Old Norse Rune Poem associates Hagalaz with the harvest and speaks of hail as the 'coldest of grains'. When hail melts it turns into water, but that metamorphosis can be painful. Therefore, Hagalaz has come to represent unwelcome external change. As an amulet, it demonstrates that such change, if used positively, can transform sorrow into happiness.

Naudhiz (Need)

This is the Rune of passion. The second Fire Rune is one of the cosmic forces that shapes the fate of humanity. It represents determination and signifies needs that are met by our own positive reactions to external hardship. Need fires were lit from early times all over Northern Europe on main festivals such as Beltane and Samhain. These fires represented the fire from within which has to be expressed externally; this Rune represents the fire sparked by friction. Such a fire is purging, and also one of new light and life, and it is this which is signified when the Rune is worn as an amulet.

Isa (Ice)

|

This Rune represents a blockage, or a period of inactivity that can be used for good, by preparing for the right moment. Isa is the second ice Rune and the fifth element in the Norse world. The single vertical mark of the Rune means that it is inherent within every other Rune. Isa can be seen as the ice of winter, an enforced obstacle to movement. Nevertheless, the period can be used positively for deliberation and development. For those who are fearful of going forward, Isa is a bridge between two ways of thinking. While change needs to be negotiated carefully, progress continues imperceptibly in the background. As an amulet, this Rune reminds us of that continuing progress.

Jera (Year)

This is the Rune of the harvest, of the results of earlier efforts. Jera represents a natural progression through the sequence of the seasons and various stages of life. It is invoked magically for fertility and achievement, a fruitful season or harvest, and for the attainment of goals through hard work. When the cyclical nature of existence slows, it is important to recognize the principles of fertility and the generosity of the deities. As an amulet, it suggests the principle of fertilization.

Eiwaz (Yew)

This is the Rune of natural endings, including death, but also promises new beginnings and rebirth. It was known that the bravest warriors would die to rise again, and Eiwaz symbolized longevity and eternal life. The yew's resinous vapour is said to induce visions, and it was also the tree of Shamans and magic. Sacred to Ullr, God of Winter and Archery, the yew tree gave a promise of better things to come; it is with this meaning that it is associated as an amulet. All things must pass, but all things must also return.

Perthro (Lot-Cup)

This is the Rune of taking a chance, of confronting what is yet not known or revealed, and of the essential self. In some ways, this is the Rune of destiny. It is the casting of this Rune that will decide one's fate, whether one looks at the situation as a gamble or whether the decision is the will of the Gods. Gambling and divination went hand in hand in the Norse communities – decisions would be made by casting lots or sometimes Runes. However, this was not a fixed fate. The gambler or diviner was expected to maximize their good fortune and take appropriate action to avoid any other potential pitfalls. It is this aspect that is used as an amulet.

Elhaz or Algiz (Elk-Sedge)

The Rune of the higher self and one's spiritual nature, this can be the most difficult to understand. The image comes from that of eel-grass, which is similar to the reed. The symbolism is that of the double-edged sword, which can both protect and damage; it can therefore be used with a degree of duality. There is the need for care and understanding in making use of such a weapon, both spiritually and otherwise. As an amulet, this Rune reminds us of our responsibilities.

Sowilo (Sun)

This is the Rune of success. As always, the Sun is seen as the most positive and potent symbol, though this time as feminine rather than masculine. Experienced often as lightning, it is the third and most powerful Fire Rune, melting the ice of winter and giving the crops a chance to grow. The longest day celebrates the inherent power of the Sun and commemorates the ideas of giving supremacy to the representations of the Sun. Potential and victory are all intrinsic in this Rune, and when you need reassurance, this is a good Rune to wear as an amulet.

THE AETT OR SET OF TIWAZ, GOD OF JUSTICE, LAW AND REASON

Tiwaz (Star)

Standing for justice and altruism (and possibly self-sacrifice), this Rune represents the pole star or lodestar. As a constant pointer, this Rune helps us to keep faith in bad times. It remains constantly visible and symbolizes justice won through fair combat. This Rune takes account of the natural imperfections we experience in life, and as an amulet it helps to keep us focused on matters in hand, but with an eye to the future.

Berkano (Birch)

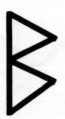

This is the Rune of spiritual regeneration, covering the arts of healing, fertility and mothering. The Rune embraces the concepts of death, birth and rebirth. Celebrating the Earth Goddess and the Goddess of the Underworld, birch is used to invoke their protection. It promises new beginnings, perhaps on a different plane to the one experienced hitherto. An understanding of the principle of the feminine and the colonization of virgin territory is inherent in this Rune. Looked at from an amuletic viewpoint, it promises growth and reintegration.

Ehwaz (Horse)

This is the Rune of loyalty and harmony. Partnership between people or inner and outer worlds, friendships, moving house or career are all associated with this Rune. Ehwaz is connected with the horse, the most sacred animal of the Vikings. It therefore represents harmonious relationships, illustrated best by that between horse and warrior. Mentioned only in the Anglo-Saxon Rune Poem, Ehwaz emphasizes the joy a horse brings to its rider, making them feel like a prince or minor God. As an amulet, Ehwaz represents the synergy that human and beast can create.

Manaz (Man)

This Rune stands for man as reflection of divinity. It is the power of human intelligence, the recognition that our lives are part of a greater whole and the ability to be compassionate and accepting of others. Celebrating the creation of the first man and woman who were given the breath of life, intelligence and a loving heart and their natural senses by Odin and his brothers, this Rune commemorates the potential of the individual and the connection to the human race. As an amulet, it reminds us of the power of the human being.

Laguz (Water)

This is the Rune of initiation into life and unconscious wisdom and intuition. Laguz is the Rune of water and the sea, and signifies birth and new beginnings. Water is frightening yet life-giving, and the Vikings used sea journeys as a symbol for a new start. The emotions will often take you into places you have never been before, provided you go with the flow. However, there is always an aspect of unpredictability about water. Wearing this Rune as an amulet reminds us of just that.

Ingwaz (The God Ing)

This Rune indicates a time of creative withdrawal in order to wait for new strength. There may be the promise of better times and a period of gestation, both human and symbolic. Ingwaz is a fertility Rune that is powerfully associated with protection, especially of the home or hearth. Ingwaz or Ing was the God of the Hearth and consort of Nerthus, the Earth Mother. It was necessary for him to die in order to be reborn, and that period of withdrawal was just as important as the time of growth. Worn as an amulet, this Rune teaches us to appreciate quiet times.

Othala (Homestead)

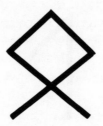

This is the Rune of the home and the sacred space. Domestic matters, family and finance are all important, for domestic tranquillity depends on material comfort. For the Norse people, stability depended on family and its continuance, so the homestead was of great importance. Being able to co-exist with others rather than living alone is an important learning experience, and belonging to a family allows us to experience such a thing. A sense of belonging and continuity comes across when this Rune is worn as an amulet.

Dagaz (Day)

This is the Rune of clear vision and awareness. It is an awakening and the coming together of two opposites. The mid-point of the day as experienced in the Norse world was dawn, at the rising of the Sun. In the Norse legends, Dagr – the son of Nott (the Goddess of Night) and Dellingr (Dawn) – was given a white horse named Skinfaxi. From his shining mane, beams of light chased away fears of the night. This Rune holds all the promise of the dawning of a new day and the enlightenment that this brings.

RITUALS FOR RUNES AND OGHAM STAVES

For the Celts, because the cycle of their year was based on fertility and associated rites, they divided their year into four segments. As we have seen in the Rituals section, within the Wheel of the Pagan Year, the Celts talked of the four 'Times' (see pages 141–2). Also, as in so many cultures that were governed by the cycle of the year, the transition point of the Celtic day was at sunset, so the times when day and night met were seen as magical. The time of sunrise was thought to bring new energy and power. Therefore, sunrise and sunset are both considered good times to carry out any ritual or blessing which you may feel appropriate both for the Runes and also for the Ogham Staves which we will consider next.

Any ritual connected with either the Runes or the Staves needs to reflect the simplicity of the images. A simple form of blessing which honours the four Elements might be, for instance:

Land, Sun, Lake and Wind,
Bless now the form of my working.

You also might like to honour the respective Gods – Odin for the Runes and Ogmios for the Ogham Staves. When working with any of the individual Runes or Staves, don't forget to pay due respect to the animals, trees and symbolism inherent in each one. By working in this way, when you wear them in amulets or use their representations in talismans, you will be linking into the intrinsic power in each Rune or Stave. When using the alphabetic equivalents in any way, also remember to allow for the energy that the letters contain. This is covered more fully in the section on talismans (see pages 244–7).

It is useful to remember that the difference between Staves and Runes is that Staves are Celtic and associated with trees or plants, whereas Runes are Nordic and more associated with light, or the lack of it, and the effect it had on peoples' lives. You may find it interesting to compare and contrast the two, and then decide to which you more naturally relate.

Next, we give the traditional meanings of the Ogham Staves.

THE OGHAM ALPHABET

The Ogham alphabet originally had 20 letters in groups of five. Each of the 20 Staves had a Sun (or marked) side and a Moon (or blank) side, giving 40 different meanings. These can be combined in many different ways for divination purposes, though today when used as amulets they are often used singly. Five more complex letters were added later, but the original form consists of straight lines notched across a straight Stave of wood. Ogham Staves were also associated with colours, birds, animals and kings.

Making your own Ogham Staves

You need to make a connection with the essential energy of each tree, so think carefully about the symbolism of each one and also about the wood from which the Staves are made, so that you can use them properly as amulets. Oak (the sacred tree of the Druids), hazel (wisdom) or ash (the tree of the All-Father) are the usual woods from which the Staves are made. Each type of tree had particular significance and symbolism for the Celts. You could make individual Staves from each of the wood types, as appropriate, or use wooden discs. Remember to mark the top clearly for easy identification.

You need 20 sticks or discs of similar size which can be marked at the top of the Stave with a small Celtic cross. If you are using twigs, you should be able to carve a symbol at the top by scraping away some of the bark. You might also use the old method of rounding the twigs at one end and making a point at the bottom, to differentiate between those that are thrown upright from those upside down, which would give a different symbol for divination (though we do not consider that here). Keep the Staves safe in a wooden box – preferably of one of the three principal woods – or inside a bag made of any natural fabric.

Ogham Staves are a potent personal tool. You can use them either to seek support with a difficulty or to gain a different perspective on life. To energize them, do the same as you did with your crystals, except that you need to go for a walk where you can touch trees in their natural habitat or place your Staves in sunlight. That way, you form a truly deep connection. The symbolism of the trees is as follows. In this list we give both the Celtic and English names.

Stave 1: Beith (Birch) Beginnings/Regeneration

The birch, linked with the Mother Goddess and the Moon, is the earliest of the forest trees (together with the elder). Symbolizing the rebirth of spring, it is used extensively in cleansing rituals – hence the use of a birch broom still used in rituals to expel evil spirits. In New Year celebrations, it expels the spirits of the old year. In ancient ceremonies of beating the bounds and marking out territories, it offers new opportunities for growth.

From an amuletic point of view, this signifies the innovator and the pioneer. It can give you the courage you need to begin afresh. When you choose to use Beith, which means 'shining', you are instigating new beginnings, opportunities based on experience and wisdom, and the removal of the old destructive patterns. Remember that you can branch out into new ventures, find new stimuli and new happiness.

Stave 2: Luis (Rowan or Mountain Ash) Protection

This tree, sacred to the Moon, is known as quickbeam, the Tree of Life, the Witch or Witch Wand. Traditionally, a rowan twig was pulled without a knife from a tree and fastened with red twine in the shape of a cross. It was – and is – used as a protective device for stables, cowsheds and outhouses, and to protect the household and its enterprises from doubt or harm. It is the tree used most against lightning and psychic attack. The rowan is also an oracular tree, often found around ancient stone circles.

This Stave signifies great intuitive abilities and inner resources. You would wear it as an amulet when you wanted to turn obstacles to advantage. When you are undertaking an important venture or delicate negotiations or doubt your own abilities, the rowan Stave might be used to remind you of the ability to overcome force by the use of intuition.

Stave 3: Fearn (Alder) Firm Foundations/Security

The alder is the Tree of Fire, known as the Tree of Bran the Blessed (see page 114). His severed head is said to be under the White Mount at Tower Hill in London, as protection so that his beloved land would never be invaded. Whistles made of this wood were traditionally used to summon and control the four winds, thereby offering security against seemingly uncontainable elements.

This Stave characterizes attention to detail and the ability to take small, steady steps towards success, and symbolizes realistic targets. As an amulet, it represents security, whether material, practical or emotional. There is reason for optimism if matters are not left to chance – any venture or relationship endures only temporary problems.

Stave 4: Saille (Willow) Intuition/Dreams

The willow is the tree of enchantment, sacred to the Moon Goddess who is the giver of moisture. It is often associated with rebirth, regeneration and the renewal of inspiration. Feelings and emotions that you experience can be a guide to right action as much as logic. As an amulet, it acts as a reminder of this.

More generally, this is the Stave of the innovator and the pioneer, and may indicate that this aspect of your personality is very strong. Saille indicates the use of imaginative faculties and suggests the need to trust intuitions and hunches, to follow your heart. Answers or directions are not clear, and yet you are aware of inner stirrings. You learn to use your dreams constructively, especially those that recur or seem especially vivid.

Stave 5: Nuinn (Ash) Expansion

Ash is a Father Tree and very sacred to the Celts. It is the Tree of the World axis (for example, Yggdrasil in the Norse tradition) and Father Gods such as Odin of the Vikings and Gwydion of the Welsh. The ash was used for Druidical magic wands, especially for astral travel. Over time, it became the tree of seafaring throughout the northern hemisphere, being associated with Poseidon-type deities of the sea. As an amulet, it brings you under the protection of that type of God.

Nuinn indicates an initiate with a thirst for knowledge and new experiences, the seeker of the truth and explorer of new territories and opportunities. This Stave can indicate an inner hunger or restlessness or, alternatively, powerful ambitions that evoke courage and confidence.

Stave 6: Huathe (Hawthorn/Whitethorn) Resilience/Courage

Whitethorn, the most common form of hawthorn, is the tree of the White Goddess (under the name Cardea), who used it to cast spells. It acts as a shield against physical or psychic harm and is sacred to Mars and other northern thunder Gods. It was set around sacred boundaries in order to deter evil. Hawthorn twigs gathered on Ascension Day are believed to have exceptional powers.

The hawthorn symbol represents the power to fight for what is right and the determination to achieve goals. As an amulet, it offers protection and tenacity. If you are feeling discouraged or need extra energy to forge ahead, Huathe is an assurance that it is possible to resist hardship and come through with courage.

Stave 7: Duir (Oak) Strength/Power

The oak is the tree of endurance and power, and was particularly special to the Druids. Equally spread between the three realms of heaven, earth and the underworld, its roots extend as far underground as its branches reach up into the sky. Oak is always the wood used for the Midsummer fire and to start the ceremonial fires of the great festivals, when the fire is lit inside the log, symbolically fuelling the Sun's power.

Duir represents leaderships, knowledge, authority and a noble spirit, as well as pure masculine power, strength and assertiveness, although these qualities co-exist with nobility, idealism and altruism. When looking for qualities of determination, patience, strength of purpose and persistence, especially in matters of career and personal happiness, this is a good Stave to use as an amulet.

Stave 8: Tinne (Holly) Fire

The original holly tree of the Celts was probably an evergreen version of the common oak tree (the evergreen scarlet oak, holm oak or holly oak). It was sacred to the Celtic God Taranis (see page 112), who carried a club made of holly. It is a symbol of the promise of the renewal of life and is also protective of the household. Holly suggests that one is in tune with life's ups and downs and therefore signifies that there is a time for action and a time for withdrawal. Holly marks a vital stage in the wider cycle of experience and suggests that however it presents itself – good, bad or indifferent – that stage is a building block for the future. As an amulet, it reminds us that better times will come if the faith is kept.

Stave 9: Coll (Hazel) Wisdom

The hazel is the Celtic Tree of Wisdom; the Druids carried a hazel rod as a symbol of authority. Hazel was also used to mark the boundaries of a court of justice, and so it can be used to represent the overall concept of boundaries. A hazel rod is used for divining for water and buried treasure. It is also associated with the sacred number nine, because the hazel takes nine years to produce nuts.

Coll is the Stave of the naturally wise person and represents intelligence, justice and recourse to traditional knowledge. When there are decisions to be made, the hazel Stave indicates that an impartial response is required, using available expertise. As an amulet, it reminds the wearer of their own inherent sense of wisdom and justice.

Stave 10: Quert (Apple Tree) Fertility/Abundance

This is the Celtic Tree of Life. Orchards have always been considered to be sacred. To encourage a bountiful, fruitful crop, not only of the orchard but also of the local land and community, apple trees were 'wassailed' (drenched in cider) and offerings were made to the Gods. Traditionally, apple wood was used for wands to cast magic circles, especially for love and fertility magic.

Quert signifies an outgoing nature with much enthusiasm for life, thus attracting new ideas or interests. Positivity and many opportunities often lead to a generosity that is out of the ordinary. This Stave allows the wearer to nurture projects that may be fulfilled over time. There is often a feeling of happiness and wellbeing associated with Quert, making it a powerful gift to give to someone as an amulet.

Stave 11: Muinn (Vine/Bramble) Joy

The vine, which was imported into Britain during the Bronze Age, has always been associated with spiritual as well as physical comfort. The native bramble or blackberry, which was the truly magical plant, was used more frequently for wine-making because it grew wild. It is said that the bramble (or vine) was the only thing that Adam and Eve were allowed to take out of the Garden of Eden.

Muinn represents unbridled joy, embracing the whole continuum of happiness, physical and spiritual, and a natural exuberance. As an amulet, it suggests personal happiness rather than success. With personal contentment comes the ability to spread joy to others, just as the vine or bramble spreads itself.

Stave 12: Gort (Ivy) Relationships/Loyalty

Ivy, traditionally regarded as the harbinger of death, was worn as a crown at the winter feast of Saturnalia. Although it was perceived to choke the tree around which it grew, it was also seen as being bound to that tree and remained evergreen – a symbol of hope. So it came to be traditionally associated primarily with fidelity and a symbol of married love and loyalty. Houses with ivy growing on them are reputedly safe from psychic attack.

Gort suggests a loyal, loving person who is supportive and does not stifle lovers or friends. When worn as an amulet, it reminds one to pay attention to love interests as well as work and other commitments.

Stave 13: Ngetal (Fern/Bracken/Reeds) Riches/Prosperity

Ngetal is an auspicious Stave to use for all money-making endeavours and questions. The reed was originally an ancient Egyptian symbol of royalty and of learning. Its association with the height of the Sun's power at Midsummer makes it a symbol of gold and riches. Ferns and bracken produce their flowers on Midsummer Eve and become golden between eleven and midnight. The scattered seed indicated hidden gold that could be recovered by effort.

Ngetal suggests a shrewd business brain that makes use of ingenious ways of increasing profits. The Stave is worth using as an amulet when you are initiating new business projects or need to consolidate business gains. Ngetal assures the success of any financial matters and money-making schemes.

Stave 14: Straif (Blackthorn) Effort/Persistence

Often seen as a tree of hardship, the blackthorn produces white blossoms on an almost black branch and is said to bloom at midnight on Christmas Eve. Straif means 'to strive', and endeavour and perseverance are fundamental to the tree and its principles. It is incredibly hardy and forms a barrier linked with physical and magical protection. Blackthorn denotes the characteristics of the individual who has not had things easy but has developed willpower and determination because of this hardship. The blackthorn-braided crown is often kept in the home as a luck-bringer. Otherwise, it is burned and scattered over the fields on New Year's Morning; blackthorn is said to ensure a good harvest in the coming year.

Straif stands for concentrated power and energy and therefore represents supreme will and determination in the face of adversity. As an amulet, it suggests that goodness of spirit will prevail.

Stave 15: Ruis (Elder) Second Sight/The Unexpected

A waterside tree, the elder has white flowers that reach their peak in Midsummer. This makes the elder another aspect of the White Goddess; it is truly the Fairy Tree. Ruis connects us to the hidden realms and our own spiritual and magical natures, giving us the art of clairvoyance.

The elder is the Stave of the visionary, someone who is as secure in the divinatory arts and mystic perception as they are in the everyday world. The elder Stave worn as an amulet will often give one a seemingly magical solution that comes in a dream or through insight. Where common sense and perception have not brought you an answer, watching the patterns in nature, such as in the growth of trees and flowers, can help you determine necessary changes.

Stave 16: Ailm (Pine/Silver Fir) Clarity/Creation

The pine was worshipped by the Celts as a symbol of fire and is one of the few trees that are androgynous. The silver fir is the tree of Druantia, the Gallic Fir Goddess, a powerful representation of birth and creation. Symbolic of the Eternal Flame, Ailm stands for an inner creation becoming manifest and new ideas being put into practice. It involves illumination, insight and communication.

As an amulet, it signifies your own natural talents and that creative energies are all around you for you to use. Clarity of communication is of importance in ensuring that things happen as they should. Make use of the amulet to move away from uncertainty.

Stave 17: Onn (Furze/Gorse) Transformation/Change

Gorse is a symbol of the early spring Sun and was associated with the Gallic Goddess of Spring. Just as spring transforms the dead world of winter and gorse transforms the drab hillsides, the Stave of Onn brings about a radical transformation in the energy available to you. In older times, gorse was a complete crop, offering food for animals and flowers for bees and, later in the year, bedding and fertilization for the next crop.

As a characteristic, Onn signifies a mind that is always open and adaptable, welcoming change. Wearing this Stave as an amulet means that you can anticipate a change for the better, though there may be some upheaval and disruption along the way.

Stave 18: Ur (Heather) Strong Emotion/Passionate Feelings

Heather is linked with the Gallic Heather Goddess called Uroica, shown sometimes as a queen bee. The heather originally bloomed scarlet at Midsummer and so came to be associated with passion and the Mother Goddess. In Romany lore, white heather, being rare, is considered especially lucky. In Celtic legend, it represents eternal love and the tears of the abandoned lover.

Ur is the Stave of the person who feels deeply and is in tune with the emotions, strong feelings and desires of others, although these emotions are unacknowledged. Used as an amulet, it reminds the wearer to follow their heart and believe that what they long for can be theirs. They have only to ask for what they most desire.

Stave 19: Edhadh (White Poplar/Aspen) Maturity/Healing

The white poplar is the Tree of the Autumn Equinox (Mabon, see pages 134 and 148), of maturity, old age and a late harvest. It stands for the achievement of final ideas and also for letting go all that is no longer valid. The aspen is said to have been the tree used in the Crucifixion and now shakes at the resulting agony. Poplar leaves are said to have magical powers.

As an amulet, it offers hope for the future based on experience of what is possible, not based on romantic dreams. Edhadh personifies the natural healer and peacemaker, with a mature and balanced view. The Stave represents the fruition of past efforts when healing can be both physical and mental. It is time to balance the books and accept what is around you.

Stave 20: Ido (Yew) Immortality/Rebirth

The yew is known as the Tree of Death throughout Europe and is a symbol of immortality because it lives so long. Associated with the Wheel of the Year and the aspect of the Triple Goddess dealing with death, Ido is the Stave of endings, transformation and rebirth. This is not pessimistic, however, but is merely an awareness of the cyclical nature of existence and the deeper meaning of life.

Ido is a Stave that you may use as an amulet at the time of a natural change or ending of a phase. The yew always symbolizes rebirth and immortality, though there may be regrets. The coming to an end of a situation is, however, almost always a positive one, often leading to new opportunities.

We have suggested here that the Staves are used as amulets and we have given individual meanings. Carried in your purse or about your person, the vibration is continually a gentle reminder of what you know already. To use two or more Staves, for instance as jewellery, not only means that you have the double reminder, but you also have available to you power squared (that is, four times the power). To use three would give you nine times the power (three times three), and so on. Therefore, choose your Staves wisely and well. You might do this by using the divinatory method of casting them on to the representation of the Cycle of the Year. We leave you to follow your own course of study.

TALISMANS

To understand the use of talismans, we have to have some kind of understanding of the principle behind them. True magicians recognized that there was a power beyond themselves that had to be anchored within the physical world. While amulets used the intrinsic power of the object, as we have seen, there had to be some way of appealing to the powers that be, and some powerful object must be used to do this. They also had to keep hidden (occult) a great deal of what they did. We can still follow the same principles today.

MAGICAL ALPHABETS

We have seen in the Runic and Ogham alphabets how the symbols used in ancient times represented certain ideas and principles. It was only later that these symbols also came to represent single letters and sounds – a kind of shorthand, if you like, an instruction. By combining those symbols in original and innovative ways, fresh ideas were put forward and new principles were discovered. The symbols were often drawn on suitable surfaces, such as rock walls, and give us a fair idea of aspects of life then.

This was a kind of ancient graffiti and holds a message for us if we can decipher it; until we can, the message remains secret and hidden. It was only later that the letters in our present-day alphabet were attributed to Runes. Most of our alphabets today, which are descended from the Phoenician system of notation, can be standardized so that we can make sense of them. It is this idea of a coded language that is greatly used in talismanic work today.

Only if we are able to decipher the symbols will we understand the purpose of a particular talisman, and only if we know what those symbols are can we convey a secret message to others in the making of our own talismans. As time has gone on, much of the original symbolism has become clouded or lost, and today we must gather up the remnants of that ancient knowledge.

As we have seen, much of the magical language that we use today has come down to us from the Kabbalah, which was primarily an oral tradition (learned through the spoken word). There were certain ideas that the ordinary layman was capable of understanding and others that only the priesthood was capable of assimilating. Knowledge was power, and that knowledge must be jealously guarded lest it fall into the wrong hands. If anything was written down, it was written so that only those with the required knowledge would be able to decipher the true meaning. The writings were therefore in code, which had a tremendous power and energy invested in them. The sense of awe and wonder they generated was phenomenal. Now, as these messages become open to interpretation, they still are able to generate that same sense of awe and wonder.

While the writings of the Kabbalah were obviously in ancient Hebrew, it was believed that the letters and numbers had very powerful vibrations. To keep the writers' intentions hidden, it was possible to substitute other phrases and letters or numbers for what was originally noted down, and it all became very confusing. Gematria, which is a method of converting phrases or words written in Hebrew into their numerical equivalents, was used to work out the hidden meanings of scripture. These numerical equivalents were then put together and transposed for another word that, when applied with the same reasoning, added up to the same number.

Once the 'code' was broken, the magical side of Kabbalah became a lot easier to interpret. Within the translation of the holy books was found the principle that the Jews believed had been applied by God. Here is a translation of what was found:

Yah, Jehovah of hosts, the living Elohim, King of the Universe, Omnipotent, All-King and Merciful, Supreme and Extolled, Who is Eternal, Sublime and Most-Holy, formed and created the Universe

*in thirty-two mysterious paths of wisdom by three Seraphim,
namely: Sfor, Sippur and Sapher ... which are in Him one and the
same. They consist of ten Sephiroth out of nothing and of twenty-
two fundamental letters. He divided the twenty-two consonants
into three divisions: Three Mothers, fundamental letters or first
elements; Seven Double; and Twelve Simple consonants.'*

The 22 Hebrew letters are divided by students of Kabbalah into
three groups: the Mother Letters, the Double Letters (so called
because they have two pronunciations) and the Single Letters
(which have only one pronunciation). The three Mother Letters are
Aleph, Mem and Shin, and they are associated with the Elements.
The seven Double Letters are associated with the seven planets
known to the Ancients, those heavenly bodies visible with the
naked eye. The twelve Single Letters are associated with the signs
of the zodiac.

Every letter of the Hebrew alphabet, in particular, can be
converted into an equivalent number ranging from 1 to 9, then
by tens (10–90) and then in hundreds, up to 400. Some of the
Hebrew letters hold different forms when used at the end of a
word; these are the letters that signify the values 500, 600, 700,
800 and 900. (We do not need these higher equivalents for our
purposes at this point.)

There are many different 'codes' that can be used for interpretation,
but here we show the Hebrew and English equivalent. It is important
to note down and be aware of these codes, as many talismans make
use of them. The following is an example of how English letters can
be transferred into numbers using Kabbalistic beliefs.

1	2	3	4	5	6	7	8	9
A	B	G	D	E	O	Z	F	T
C	K	Gh	Dh	H	U		P	Tz
I	Kh	M	M	N	V		Ch	
J	R	S	Th		W		Ph	
Q		Sh			X			
Y								

Below we show some other alphabets and their equivalents. In theory, there is nothing to prevent you from mixing up your alphabets in the making up of a talisman, though the purists among us will cringe at such an idea.

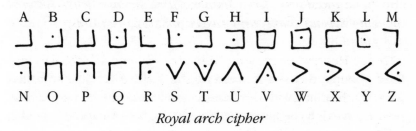

Royal arch cipher

Hebrew alphabet

Greek alphabet

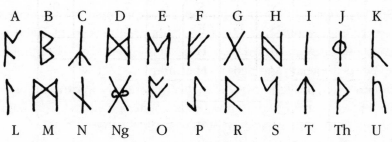

Futhark (Runic) alphabet

247

NUMERICAL SIGNIFICANCES

We know that the Kabbalah recognized the esoteric significance of numbers and have seen that each planet has traditionally had a number assigned to it. Following the principle that number is also an important part of magical working, we give below some of the significances that have grown up throughout the years from various traditions.

One This number is a representation of the individual and their potential. Working with this number could make anything possible, but care needs to be taken that you do not become too involved in self-interest. Magically, it is used for personal work.

Two Partnership and the feminine are epitomized by the number 2. Attributes such as peacefulness, compromise and softness are represented by this number, as is duality. Signifying receptivity rather than action, magically it must be used with care.

Three Enterprise and fertility come to the fore with this number. However, pride and arrogance also show themselves in the number 3. It comes into its own when undertaking new beginnings, as it is the number of pregnancy in the sense of a waiting period while a matter incubates. In spell-working, it is good to use for new undertakings.

Four Stability and logic are the main attributes of the number 4. It is the main grounding number to do with giving form to matter, and is traditionally the number of protection and guardianship for people who seek it. It is a protective number.

Five Freedom and sexual expression show themselves in this number. The need to exhibit, and indeed show off, are shown in the number 5. Used to effect change, this number is very creative, and if used correctly, can be used in sexual spells.

Six To people to whom this number is special, the home and family is very important. Trust is also very important, as is the need to communicate one's thoughts to others. The use of this number cements domestic and personal harmony.

Seven Often thought to be lucky, this is also a very spiritual number. People who have 7 as their number are quite secretive – a reflection of the 'hidden guardianship' of this occult number.

Eight This number is a combination of spiritual success and material attainment. Personally, number 8 indicates toughness and single-mindedness. Magically, it can be used in the areas of finance, career and business.

Nine This is the number of compassion and charity. In the individual, it shows a passionate seeker of the truth. In magical workings, number 9 is used to manifest spiritual love and suggests that one is working on behalf of groups of people.

Eleven From a personal viewpoint, number 11 is sometimes a difficult number with which to work. It suggests a person who is capable of accepting great responsibility. When capable of working at a high vibration it works well, but when out of control it can result in chaos. It is the first master number and will revert to two when not worked as a master number.

Twenty-two This is the number of 'the master builder' and suggests the manifestation of something of lasting value. The number 22 must not be used for selfish ends. When not used properly, it reverts to the simpler 4 (2+2).

Thirty-three This number is probably too powerful to work with in simple magic. It signifies the adept or spiritual leader, someone who has accepted the responsibility for making major changes in the world in which we live. It is unlikely that it can be worked with unless such responsibility has been accepted, since it will usually revert to the number 6, its simplest form. It normally requires acts of great sacrifice (making life sacred).

MAKING A TALISMAN

Let us suppose that we are making a talisman to help a new business get on its feet. We might use the number 3 and have three 'success' symbols to signify the new undertaking. In addition, we might have five repeated symbols to indicate the ability to stand out from the crowd, giving eight symbols in all. This would mean that we were also signifying the energy necessary to create our business and spiritual success.

You can see that you can be as simple or as complicated as you wish in your making of the talisman, and those in the know can interpret what you are representing. When you begin to put all the information together, the talisman becomes more and more powerful.

A POWERFUL SUCCESS TALISMAN

Below is a number talisman known as the Table of Jupiter; it is also known as a Magic Square. All of the lines add up to 34.

4	14	15	1
9	7	6	12
5	11	10	8
16	2	3	13

It should be inscribed on a piece of parchment and, according to the correspondences for the planets (see below), be placed with an amethyst crystal and kept in the pocket or a talisman bag made of purple velvet. It might alternatively be inscribed on a metal (tin) tablet. It would also have diagonal double lines across it, linking 4, 7, 10, 13 and 16, 11, 6, 1, each adding up to 34. Jupiter's principal number is 3 and the number of manifestation is 4, which anchors Jupiter's qualities. The talisman is said to bring riches and peace. For maximum effect, the talisman would be written on a Thursday at the hour of Jupiter, according to the planetary hours.

PLANETARY CORRESPONDENCES

In the section on amulets, we briefly spoke about some planetary correspondences (see page 216). Over the next few pages, we bring together further information so that you will be able to start thinking about some simple talismans. The seven 'popular' planets are linked with the characteristics and personal nature of the deities that represent them. As you will see, each planet rules over – and relates to – various attributes. In our list, we have taken the most common correspondences. As time goes on, you will find that you are accruing more and more knowledge of what attributes fit with each planet, and your talismans will thus begin to take on more and more meaning.

To take the first entry of the Sun as an example, you can see that the Sun makes us think of gold (both the colour and the metal), its Element is Fire and it is associated with the laurel bush. It is connected with the number 1, so if we wish to fashion a talisman with these correspondences, we would choose a gold disc and have on it a representation of one laurel wreath. On the obverse (or back), we might etch a flame with a lion's head. We would make it on a Sunday. These links are the core meaning of the 'talisman' and are used to strengthen the union between the wearer and the power it symbolizes.

When you are making talismans, some meanings have more significance than others and expand and enhance the information that is given elsewhere. As you peruse the list that follows, be aware that it is the most commonly accepted list of relations that have been used; you will add to it as your knowledge increases.

The Sun

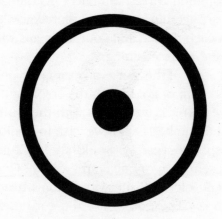

Day	Sunday
Number	1
Colour	Gold, Orange, Deep yellow
Metal	Gold
Gem/Mineral	Diamond, Amber
Tree/Shrub	Juniper, Laurel
Flower/Herb	Marigold, Saffron
Wood	Walnut
Fabric	Brocade
Animal/Bird	Lion, Hawk
Element	Fire
Zodiacal sign	Leo

The Sun is generally associated with strength, determination, vitality and self-expression. It also relates to the arts, banking, corporate bodies, fame, fatherhood government office, health, honour and esteem, influence, leadership, nobility, organization, public acclaim, rulership and teaching.

The Moon

Day	Monday
Number	2
Colour	Silver, Pastel shades
Metal	Silver/Aluminium
Gem/Mineral	Moonstone, Pearl
Tree/Shrub	Willow, Hawthorn
Flower/Herb	Convolvulus, Watercress
Wood	Birch
Fabric	Silk
Animal/Bird	Crab, Owl
Element	Water
Zodiacal sign	Cancer

The Moon generally rules over domesticity, emotional responses, fluidity, inspiration, instinct and sensitivity. It also rules over feeling and rhythm. It relates to antiques, commitment, inevitability, introspection, isolation, karma, maturity, mining, morality, property management, social welfare and tenacity.

Mercury

Day	Wednesday
Number	5
Colour	Sharp yellow, Mixed hues
Metal	Quicksilver, Zinc
Gem/Mineral	Citrine, Agate
Tree/Shrub	Hazel, Forsythia
Flower/Herb	Bittersweet, Fern
Wood	Beech
Fabric	Linen
Animal/Bird	Monkey, Magpie
Element	Air
Zodiacal signs	Gemini and Virgo

Mercury rules communication, healing, hyperactivity, the intellect, shrewdness and versatility. It relates to accountancy, curiosity, impressionism, invention, land or air travel, language, learning, mathematics, the media, public speaking, publishing of all types, vehicles and wit.

Venus

Day	Friday
Number	6
Colour	Light blue, Green, Pink
Metal	Copper, Bronze
Gem/Mineral	Jade, Lapis lazuli
Tree/Shrub	Peach, Pear
Flower/Herb	Rose, Carnation
Wood	Sycamore
Fabric	Satin
Animal/Bird	Cat, Dove
Element	Air
Zodiacal signs	Taurus and Libra

Venus correlates to harmony, growth and development, as well as love and marriage. It also extends to aesthetics, the affections, dance and music, fashion, femininity, materialism, personal finances, pleasure, relationships, sexuality and union.

Mars

Day	Tuesday
Number	9
Colour	Strong reds, Autumnal shades
Metal	Iron, Steel
Gem/Mineral	Ruby, Bloodstone
Tree/Shrub	Monkey puzzle, Heather
Flower/Herb	Nasturtium, Nettle
Wood	Mahogany
Fabric	Tweed
Animal/Bird	Tiger, Falcon
Element	Fire
Zodiacal signs	Aries and Scorpio

Mars symbolizes competition and confrontation, determination, focus and masculinity. It is also related to an adventurous spirit, the armed forces, courage, engineering, the fire service, forcefulness, male sexuality, metalwork, speed of reactions and sports.

Jupiter

Day	Thursday
Number	3
Colour	Purple, Deep blue, Indigo
Metal	Tin, Antimony
Gem/Mineral	Amethyst
Tree/Shrub	Cedar, Ash
Flower/Herb	Sweet William, Sage
Wood	Oak
Fabric	Velvet
Animal/Bird	Horse, Eagle
Element	Fire
Zodiacal signs	Sagittarius and Pisces

Jupiter covers charity, majesty, mental and physical searchings, might and wisdom. It then covers friendships, good judgement, knowledge and understanding, legal matters, philosophy, theosophy, travelling abroad and any other long journeys.

Saturn

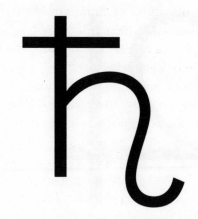

Day	Saturday
Number	8
Colour	Black, Dark shades
Metal	Lead
Gem/Mineral	Jet, Onyx
Tree/Shrub	Yew, Cypress
Flower/Herb	Fuchsia, Thrift
Wood	Ebony
Fabric	Hessian
Animal/Bird	Goat, Vulture
Element	Earth
Zodiacal signs	Capricorn and Aquarius

Saturn signifies concentration, conversation, destiny, experience and perseverance, as well as providing a facilitating energy that helps us get things done. It relates to agriculture, career status, discovery, economy, endurance, farm workers, housing, maths, sacrifice, structure, tests and transformation.

You will see that all the planets (apart from the Sun and the Moon) rule two signs of the zodiac. This is because when the system was first inaugurated in the mists of antiquity, Pluto, Neptune and Uranus had not yet been discovered. It was only during the 20th century that Pluto, Neptune and Uranus were handed rulership over Scorpio, Pisces and Aquarius.

Because our ancestors needed a simple form of classification, they decided that the Sun was assertive, positive and (in their view) masculine, whilst the Moon was retiring, negative and passive and therefore feminine. Continuing with that method of classification, they then decided that the other planets also had masculine (positive) and feminine (negative) qualities. These are reflected in the zodiacal signs. Incidentally, even today we still refer to the 12 signs as being positive or negative. This knowledge need not particularly impinge on your making of talismans, unless you become very proficient or need the information to ensure that your herbal and other correspondences do not conflict.

When you cannot use the correct metal for the planet, you may, if you wish, use the correct wood. In the table of planetary jewellery (page 216) we have said, for instance, that you should not wear lead next to the skin. You could, however, make your Saturn talisman from ebony and still be perfectly correct. You may also discover that other woods are appropriate for you.

PLANETARY MINERALS

Stones and gems have long been linked with the planets and have forever been acknowledged as having great talismanic elements. While it is often a good idea to carry around a particular stone or mineral that has meaning for you, if you then inscribe it with a symbol, it becomes an amulet. If you take the process one stage further and inscribe it with a design that fits in with talismanic principles – a circular design which calls on powers above and beyond itself – you have turned it into a talisman.

Because the seven metals associated with the planets – silver, iron, copper, gold, quicksilver, lead and tin – are not necessarily available to all, it may be that you have to use an alternative with the same mineral content, or an alloy, for the purposes of a talisman.

Below is a list of stones and minerals from which talismanic jewellery can be made, with particular relevance to the planets. Some are obviously too soft to be inscribed but might be utilized in other ways, such as in the centre of another metal. The negative and positive aspects of each stone is listed and should provide guidance to anyone wishing to have the appropriate items in their talismanic bag!

THE SUN

Aventurine Promotes health, vigour and cheerfulness; promises emotional moral support in new commercial undertakings; gets rid of doubt, diminishes anxiety and eases bodily aches and pains; strengthens resolve against hardship.

Citrine Linked with boldness, courage and mastery; promises victory over sporting, business or romantic rivalry; wards off infections and any unwanted attention; prevents accident or injury, especially on journeys.

Diamond Heightens awareness, encourages enterprise and strengthens resolve; brings personal progression and acclaim; affords relief from mental or emotional stress; confounds enmity and protects from physical dangers.

Heliodor Gives the advantage to speculators, gamblers and sportsmen; promotes prosperity and happiness; prevents deception and disillusionment; lifts depression and helps the body to recover and recuperate.

Topaz Bestows courage, determination, desire, confidence and judgement; promises health, joy and prosperity; improves physical fitness and raises the spirits; overcomes envy and malice.

Tourmaline Brightens the imagination and sharpens the intellect; promotes harmony and brings financial reward; defends the home from theft; improves vision, relieves tension and lifts depression.

Zircon Energizes the body; heightens awareness and sharpens the intellect; brings rich rewards; overcomes obstacles or opposition; strengthens the constitution; safeguards travellers and property.

THE MOON

Chalcedony Attracts public favour, recognition and financial reward; increases popularity, enthusiasm and fitness; dispels gloom, despondency, envy or anger; affords protection to travellers; helps nursing mothers.

Feldspar (also **Felspar**) Strengthens bonds of affection and promotes marital happiness; associated with fertility; mitigates quarrels and poor situations; protects from sunstroke, headaches and nosebleeds.

Flint Expands consciousness and prompts prophetic dreams; improves memory and heightens intellectual capacity; helps ward off physical danger and dispels melancholy; aids the union between children and parents.

Gypsum Signifies hope and youthfulness; benefits children and adults wanting to 'go it alone'; reduces swellings and aids digestion; averts the envy of others; brings peace of mind.

Labradorite Brings prophetic visions and expands consciousness; promotes harmonious relationships; dispels anxiety, enmity and strife; gives relief from nervous disorders.

Magnesite Clarifies vision, both literally and figuratively; improves profitability and wins admiration and respect; provides freedom from adversity; aids digestion; releases emotional stress.

Moonstone Affords vitality and fertility; awards success to artistic and creative efforts and new commercial projects; heals relationship rifts; protects crops; aids digestion and concentration.

Morganite Induces love, devotion and friendship; promises career advancement or improved financial viability; reconciles differences of opinion and dispels anger; offers safety to travellers in any dimension.

Pearl Rewards charitable deeds and selfless actions with love and respect; promotes harmony and understanding; protects those travelling over water; eases muscular tension; lifts depression.

Pumice Linked with purity, vision, truth and development; helps sociability and personal gain; bestows success on long-term ventures; guards against illusion and delusion; brings comfort to a troubled mind or spirit.

Rock crystal Represents purity, hope and chastity; expands conscious awareness and prophetic visions; promotes trust and harmony; dispels bad dreams, delusion and illusion; safeguards the very young and astral travellers from harm.

MERCURY

Agate Promotes good health and fortune; increases physical stamina; brings benefits through wills or legacies; repels anger, mistrust and enmity; affords protection against rumour and gossip.

Chrysoprase Brings joy to the wearer; sharpens the intellect, opens up new areas and rewards initiative; gets rid of envy, jealousy and complacency; dispels anxiety, lifts depression and helps insomnia.

Onyx Attends to business shrewdness; vitalizes the imagination and increases stamina; dispels nightmares and eases tension; brings emotional and mental relief.

Sardonyx Inspires love, romance and vitality; helps confidence and fitness; ensures a result in contractual difficulties; wards off infectious disease; improves vision; heals fragile relationships.

Serpentine Attracts respect and admiration; sharpens the intellect; rewards innovation and creativity; offers the wearer protection from hostility, jealousy or rivalry; improves the effect of medicine.

Tiger's eye Defeats the opponent and ensures victory in any competitive situation; commands love and loyalty; offers protection from treachery and deception; increases the body's immune system.

VENUS

Almandine Linked with achievement, improvement, self-confidence and determination; enhances psychic ability; makes existing problems or difficulties clear; overcomes rivalry and obstacles in the form of human behaviour.

Aquamarine Encourages hope; promotes youthfulness and physical fitness; provides a powerful token of love and friendship; eases digestive or nervous disorders and mental distress; renews confidence and energy; relaxes fear.

Azurite Commands social success and friendship as well as constancy in love; improves vision, both physically and psychically; provides protection from deceit and disillusion; affords help to those faced with generative difficulties.

Beryl Represents hope, friendship and domestic harmony; sharpens the intellect and favours new commercial projects; clarifies and resolves problems; reduces susceptibility to deception or disillusionment.

Cat's eye Encourages success in speculative ventures or competitive sport; strengthens ties of love or affection; protects the home from danger; brings relief to those with respiratory problems.

Coral Helps vitality, good humour and harmonious relationships; expands horizons and helps encourage development; prevents damage to crops and property; protects travellers, mariners and small children.

Emerald Favours love and lovers, promising constancy and fidelity; inspires confidence and emotional fulfilment; strongly protective, especially against deceit or delusions; ensures safety of travellers and expectant mothers.

Jade Promotes good health and good situations; favours artistic and musical endeavours; dulls pain and helps soundness of sleep; improves a poor memory; strongly protective.

Lapis lazuli Inspires confidence, courage and friendship; helps the wearer to succeed – anywhere. Averts danger and preserves travellers and expectant mothers from harm; eases circulation problems.

Malachite Wins favourable judgements in lawsuits or legal actions; enhances social standing and increases prosperity; lifts depression, induces sound sleep and serenity; affords protection against infection.

Opal Signifies fidelity and friendship; highlights psychic and prophetic talents; stimulates memory and intellect; improves vision, digestion and resistance to stress; safeguards property against theft.

Rose quartz Enhances psychic awareness and creative talents; sharpens intellect; preserves the home and family; heals rifts; brings peace of mind and understanding.

Turquoise Inspires health, wealth and happiness; affords a successful conclusion to any constructive enterprise; counteracts negative influences; wards off harmful psychic or physical harm.

MARS

Bauxite Enlivens personality and strengthens the will to succeed; encourages wise investment and fruitful speculation; lifts flagging spirits and speeds recovery from illness; negates strife and reconciles parted lovers.

Bloodstone Promotes eloquence, trust, loyalty and devotion; boosts courage, vitality and the ability to earn money; heals discord; relieves digestive orders or stress; strengthens recuperative powers.

Carbuncle Increases energy, determination and confidence; boosts income and social standing; maintains physical fitness and fights infection; reconciles differences between friends.

Haematite Promotes successful legal action and official contracts; increases sexual drive and fitness; helps overcome nervousness and irritability; improves circulation.

Jasper Helps in psychic development; inspires confidence, friendship and loyalty; defends home and family; inhibits and is said to discourage unwanted pregnancy.

Magnetite Prompts respect of others, loyalty and devotion; increases stamina and virility; promises success and happiness; brings relief from stressful situations; helps to speed recovery from illness or depression.

Ruby Highlights vitality and virility, bringing pleasure and prosperity; good for property development; protects crops and offers security to descendants; dispels strife and dissent.

JUPITER

Alexandrite Refreshes the body and mind; brings hidden talents to the fore; strongly protective, especially against deceit or treachery; awards relief from imaginary fears or phobias.

Blue John Attracts honours, wealth, prestige and social success; improves business and personal relationships; guards the wearer against injury or accident while travelling; mitigates the envy of others.

Calamine Favours visionary and human undertakings; affords success to joint ventures, especially overseas; calms skin irritation and deflates fever; dispels parental anxiety and helps with uneasy consciences.

Carnelian Helps with peace, pleasure and prosperity; brings joy to those going on a long journey or moving house; offers protection to travellers and expectant mothers; assuages strife, anger and disappointment.

Obsidian Encourages boldness, determination and vigour; overwhelms opposition and promotes personal achievement;

strongly protective against psychic attack, accident or injury; strengthens weakened spirits or tiredness of the body.

Sapphire Affords good health, strength and efficiency; heightens perception; rewards commercial and social efforts; strongly protective against antagonism and malice; effects reconciliation between lovers.

Spinel Enhances speculative powers and creativity; improves financial prosperity and social prestige for efforts made; guards against psychic attack, mental stress and emotional blackmail; ensures safety for travellers.

SATURN

Alabaster Brings success in litigation, official and contractual disputes; wins respect, recognition and reward; heals rifts; offers protection against loss of status; inhibits disease.

Alunite Attracts good fortune, health and happiness; helps understanding and domestic harmony; speeds recovery from illness; protects home and property against physical and psychic danger.

Borax Inspires confidence, perseverance and determination; helps to make bad situations good; overcomes fear, hesitation and self-doubt; improves circulation and offers relief from migraine, indigestion and/or gout.

Garnet Helps with devotion, humour and loyalty; increases drive, determination and physical fitness; wards off thunder and lightning; protects travellers from injury or contagious disease.

Granite Wins friendship and fortune; helps with confidence, particularly in the areas of examination-sitting or employment; eases depression; resolves conflict and helps find practical solutions to current problems.

Jet Strengthens determination and focus; affords success to those seeking success or heading into business; eases childbirth and dispels fever; offers protection against gossip and harmful actions.

Marble Improves financial position and status in the community; commands respect and admiration; relieves headaches and stress; preserves home and property from fire, flood and storms.

Meerschaum Benefits philanthropy and investment; favours those working in big organizations; clarifies problems and provides practical solutions; relieves anxiety, depression and nervousness.

Scheelite Highlights diplomacy, business acumen and self-assurance; promises commercial and domestic happiness; alleviates strife and envy; handy for nervous disorders and nursing mothers.
Sulphur Highlights clear expression and physical fitness; professional acumen is rewarded with public acclaim; powerful against malice; purifies the blood and relieves menstrual tension.

By now, you will be beginning to have a fair idea of what you need to start constructing your talismans. Before we do this, however, we need to crank up the energy a little. For simple talismans, the method of casting a circle shown on pages 41–2 is quite sufficient, but when you begin to take more complex energies into account, you need to be much more aware of the Higher Powers that can be used. The ritual given over the next few pages has been used for many centuries to do just this.

The Lesser Banishing Ritual of the Pentagram

This two-part ritual can be performed to purify a room for further magical work or meditation, and can also be used for protection. It has a much higher vibration than simply casting a circle, however, and, in addressing the Archangels, appeals to the highest authority for protection and assistance. Rather than appealing to the Elements, we now go to those beings or energies that are in charge of the Elements and make a direct appeal to them.

The first part of the ritual, that of the Kabbalistic Cross, is used by the practitioner to open themselves to the powers of the universe and to state that they are present and ready for work. By calling the energy of the universe into the practitioner through the centre of their being, the mind, body and soul are energized and in alignment with the cosmic forces. The practitioner is then able to direct these energies with wisdom and at will.

It is suggested that you perform at least the first part of this ritual – which deals with the personal self – every day.

KABBALISTIC CROSS

METHOD

Stand facing East and perform the Kabbalistic Cross as follows:

Touch your forehead with the first two (or index) fingers of your right hand and
visualize a sphere of white light at that point.
Chant:

Atah
(This translates roughly as 'Thou art')

Lower your hand to your solar plexus and visualize a line of light extending down
to your feet and chant:

Malkuth
(The Kingdom)

Raise your hand to touch your right shoulder and visualize a sphere of light
there and chant:

Ve Geburah
(And the power)

Extend the hand across the chest, tracing a line of light, and touch your left
shoulder where another sphere of light forms and chant:

Ve Gedulah
(And the glory)

Clasp your hands in the centre of your chest at the crossing point of
the horizontal and vertical lines of light.
Bow your head and chant:

Le Olam, Amen
(For ever, Amen)

The second part of the ritual brings about a quiet mind free of 'chatter'
from the everyday world. This is useful in meditation, and also in spell-
working when concentration is needed. In the making of talismans, this

quiet mind is of extreme importance so that the correct energies can be focused properly into the object. Whereas before we have used English words in our rituals, now we are beginning to use words which, through long usage, have become Words of Power. We acknowledge the Archangels in their proper place and create a very positive space in which to work.

The effects of the whole ritual are first and foremost on the Astral (more subtle) energies, though it uses the Earth pentagram (5-pointed star traced on the body, see below) as a sign that the practitioner recognizes their place on Earth as Human. There is, in effect, a stepping down of the energies to make them usable, though you should also understand that the practitioner's own power is raised or enhanced at the same time. The protection that the pentagrams give is to banish any negative energy that may be present on any level whatsoever. In previous times, it was thought that the magister or practitioner had mastery over the power he or she was using. Today, we would rather think of it in terms of a collaborative effort between spiritual or magical energies and the practitioner. This does not mean there is any less respect.

FORMATION OF THE PENTAGRAM

METHOD

Facing East and using extended fingers, trace a large pentagram with the point up, starting at your left hip, up to just above your forehead, centred on your body, then down to your right hip, up and to your left shoulder, across to the right shoulder and down to the starting point in front of your left hip.

Visualize this pentagram in blue flaming light.
Stab you fingers or dagger into the centre.
Chant:

YHVH (Yod-heh-vahv-heh)
(This is the Tetragrammaton, a four-letter word of power –
translated into Latin as 'Jehovah')

Turn to the South.
Visualize the blue flame following you fingers, tracing a blue line from the pentagram in the East pentagram to the South.

Repeat the formation of the pentagram while facing South.

This time, chant:

Adonai
(Another name for God, translated as 'Lord')

Turn to the West, tracing the blue flame from South to West.
Form a pentagram again, but this time chant:

Eheieh (Eh-hay-yeah)
(Another name for God, translated as 'I am' or 'I am that I am')

Turn to the North, again tracing the blue flame from West to North.
Repeat the tracing of the pentagram and chant:

AGLA (Ah-gah-lah)
(A composite of 'Atah Gibor le olam Amen')

Return again to the East, tracing the blue flame from North to East.
Stab the fingers back again into the same spot as you started from.

You should now visualize that you are surrounded by four flaming pentagrams
connected by a line of blue fire.

Visualize each Archangel standing guard at each station and extend your
arms out to your sides, forming a cross.
Chant:

Before me, RAPHAEL (Rah-fah-ell),
Behind me, GABRIEL (Gah-bree-ell),
On my right hand, MICHAEL (Mee-khah-ell),
On my left hand, URIEL (Ooh-ree-ell or sometimes Aw-ree-ell),
Before me flames the pentagram, behind me shines the six-rayed star.

Repeat the Kabbalistic Cross as you did at the beginning and chant:

Atah
Malkuth
Ve Geburah
Ve Gedulah
Le Olam, Amen

As can be seen, Raphael is in the East, Gabriel in the West, Michael in the South and Uriel in the North. Sometimes Michael and Uriel are transposed by practitioners. Looking back at the work we have already done, it can be seen that these four guardians of the Directions now have names and, as we said in Casting a Circle (pages 41–2), we can begin to think of them as old friends whom we can invite into our sacred space.

Before we do that and ask them to help us to create our talismans, we should get to know them better.

THE ARCHANGELS

The four Archangels can be found in a variety of protective incantations and invocations. Their purpose is, as we have seen, to guard the four quarters or cardinal points. They are an almost universal symbol that can turn up in many different aspects, from nursery rhymes to the Guardians of the Dead.

For our purposes, they might be thought of as extra help in living our lives successfully, not just at times when we make talismans, but also as an ever-present boost to us. Think of yourself making a connection to Michael for love, so that you can love more fully; Raphael for healing all your ills; Gabriel for strength, to fill you with power for the next day; and Uriel for suffusing you with the light of the mind or understanding. When you are having a hard time, you can send a brief prayer or request to whichever one is appropriate.

Generally there are, in fact, considered to be seven Archangels, and it will depend on your own teaching as to which school of thought you choose to follow in naming them. Because the teachings were initially by word of mouth, there are many different lists of Archangels deputed to help the world upon its way. The four we consider here are the ones who appear consistently in most lists and are therefore the best known universally. They are the ones most often called upon in magical workings. The only problem is that sometimes Michael and Uriel appear to swap places in some traditions, which can be confusing. We suggest, therefore, that if the attributions given here do not feel right, try the ritual the other way around and change the words accordingly. Do ensure that you still call upon all four Archangels, however. So now to meet our guardians.

Michael, which means 'Who is as God' in Hebrew, is one of the seven Archangels and also chief of the four closest to God. The Roman Catholic Church regards Michael in much the same light as the Catholic Church, his festival – Michaelmas – being held on 29 September. He is known in mythology as the one who attempted to bring Lucifer back to God. In Ezekiel's vision of the Cherubim, or the four sacred animals, he is the angel with the face of the lion. Michael is often visualized as a masculine Archangel dressed in robes or armour of red and green. He stands in the attitude of a warrior amid flames. Bearing either a sword or a spear, Michael is the guardian against evil and the protector of humanity. He is stationed in the South.

Raphael is one of four Archangels stationed about the throne of God; his task is to heal the Earth. Initially, he was pictured with the face of a dragon, but this was changed in later imagery to the face of a man. He is often visualized as a tall, fair figure standing upon the clouds in robes of yellow and violet, sometimes holding the Caduceus of Hermes as a symbol of his healing powers. He is God's builder or composer and has the task of building or rebuilding the Earth, which the fallen angels have defiled. Raphael's name in Hebrew means 'Healer of God' or 'God has Healed'. Raphael Ruachel ('Raphael of Air') is stationed in the East.

Gabriel means 'Strong One of God' in Hebrew. He was one of the four Archangels who stand in the presence of God, and was sent to announce to Mary the birth of Jesus. In Ezekiel's vision of the four sacred animals, he has the face of an eagle. Gabriel is often visualized as a feminine Archangel holding a cup, standing upon the waters of the sea, and wearing robes of blue and orange. Gabriel is also at one with the higher ego or inner divinity. Gabriel Maimel ('Gabriel of Water') is stationed in the West.

Uriel Uriel's (or Auriel's) name in Hebrew means 'Light of God'. Specifically, he is the angel or divinity of light – not simply of physical light, but of spiritual illumination. Also referred to as 'The Angel of Repentance', he is the angel of terror, prophecy and mystery. He was sometimes ranked as an Archangel with Michael, Gabriel and Raphael, and believed to be the Angel who holds the keys to the gates of Hell. He is also often identified as the Angel who drove Adam and Eve from the Garden of Eden, and was thought to be the messenger sent to warn Noah of the forthcoming floods. As 'Uriel Aretziel' ('Uriel of Earth'), he is stationed in the North. He is often seen rising up from the vegetation of the Earth, holding stems of ripened wheat and wearing robes of citrine, russet, olive and black.

THE ELEMENTALS

Each Archangel of the Elements has as his servant one of the kings of the Elemental Kingdoms. They are:

Air Paralda, King of the Sylphs, who appears to the clairvoyant vision as a tenuous form made of blue mist, always moving and changing shape. He accompanies Raphael.

Fire Djinn, King of the Salamanders, who appears as a Fire giant. He is composed of twisting living flame surrounded by sparks that crackle and glow. He accompanies Michael.

Water Nixa, King of the Undines, is seen as an ever-changing shape, fluid with a greenish-blue aura splashed with silver and grey. He accompanies Gabriel.

Earth Ghob, King of the Gnomes, seen traditionally as a gnome or goblin, is squat, heavy and dense. He accompanies Uriel.

You do not necessarily have to call on these Elementals specifically in your rituals, but you should be aware of their energies in that they are the servants of the Archangels, and not yours.

THE CREATION STORY

According to Kabbalistic doctrine, the physical world was created from the top down – from the heavenly realms down to the earthly. The first world created was fiery (red), the second was watery (blue), the third was airy (yellow) and the fourth and final world, which arose out of the other three, was earthly Assiah (black).

It is said that God selected three letters from the simple ones we have already seen, sealed them and formed them into a Great Name, I H V (in English, 'Jehovah'), thus giving himself a name or vibration with which to work. With this name, he sealed the universe in six directions:

He looked above, and sealed the Height with I H V.
He looked below, and sealed the Depth with I V H.
He looked forward, and sealed the East with H I V.
He looked backward, and sealed the West with H V I.
He looked to the right, and sealed the South with V I H.
He looked to the left, and sealed the North with V H I.

Following this doctrine, it is possible to see that the idea of creating seals as actual physical objects would be the next logical step for humans. The first talismans, therefore, were actually representations of these variations of the correct sounds to be made when opening the directions – the keys. The seals gradually became more and more complex, and contained more and more information that would remind the practitioner of the correct way to use their keys.

It would not be too fanciful to appreciate that a talisman was a concrete record of the ritual that needed to be performed in order to use or manifest a particular energy or power. The magical practitioner would use whatever knowledge and aspects of their physical world they had around them to remind themselves of what needed to be done. In this way, the correspondences that we see on pages 250–1 were born.

Whatever system of magic we choose to use, we now have a huge compendium of records, both physical and otherwise. Some magicians would use symbols, others would use pictures, and yet others would substitute different letters for what they were trying to remember, in the belief that the Ultimate Power in its infinite knowledge would recognize what was needed. To make our talismans, we must first go back to simplicity and follow their original reasoning:

• The seal or talisman would first of all have to be round. This is because a circle was the closest written representation that could be given for totality.
• Then it would have to have represented on it the four worlds, giving particular significance to the one that the magician was petitioning. Here arises the idea of the four quarters, with each quarter circle showing the significance that was placed on it.
• In each quarter was placed a representation of an idea or need.

• Finally, the article would be sealed by Words of Power which would be placed around the edge in order to draw the correct energy inwards towards the seal. This is why we can differentiate between talismans and amulets; talismans are designed to draw power towards the object for use by the practitioner – the practitioner has taken deliberate action to have this happen.

• The centre of the talisman would be the most important point of power, so the easiest way initially would be to construct the talisman from that point.

• On the obverse (back) of the talisman would be placed an acknowledgement of the power of the planet or Element being petitioned.

As a rough rule of thumb, you would keep the front of the talisman for anything to do with the outer or public workings, with anything personal on the back. You might, for instance, have your own name on the obverse to represent your own personal link with the heavens. You might represent your own astrological sign or its Glyph (symbol).

DESIGNING AND CONSTRUCTING A TALISMAN

To do this, you must have as much information as you can about its purpose and the person for whom it is intended. You can keep the essential talisman very simple. To make it easy, let us suppose that we are making a talisman for a friend. This person's initial is M, she is a Gemini and wishes to obtain a job in publishing.

Referring to the list on page 254, we see that fortunately her zodiacal sign is ruled by Mercury, which also looks after publishing of all types; her Element is Air, her number is 5 and her colour is yellow. Unfortunately, her metal is quicksilver or zinc, which makes it somewhat difficult, because you cannot make a talisman from quicksilver. We must therefore find another material for our talisman. Scanning the list quickly, we see that her fabric is linen, which is very useable as a surface on which to inscribe the talisman. Air is ruled by Raphael, so he is the Archangel we must use. His direction is East, so we can use the information we now have and incorporate the Word of Power from that direction, which is HIV (the Word of Power in this context has nothing to do with viruses).

Broadly, anything above the East–West horizon is to do with spiritual matters, while anything below is to do with the physical world. We want security for our friend, so we might incorporate a square around the centre, representing the material plane of existence. We will incorporate a symbol for each of the four guardians in each of the triangles so formed. In the Eastern quarter outside that square we will put three symbols for Air (see page 278) and two more in the Western quarter – that way we have five in all. We have therefore requested enterprise and some arrogance in her new beginning, which should help her confidence, but have also put in some emotional softness and receptivity in the West.

Obliquely, we have also wished her happiness in partnership in these two symbols in the West. We have also used five, which effects change, but we must also remember that this gives sexual freedom, so we must be sure that our friend is ready for this should it come along. For the moment, that is probably enough information to include within the centre. Around the outer circle of the talisman we can include one of the holy names, so let us choose Elohim, which is one of the names of God. We might inscribe it in Hebrew letters if we so choose, and intersperse the 'call sign' or seal we already have for Raphael, which is HIV. This also might be in Hebrew.

On the obverse (shown overleaf) we could include the Table of Jupiter (see page 250) and our friend's initial, perhaps pointing in the four directions. Around the outside we might inscribe a favourite saying, interspersed by the symbol for Gemini.

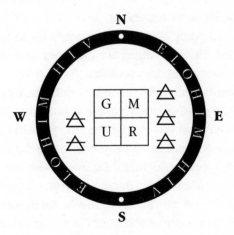

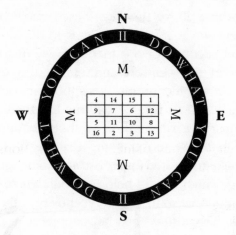

You can see that with only a little knowledge, we have made quite a powerful design for our friend.

Now, we must inscribe this design on our piece of linen; it would be for you to decide whether you wish to make a picture that she might frame and put on her wall, or whether you will make her a talisman bag. Whatever you do, you could either make the linen yellow or use yellow ink or fabric paint to inscribe your gift. It doesn't matter if the back of the talisman is not seen. You have still put the power into the representation.

We have kept things very simple in the above design, but there are other representations of numbers that it might be useful to know. These are shown below.

Essential symbolism of talismans

The dot, line and circle are basic symbols from which many others have developed. Despite differences in language, they have come to have universally accepted meanings.

The circle symbolizes infinity, totality and eternity, as well as the abyss or 'no-thing'; the dot signifies unity and a beginning; the vertical line suggests the vibrant, energetic principle; the horizontal line is the passive, more fixed principle. All of these basic symbols can be joined together in many different ways to enhance their meaning and to indicate broader, equally important concepts that are used in talismanic work. There are so many variations that we have only given brief explanations of the more common examples.

A dot within a circle; centre of infinity; manifestation; the Sun; the eye of God; perfection; the cosmos.

The circle divided equally in two by a single line forms the basis of all lunar symbols. The Moon is said to represent the soul; it also reflects the light of the Sun as the earthly soul reflects the Divine. The crescent or half-circle symbolizes the feminine, passive, receptive principle.

The primal ternary, or basic three-figure, embodies the idea of structure and development, as it originates from the (dot) centre above or below the horizontal line. It therefore takes two basic forms – the active and the passive – downward pointing and upward pointing, which connect with the Elements of Fire (active and masculine) and Water (passive and feminine).

The introduction of a second horizontal line within the primal ternaries produces the symbols for Air (active) and Earth (passive).

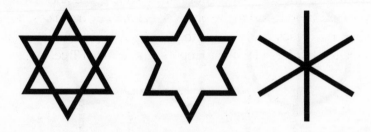

Putting the two triangles together gives us a star, one of the most recognizable symbols showing the four physical elements surrounding the invisible Element of Spirit. As a shining light, the star also suggests Divine order, one's destiny or purpose.

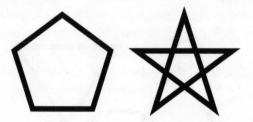

Five is the next prime number after three, and all five-sided figures suggest the five physical senses and the five Elements, no matter what form they take. The five-pointed star has already been mentioned when working with a pentacle (pages 39 and 45), and is a symbol for the Cosmic or Perfect Man.

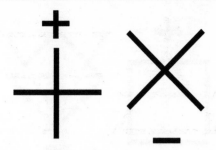

The primary four-sided figure takes two forms: the neutral and the active. It is formed from two lines intercepting at right angles – a cross. This suggests the four aspects of humans' existence and the many ways of manifesting within the physical realm. Known as a cosmic axis symbol, it signifies equilibrium, the union of opposites, integration and manifest order. It is used to represent the World Tree.

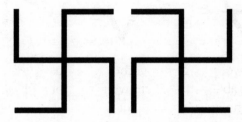

One simple but very ancient variation of the basic equal-armed cross is the swastika, which has gained notoriety as a symbol of the Nazi movement. It actually equates symbolically to the cosmic Wheel of Life. The arms may point in a clockwise or anticlockwise direction. Both the swastika (clockwise) and the fylfot (anticlockwise) incorporate the four-fold principle of manifestation.

A cross inside a circle signifies all those things that are cyclical and creative. Any symbolism to do with the world of matter within the cosmic sphere is symbolized in this way.

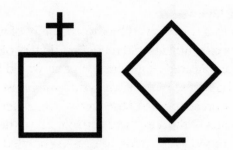

The other basic quaternaries are formed by joining the cross points to represent the four-fold nature of the physical universe; the material plane of existence; the Earth; the manifest world; order and development. Again, there are two basic forms of this primal symbol, the active and the neutral, and both figures incorporate the principle of a double ternary.

When we consider that the 22 letters of the Hebrew alphabet are said to be the primeval energy patterns of creation, ultimately we have, by multiplication, 22 x 21 x 20 x 19 x 18 x 17 x 16 x 15 x 14 x 13 x 12 x 11 x 10 x 9 x 8 x 7 x 6 x 5 x 4 x 3 x 2 x 1, giving 1,124,000,728, 000,000,000,000 different forms. The tremendous versatility of form seen in the natural world is only one consideration. Starting with the primal symbols, we can develop or combine the symbols we have given above to represent some quite complicated concepts. Breaking them down to their simplicity is one way of discovering what the makers of talismans are actually attempting to convey.

SIMPLE BLESSING OF THE TALISMAN
Now you may simply bless and dedicate your talisman to the purpose for which it is intended. The technique that you used for dedicating jewellery will, for simpler amulets and talismans, be quite sufficient. However, now you have a degree of knowledge of the Archangels and their powers, you may wish to use a more comprehensive form, and this requires a more complex ritual and understanding.

THE TREE OF LIFE

Having been totally overawed by the enormity of what is possible, we come back to simplicity and recognize that, of old, there needed to be an uncomplicated representation that would help the initiate understand the nature of the Powers they might use. This was done through the representation of the Tree of Life. Later, the 22 cards of the major arcana of the Tarot were attributed to the Paths.

There are ten sephiroth or attributes needed in life, in the manifestation of magic and in the understanding of the meaning of life. Below we give the anglicized forms of the names they were given by Kabbalists. They move from the spiritual into the physical down the Tree, and might be thought of as the seals we spoke of earlier.

Kether	Crown
Chokmah	Wisdom
Binah	Intelligence, Understanding
Chesed	Love, Mercy
Gevurah	Justice, Judgement, Severity
Tiphareth	Beauty
Netsach	Steadfastness, Eternity, Victory
Hod	Splendour, Majesty
Yesod	Foundation
Malkud	The Kingdom

There is an eleventh seal known as Da'ath – also called Ultimate Knowledge – but for the moment we are looking at the Tree of Life as a way of understanding the process of anchoring the power and energy available to us. The two outer pillars represent Force and Form, and the Middle Pillar signifies Balance and Equilibrium – a state to which we all aspire. The following is a ritual that helps us to achieve that state of equilibrium before we bless and consecrate our talisman.

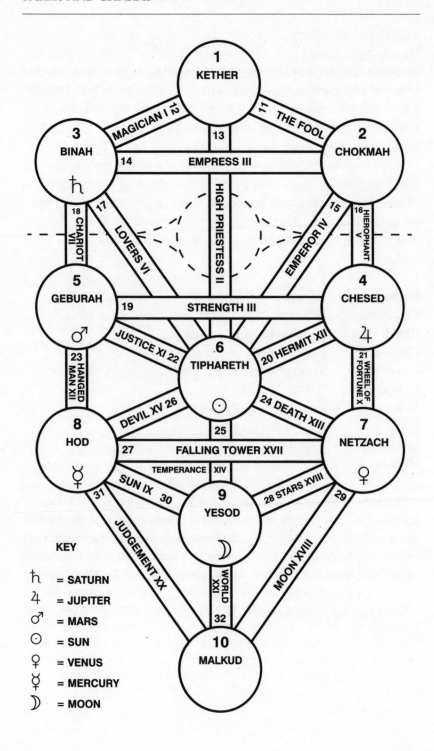

KEY

ħ	=	SATURN
♃	=	JUPITER
♂	=	MARS
☉	=	SUN
♀	=	VENUS
☿	=	MERCURY
☽	=	MOON

Middle Pillar Ritual

Remembering the representation of Perfect Man we used in A Ritual of Gestures on pages 94–5, see if you can visualize that Perfect Man laid out on a representation of the tree. This will give you some idea of the placings for each of the sephiroth (seals) in relation to your own body.

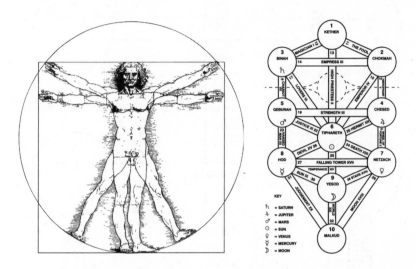

The following Middle Pillar exercise is used to ground the practitioner, to give you a connection to the Earth. You use your will to direct the Energy of the Universe down into Kether and through the middle of the body to create a permanent energy flow that connects you to the Earth. It is similar in many ways to the ritual you performed for Ostara (pages 145–6).

This is not an easy exercise to become proficient at, but it is very powerful and can bring enormous benefits. It should not be performed when you have other things on your mind, since it requires concentration and full awareness as you work. It should be performed before any major magical workings. If you have not previously done so, we suggest that you perform The Lesser Banishing Ritual of the Pentagram first (pages 266–9).

Prepare yourself by lying down on your back or sitting comfortably. Find a comfortable position and relax completely. Continue to breathe deeply, slowly and rhythmically. Do so throughout the entire ritual. Ideally, each part of the ritual should be repeated at least three times and up to nine times, but you may find you need to work up to that over a period of time. Keep to the same number of repetitions for each section, however (e.g. two sets of three).

METHOD

Visualize a sphere shining just above your head, about the size of a football.
It has a mist of opalescence around it (like the Moon on a hazy night).
Inhale, continuing to visualize the sphere above your head.
As you exhale, see how the sphere grows more brilliant as you do so.
If it feels right to you, chant:

AHIH

Repeat this process nine more times.
Relax for a few minutes and feel the Energy pulsating throughout your body.

Visualize a shaft of white light coming down through your head from the sphere
above you, to your throat.
Inhale and visualize a second smaller sphere in the middle of your throat.
As you breathe out, watch again as this sphere brightens.
At the same time, chant:

Jehovah Elohim

Repeat this process nine more times.
Relax and feel the Energy begin to pulsate in your body.

Visualize a shaft of light coming down through your chest from the sphere in your
throat to the area around your heart and solar plexus.
Inhale and visualize a third sphere at your heart and solar plexus area.
The sphere brightens as you exhale while chanting:

Jehovah E lo VeDath

Repeat this process nine more times.
Relax for a few minutes and scan your body, noticing any changes and feeling the
pulsation of the Energy.

Visualize a shaft of light coming down from your chest to your pelvic area.
Inhale, completely filling your lungs, and visualize a fourth sphere
around your genitals.
The sphere brightens as you exhale while chanting:

Shaddai El Chai

Repeat this process nine more times.
Relax for a few moments and just sense your body and how it vibrates.

Now visualize a shaft of light coming down from your pelvis to a point
beneath your feet.
Inhale deeply and visualize another sphere beneath your feet.
The sphere takes on more light as you exhale while chanting:

Adonai Hah-Aretz

Repeat this process nine more times.
Be aware of your body once again, noticing whatever is happening there and
feeling the Energy as it courses through your body.

At this point, focus your attention on the sphere above your head.
As you exhale, bring a ball of light down your left side to the sphere beneath
your feet.
Inhale and bring it back up your right side to the sphere above your head, forming
a circle of brilliant light.
Repeat this process nine more times.

Again, focus your attention on the sphere above your head.
Exhale and bring a ball of light down the front of your body to the sphere beneath
your feet.
Inhale and bring it back up behind you to the sphere above your head.
Form a circle of brilliant light.
Repeat this process nine more times.
Relax for a few moments and feel yourself inside a sphere of white light that
envelops your entire being.

Focus your attention on the sphere beneath your feet, which should now be
glowing considerably.
Inhale and pull a brilliant shaft of light through your body and up your spine to the
sphere above your head.
While exhaling, visualize a light breaking into many fragments and raining gently
down around you, and return to the sphere beneath your feet.
Repeat this process nine more times, making sure you finish at the top.

Scan your body once again, noticing whatever is happening there and feeling
the Energy for as long as you wish, while you consecrate your talismans or
perform other magical works.

The above ritual is very similar to some techniques used in Eastern disciplines, so it has been given here in its entirety in order that you may judge for yourself as to how you wish to use it. Not only is it used in Magic, it is also used in understanding the Mysteries and brings in its wake a much more profound understanding of the world in which we live.

It can make you somewhat disorientated and a little dizzy when you first start performing it. It takes time to carry out, so make sure you are not likely to be disturbed during the ritual. Do be sure that when you have finished your workings, you acknowledge the Power that you have used and return the Energy to its source with a blessing. A simple visualization of the light returning to the larger sphere above your head will suffice.

MAKING YOUR TALISMAN

When you are making a talisman, you should gather up all the materials you need and assemble them within your sacred space. The materials should be dedicated in the same way that you dedicated your ritual tools. You will have:

• Your core, which will usually be a circle of the metal or wood belonging to the particular planet, deity or Archangel you are using. It does not matter if the metal is not pretty, because it will probably be covered by the design.
• Your design, which you have previously worked out.
• Tools for inscribing the design, including pens with coloured ink.
• Any other paper or parchment you might need.

You should assemble your talisman in the following manner:

• Inscribe the front design – to a size that fits the core material – on a circular piece of parchment or paper that is slightly larger than the front of the talisman.
• Inscribe the design for the back to a size that exactly fits your circle of core material.
• Snip the edges of the paper for the front, so that it can be neatly folded around your core material and stuck in place.
• Stick your design for the back in place.

CONSECRATING YOUR TALISMAN

Next you must consecrate your talisman. You can do this in any way that suits you best. You might use A Ritual of Gestures (see pages 94–5), finally presenting your talisman for blessing at the end of it. You might use the ritual for dedicating jewellery – again modifying your own words to suit your purpose – or you might use an invocation to each of the Archangels and Elements in turn with a form of words such as:

Archangel [name], bless now my working in constructing this talisman,
May you and your Spirits and helpers lend the power of [Element] to it today.
Let that Power be used only for the purpose of good for which it was intended.
So be it.

Finally, present your talisman to your deity or deities with an appropriate form of words such as:

May the Gods bless this symbol of Power and protection and keep the owner safe from all harm.
May it be used for the Greater Good and for nothing else.

Now make a circle three times over it with your power hand and put it in a safe place until you can present it to the person for whom it is intended. Obviously, if it is for yourself, you will place it where you consider it to be most effective.

DISPOSING OF YOUR TALISMAN

When you no longer have any need of the talisman, i.e. when you have had success with what it was intended for, you can dispose of it. However, it cannot simply be thrown away. It should be 'uncharged' – which means that the Power must be returned to its original source.

The undoing process should be done in reverse order to the order in which the talisman was put together. Therefore, having constructed your sacred space in whatever fashion was appropriate for you, you now call upon your deity or deities and thank them for the use of the Power that was given. Ask them to withdraw the Power that has been used. You might say:

> *I thank you now for the assistance you have given me.*
> *I ask that, its purpose fulfilled, you return*
> *this object to its natural state,*
> *Powerful as that is.*

You then acknowledge the help that you have had from the Archangels, the Elementals and the helpers. You can now dismantle the talisman and return it to its constituent parts.

Think very carefully about what you made it from and dispose of it accordingly, in line with the Elements. For example, metal might be buried in the earth, paper or parchment burned, and wood either buried or burned. Always perform these acts with either a silent or spoken acknowledgement.

Obviously, if your talisman has been made for you or if you have made it yourself – for instance, from semi-precious metal – you will not want to throw it away. Then it can be cleansed in the same way that you treated your crystals (see page 161) and your altar objects. It could also be buried for a short period to allow the earth to cleanse it, provided you remember what you have done with it. (Incidentally, if you have a fondness for old jewellery, you might clear their vibration in the same way.) Never reuse in a talisman any material taken from an old talisman. This is because a talisman can only be used for one person and for one purpose. To guard against the possibility of it being reused, it is always better to bury the core material or throw it in running water, a river, a stream or out to sea.

You now have all the basic information you need to make, use and dispose of talismans. We suggest that you start simply and experiment until what you are doing feels right. As with any magic or ritual, if it is done with the right intention, neither you nor the recipient can possibly come to any harm. If, however, your intention is malign, then we can only warn that, in accordance with most spiritual belief, the negative intent is usually put to the test three times. There is no advantage! Spell-making and magical practices are there for a purpose – to help the world function in the best way possible.

SIMPLE MAGIC

To complete a full circle and make things as easy as possible, we give here a simple way of classifying information helpful in your spell-making and magic practice.

In the modern day we have, of necessity, moved away from a true celebration of the Wheel of the Year. Rather than having to remember when all the Sabbats fall, it is sometimes easier to work with the modern-day calendar and remember the correspondences for each month rather than each Moon. We give here some of those correspondences, beginning with the essential energy of each month.

POWER FLOW

Each calendar month brings into sharp focus certain feelings, energies and concerns which can usefully be worked on during that time. The following are some suggestions you might find interesting. The simpler you keep your rituals when working with the flow of power, the better. Asking the Archangels or Gods and Goddesses to help you in managing your life as successfully as possible is usually enough. This is one way of ensuring that you, the instrument of power, are as clear as possible.

The Blue Moon in pagan times, when the lunar calendar was more important, was a thirteenth month. For many nowadays that time is much shorter, being a time of adjustment and realignment.

January

Beginning and planning. Protection and reversing spells. Conserving energy that is sluggish and below the surface means that you work on personal problems that involve no one else. You need to get your various subtle bodies to work together towards the same goals.

February

Purification, growth and healing. Loving the self. Energy working toward the surface suggests that you take responsibility for past mistakes. Forgiveness of oneself and making plans for the future are the prime tasks.

March

Growing, prospering. Exploring. New beginnings. Energy breaks into the open and gives a balance of dark and light. The task is to break illusions and find the truth, no matter the pain it causes.

April

Change, self-confidence and self-reliance. Taking advantage of chances. Energy is put into creating, producing and returning a balance to the nerves. The task is to work on temper and perhaps emotional selfishness.

May

Propagation and intuition. Creative energy is rising now. Should you wish, contact with the supernatural and Nature Spirits is easy. Learning to have empathy with others is the task at this time.

June

Protection, strength and prevention. The energy is total but restful at this time of light. It is a time for decision-making and taking responsibility. There are rewards for positive action, so you need to work on personal inconsistencies.

July

Relaxation, preparation and success. The energy is suitable for dream work, divination and meditation. You should consider your objectives, especially the spiritual ones.

August

Vitality, health and friendship. Energy is put into the harvesting and gathering of just rewards. The task is to learn how to appreciate what you have.

September

Balance of light and dark. Organization. Energy is resting after hard work. The task is to clear and realign physical, mental, emotional and spiritual confusion.

October

Justice, balance and inner harmony. Energy is concentrated on letting go and inner cleansing. The task is to consider the laws of karma (cause and effect) and those of reincarnation and rebirth.

Blue Moon (27 October – 1 November)

Prophecy and communication with the dead. Energy is used for releasing and remembering the past. The task is to let go of negative memories and emotional baggage.

November

Transformation. The energy is designed to allow one to put down roots and prepare for the new. The task is to open up channels of communication with your personal deities and guardians.

December

Darkness and personal magic. Energy is concentrated on enduring, ending and rebirth. As the Earth tide turns, you can reach out to friends and family, the lonely and needy. It is often a time of finding your own spiritual path.

ANIMALS

The following are the power animals for each month.

January: Fox
February: Otter, Unicorn
March: Hedgehog, Boar
April: Bear, Wolf
May: Cats, Leopard
June: Monkey, Butterfly, Frog, Toad
July: Crab, Turtle, Dolphin, Whale
August: Lion, Phoenix, Sphinx, Dragon
September: Snake, Jackal
October: Stag, Elephant, Jackal, Ram, Scorpion
Blue Moon: Bat, Wolf, Sow, Dog, Snake
November: Unicorn, Scorpion, Crocodile, Jackal
December: Mouse, Deer, Horse, Bear

BIRDS

Here are the birds that are particularly appropriate for each month.

January: Pheasant, Blue jay
February: Eagle
March: Seagull
April: Hawk, Magpie
May: Swallow, Dove, Swan
June: Wren, Peacock
July: Starling, Swallow
August: Falcon, Crane, Eagle
September: Sparrow, Ibis
October: Heron, Crow, Robin
Blue Moon: Owl, Raven, Falcon
November: Owl, Goose, Sparrow
December: Rook, Robin, Snowy owl

COLOURS

Here are the colours associated with each month.

January: Brilliant white, Blue-violet, Black
February: Light blue, Violet
March: Pale green, Red-violet
April: Crimson red, Gold
May: Green, Brown, Pink
June: Orange, Golden Green
July: Silver, Blue-grey
August: Yellow, Gold
September: Brown, Yellow-green, Yellow
October: Dark blue-green
Blue Moon: Black, White, Purple
November: Grey, Sea green
December: Blood red, White, Black

FLOWERS

The following are some flowers which may be placed on your altar or in your home (or even given as gifts) as a reminder of the natural energy around us.

January: Snowdrop, Crocus
February: Primrose
March: Jonquil, Daffodil, Violet
April: Daisy, Sweet pea
May: Lily of the valley, Foxglove, Rose, Broom
June: Lavender, Orchid, Yarrow
July: Lotus, Water lily, Jasmine
August: Sunflower, Marigold
September: Narcissus, Lily
October: Calendula, Marigold, Cosmos
Blue Moon: White lily, Dahlia, Chrysanthemum
November: Blooming cactus, Chrysanthemum
December: Holly, Poinsettia, Christmas cactus

NATURE SPIRITS

As we saw on pages 47–8 and 50–2, Nature Spirits can be important allies. Each month is cared for by particular entities, as below.

January: Gnomes, Brownies
February: House fairies (both of the home itself and of houseplants)
March: Mer-people – these are Air and Water beings which are connected with spring rains and storms
April: Plant fairies
May: Fairies, Elves
June: Sylphs, Zephyrs
July: Hobgoblins, Fairies of harvested crops
August: Dryads
September: Trooping fairies
October: Frost fairies, Plant fairies
Blue Moon: Banshees and other beings who carry messages between worlds
November: Subterranean fairies
December: Snow fairies, Storm fairies, Winter tree fairies

STONES

We have given the qualities of many stones throughout the book. This list is simply included for easy reference.

January: Garnet, Onyx, Jet, Chrysoprase
February: Amethyst, Jasper, Rock crystal
March: Aquamarine, Bloodstone
April: Ruby, Garnet, Sard
May: Emerald, Malachite, Amber, Carnelian
June: Topaz, Agate, Alexandrite, Fluorite
July: Pearl, Moonstone, White Agate
August: Cat's eye, Carnelian, Jasper, Fire agate
September: Peridot, Olivine, Chrysolite, Citrine
October: Opal, Tourmaline, Beryl, Turquoise
Blue Moon: Obsidian, Onyx, Apache tear
November: Topaz, Hyacinth, Lapis lazuli
December: Serpentine, Jacinth, Peridot

TREES

We saw in the section on Ogham Staves how important trees were in magical workings. We give here the correspondences for modern-day use of such energy.

January: Birch
February: Rowan, Laurel, Cedar
March: Alder, Dogwood
April: Pine, Bay, Hazel
May: Hawthorn
June: Oak
July: Oak, Acacia, Ash
August: Hazel, Alder, Cedar
September: Hazel, Larch, Bay
October: Yew, Cypress, Acacia
Blue Moon: Pine, Cypress, Yew, Elder
November: Alder, Cypress
December: Pine, Fir, Holly

CONCLUSION

So, we must now bring this book to a close. We started off with some very simple work where you learned the 'why' of magic – that people have always felt the necessity to control their environment and to make use of the power and energy around them. You learned to create a magical space for yourself and how to consecrate your tools and artefacts in a simple, efficient way.

Then we explored the true meaning of spells, the use of sound to manifest what is felt to be necessary in your lives, and learned to use simple spells. Love and money are two aspects of life that give everybody great concern, and simple magic can be a great help in maximizing the potential of what we have been given. You discovered the way in which ritual and the various forms of magic which have been in use for centuries can help us in that process of maximization; we also found how we can be in harmony with nature by following the simple structures of the Wheel of the Year. In honouring this cyclical aspect of Mother Nature in the modern day, we saw that there were other ways of using the magical powers, and you learned how to choose the appropriate vehicle in the use of charms and amulets. Not only can we use the broader viewpoint of the seasons, but we can also utilize the diurnal round to use energy more specifically and to accomplish a great deal through using the influences of the planets.

Finally, having gone full circle, as it were, we learned how, even in the modern day and given the correct method, we can protect ourselves from harm and make things happen through the use of talismans. We can use their focusing of very subtle but powerful energies to live life with some effect.

Because we have deliberately not concentrated on one school of thought, you have hopefully learned from very simple beginnings to understand a little more of the energies around us, and so can pick and choose the ways that work best for you. It simply remains to remind you of the main principle behind the working of any magic. This is the Law of Knowledge.

With understanding comes control and power, but the paradox is that the more you know, the less power you need to use to control it.

We leave you with this blessing:

May your Gods support you in all that you should.
May all that you do be done for good.
May love, life and happiness be all that you would.

SOURCES

Alderman, Clifford Lindsay *A Cauldron of Witches: The Story of Witchcraft* Bailey Bros. and Swinfen, 1973

Andrews, Carol *Amulets of Ancient Egypt* British Museum Press, 1994

Ball, Pamela *10,000 Dreams Interpreted* Arcturus Publishing, 1996

Ball, Pamela, *10,000 Ways to Change your Life* Arcturus Publishing, 1997

Barrett, Clive *The Egyptian Gods and Goddesses* Diamond Books, 1996

Bloomhill, Greta *Witchcraft in Africa* Bailey Bros. and Swinfen, 1962

Cabot, Laurie *Love Magic* Delta, 1998

Cavendish, Richard *A History of Magic* Weidenfeld and Nicolson, 1977

Conway, D. J. *Moon Magick* Llewellyn Publications, 1998

Cooper, Rabbi David A. *God is a Verb: Kabbalah and the Practice of Mystical Judaism* Riverhead Books, 1998

Cunningham, Scott *Cunningham's Encyclopaedia of Magical Herbs* Llewellyn Publications, 1986

Denning, Matilda & Phillips, Osbourne *The Magical Philosophy* Llewellyn Publications, 1974

Eason, Cassandra *A Complete Guide to Divination* Piatkus Books, 1998

Flints, Valerie I. J. *The Rise of Magic in Early Medieval Europe* Clarendon Press, 1991

Frost, Gavin and Frost, Yvonne *A Witch's Grimoire of Ancient Omens, Portents, Talismans, Amulets and Charms* Parker, 1979

Gilfond, Henry *Voodoo; Its Origins and Practices* F. Watts, 1976

Ginsburg, David Christian *The Essenes: Their History and Doctrines*

–   *The Kabbalah: its Doctrines, Development and Literature,* Routledge & Kegan Paul, 1955

Hodges, Doris M. *Talismans and Amulets in the History of Healing* Venton, 1987

Howard, Michael *Candle Burning: Its Occult Significance* The Aquarian Press, 1980

Hultkrantz, Ake *Native Religions of North America* Harpers and Row, 1987

Kemp, Gillian *The Good Spell Book: Love Charms, Magical Cures and Other Practical Sorcery* Orion Books, 2000

Logan, Jo *Prediction Book of Amulets and Talismans* Javelin Books, 1990

Meaney, Audrey L. *Anglo Saxon Amulets and Curing Stones* British Archeological Press Reports, 1981

Persall, Judy and Trumble, Bill (eds) *The Oxford English Reference Dictionary* Oxford University Press, 1995

Vinci, Leo *Talismans, Amulets and Charms. A Work on Talismanic Magic* Regency Press, 1997

Waite, A. E. *The Holy Kabbalah: A Study of the Secret Tradition in Israel* Whitefriars, 1924

Worwood, Valerie Ann *The Fragrant Heavens* Bantam Books, 1999

Internet:
http://www.donnachaidh.com
http://www.eggmac.demon.co.uk
http://www.themystica.com
http://www.newmoon.uk.com
http://www.religioustolerance.org
http://www.spiritonline.com
http://www.teleport.com
http://www.wicca.com

Any other sources from which we have, at any time, taken information and inadvertently omitted to include here are acknowledged without reservation. We also acknowledge with gratitude the help we have received from many friends and colleagues in the writing of this book.

LIST OF SPELLS, RITUALS AND TECHNIQUES